EYE TO EYE
THE CAMERA REMEMBERS

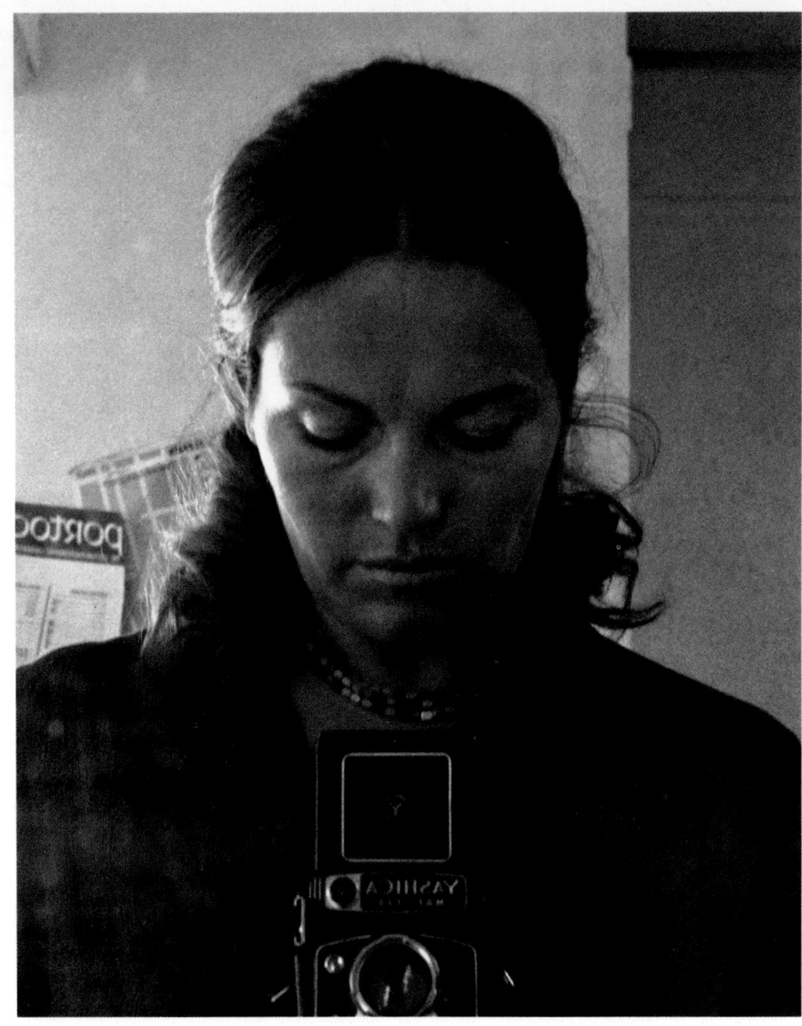

Renate Ponsold   1971

PORTRAIT PHOTOGRAPHS BY

RENATE PONSOLD

EYE TO EYE
THE CAMERA REMEMBERS

FOREWORD BY
DORE ASHTON

AFTERWORD BY
ROBERT MOTHERWELL

HUDSON HILLS PRESS, NEW YORK

First Edition

© 1988 by Renate Ponsold Motherwell
Introduction © 1988 by Dore Ashton

All rights reserved under International and Pan-American
Copyright Conventions. Published in the United States
by Hudson Hills Press, Inc., Suite 1308, 230 Fifth Avenue,
New York, NY 10001-7704.

Distributed in the United States, its territories and
possessions, Mexico, and Central and South America by
Rizzoli International Publications, Inc.
Distributed in the United Kingdom, Eire, Europe, Israel,
and the Middle East by Phaidon Press Limited.
Distributed in Australia by Bookwise International.
Distributed in Japan by Yohan (Western Publications
Distribution Agency).
Distributed in South Korea by Nippon Shuppan Hanbai.

Editor and Publisher: **Paul Anbinder**
Senior Editor: **Virginia Wageman**
Designer: **Nai Y. Chang**
Composition: **Trufont Typographers, Inc.**

Manufactured in Japan by **Toppan Printing Company**

Library of Congress Cataloguing-in-Publication Data
Ponsold, Renate.
 Eye to eye.
 Includes index.
 1. Photography—Portraits. 2. Artists—Portraits.
I. Title.
TR681.A7P66 1988   779′.2′0924   88-12783

ISBN 1-55595-004-3 (alk. paper)

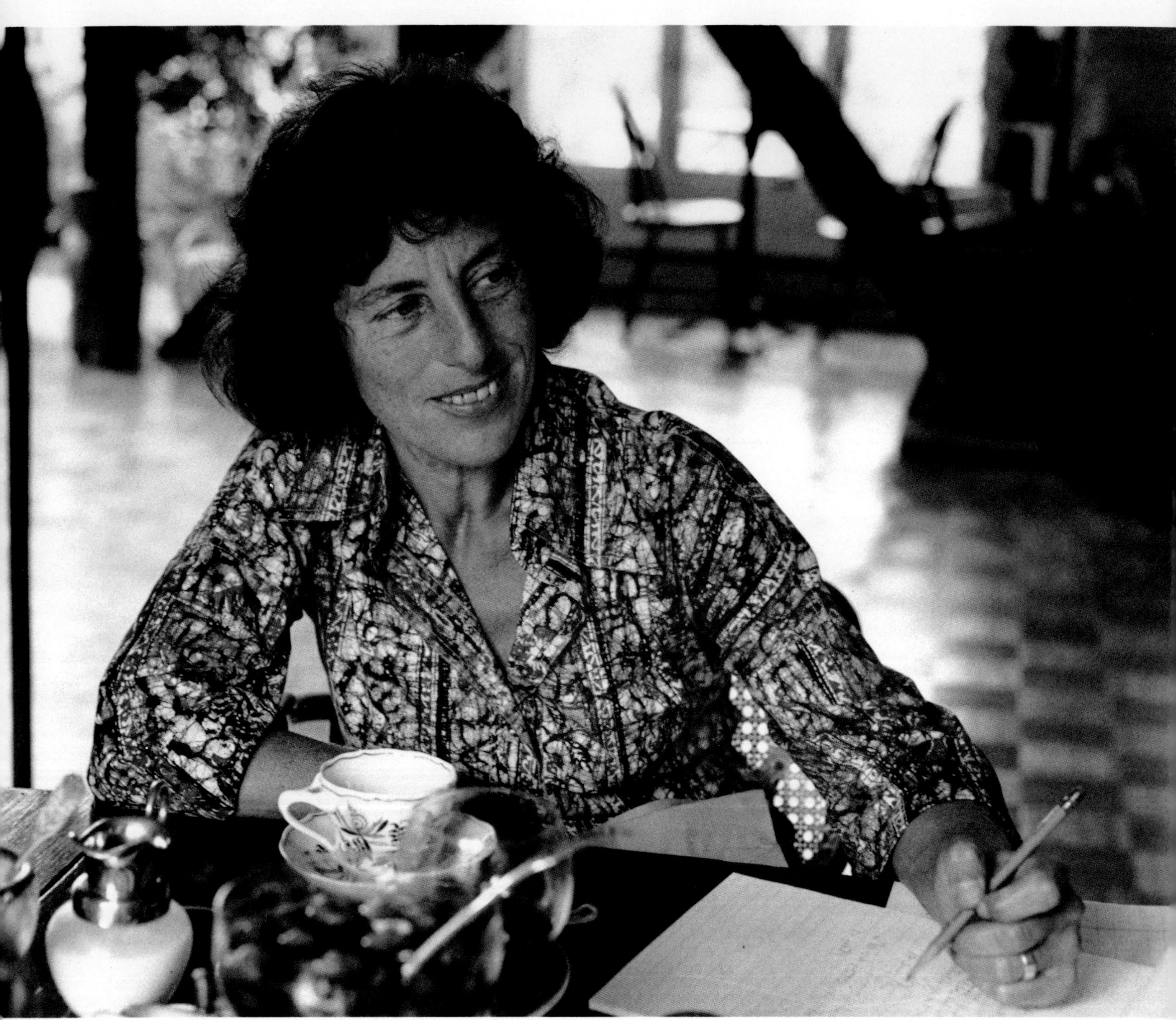

Dore Ashton   1974

FACING A MILIEU

by DORE ASHTON

The search for the origin, the real initiation of our interest in the photographic portrait, can be vexing. On the most elementary level, it appears that the portrait photograph commands our attention simply because we are human. Despite centuries of speculation bolstered by increasingly scientific explorations of what is human in us, there is as yet no definitive vision. In this perplexing search for definition, any means is welcome. We peer at faces on the printed page and speculate, make hypotheses, try to read hidden codes, try, in short, to sum ourselves up, the one in the many. "One of the fascinating things about portraits is the way they enable us to trace the sameness of man," Henri Cartier-Bresson wrote.

There is a considerable body of literature verging on the philosophic concerning the photographic image, and it is not my purpose to review it. But I think it is worth pointing out that nothing serious has ever been written about photography that does not, in one way or another, concede that any photograph is only part of a truth. In the exceedingly interesting struggle to define just what photography is, most commentators have sooner or later come up against the problem of interpretation. They have discovered that the photograph, once thought to be the most faithful of representations of something called reality, is just as dependent on conventions of seeing and epochal conditioning as is the nonmechanical work of art.

The question that occurs to me when I think about photographs of people is why in the first place we are all curious about the others. Why do we want to see faces and more faces? When I study the art and literature of the nineteenth century, I am avidly interested in what the people looked like. I always turn first to the illustrations, seeking to find photographic portraits, gazing and guessing. More than that: I find that I am drawn to photographs of the past, even to those figures whom I cannot identify, those whose histories are lost or insignificant. The lure of the photograph, it seems, even to someone as profoundly intellectual and inquisitive as Roland Barthes, lies somewhat in its magic.

It appears to me, in my wayward thoughts about the photographic portrait, that there are at least (and that is an understatement) two ways of looking. When we see members of some unknown family arrayed on the page,

perhaps dimmed and distanced by their postures, costumes, and household attributes, we are not only confronting the notion of pastness but are instigating a process of fabulation. One of the unintended functions of the portrait photograph is to cater to the overweening human instinct to tell stories. We pretend to ask ourselves: Who are these people, how did they live, who is that child, what ever became of him? But all the while we have already begun the fable of their lives in our imaginations. The other way of looking is when we seek confirmation. We have already formed an idea and turn to the photograph only to congratulate ourselves on our prescience.

An example: Like many art historians I have turned my attention at one time or another to Nadar's portraits of nineteenth-century artistic and literary celebrities. Some have remained vivid in my memory, such as, for instance, the portrait of Alexandre Dumas. Nadar, with his usual instinct for the expressive detail, was at pains to highlight Dumas's crinkly gray hair—his mixed blood being part of his myth—and to show him in rumpled, bohemian, informal dress. I had already formed an impression of Dumas, having read nineteenth-century memoirs, and Nadar confirmed it. The same is true of his tragic portrait of Charles Baudelaire, whose anguished life was expressed in his poetry and seemed to me (as I made my own fable) to be reflected in the photograph; and also of the portrait of Gustave Doré, whose dandyish appearance seemed to me, despite his hellish illustrations, to reflect the very essence of his personality.

Beyond the fact that there are various functions the photographic image initiates, there is its mystery. In the beginning, in the mid-nineteenth century, photography was the province of intellectuals and artists. They were highly ambivalent in their responses, but not indifferent to the magical properties of the printed image. When Eugène Delacroix became a member of the Société Héliographique, he undoubtedly approved of the motto of its founder, B. R. Monfort: "Nothing is so beautiful as the truth, but one must choose it." Truth to detail was a large issue in the mid-century, and the camera, it seemed, would go far toward what was called realism in art. But if we look at the literary enthusiasts who actually utilized photography—first Théophile Gautier in 1840 and then Gustave Flaubert in 1850—it is striking that both had at once a mystical and a practical side in their own works, and both were excited by the magic of the photograph. Photography is inherently magical, as any photographer who has labored in the darkroom can attest. When William Henry Fox Talbot, otherwise apparently a calm and scientific man, discovered that "the impression is latent and invisible" in its initial stage, even he was excited. That small detail leads to a wealth of discourse around the premise that between the idea and the act falls the shadow, that the unpredictable emerges as the print is submerged. Ghost images are always with us. Photography, then, began in the province of artists and intellectuals and it has done its full circuit.

The initial question of interpretation has another aspect—one that is germane to the discussion of Renate Ponsold's photographic chronicle—and that is the degree to which the viewer is subjected to the latent images of his general culture. Ponsold's portraits are in several respects a record of a certain culture—my culture. They are at once memories and facts. They function both as a family album might (and I like to look at family albums, even those of people I don't know or could never know) and as a historical record. But as Goethe maintained, no one can assess an epoch from within that epoch. Once the general lineaments of Ponsold's notable faces are discerned, we are off on a maddening round of speculation about what in fact they represent. Do they reflect a certain culture? But then, how to define culture? Jean-Paul Sartre said in *The Words*: "Culture doesn't save anything or anyone, it doesn't justify. But it is a product of man: he projects himself into it, he recognizes himself in it; that critical mirror alone offers man his image." How, in this procession of distinctive faces, do we form our image of our culture, our milieu? Ponsold's photographic essays are representatives of an international village, and we are the idle gossipers at the well. We peer at them and guess ourselves to be their contemporaries, their beneficiaries (if we believe they have helped to shape our image of our world), or their critics. Whatever our own personality, we are participants in the epoch she has set off in the brackets of photographs-of-record, in her boundary markers of time. These images are both products of and producers of that image of which Sartre speaks. Perhaps that is what Gabriella Drudi, herself a fine photographer and writer, meant when she wrote of Ponsold's portraits: "A portrait of an artist is the portrait of a portrait. . . . It portrays what his own creative images have long since revealed to us."

Whatever may be said about Ponsold's images, it is clear that behind her camera she is a warm, responsive inquirer and is as much puzzled by the endless mystery of the human visage as any intellectual. The human face, Marcel Proust maintained, is like "those Oriental gods: a whole group of faces juxtaposed in different planes; it is impossible to see them simultaneously." It is a truism that each of us composes his or her mask, and certainly artists are specialists in the procedure. As I look through Ponsold's treasury of faces I have known, I pause before the image of a beloved friend, Octavio Paz, and remember one of his most haunting poems:

"El Otro"

Se inventó una cara.
     Detrás de ella
vivió, murió y resucitó
muchas veces.
    Su cara
hoy tiene las arrugas de esa cara.
Sus arrugas no tienen cara

("The Other"

He invented a face for himself.
     Behind it,
He lived, died and was resurrected
Many times.
    His face today
Has the wrinkles from that face.
His wrinkles have no face—
Tr. by Eliot Weinberger)

In the surpassingly ambiguous concision of this little poem I find consolation for the unanswerability of so many questions the human face raises. Ponsold is totally unassuming. As chronicler, archivist, diarist, she has hoped—and only hoped—to find the mask that reveals the mask, and in numerous cases her very modesty has summoned a truth.

Since I am writing from within Ponsold's epoch—that is, I have known almost all of the people she has photographed, either well or fleetingly—I am at both an advantage and a disadvantage. I see her photograph of a monument of art history to whom I also made a pilgrimage, Man Ray, and I say to myself, oh yes, that is how he was. I see another image and ask myself, is that how he was? Always the "I" intervenes. (But need I feel embarrassed? All of the theoretical writing about photography of the past few years asserts that such intervention is inevitable.) I look at the face of a once-dear friend, such as the late Jack Tworkov, and believe I can read his character there, even hear his hesitant beginning of a sentence, a long *uuuuuh* that trails off. But immediately I remember reading a review by Neil Ascherson of a book about Nazi doctors whose photographs, he suggested, revealed nothing of their criminality.

For all that, I *recognize* many of these people as Ponsold presents them: re-cognize. This is because she has caught them in characteristic moments. A photograph may reveal little, but it may also characterize if the photographer and the subject share a culture, or at least a moment of culture. That, it seems to me, is Ponsold's strength. She has enabled her subject to enter into the process, sometimes even before he has had time to reassemble his mask. The spontaneous quality in Ponsold's work is of course a function of her personality. Her own biography resides in these photographs as well as the cumulative experience of the sitter, the formation of her personality.

Browsing among these mementos of a rich past, it is clear that the principle that reigned in Delacroix's photographic society—that of choosing—was at work at a strong instinctive level from Ponsold's early youth. Even as a student, Ponsold, who spent two years in the late 1950s studying photography in Munich, put herself into the position of an open, inquiring spirit, awaiting the moment—which could never be prepared beforehand—to choose. The earliest photographs in this book attest to her curious mixture of boldness and diffidence. I am sure that the unstinting smile on Louis Armstrong's face was a response to the young girl who despite her shyness had managed, finally, to push her way through the crowd to record a special moment. That young girl was already drawn to the haunts of artists and the special atmosphere they generated, as we see in her portrait of Wilma, a now legendary proprietress of an artists' café in Berlin. In those days the artists of Berlin were attempting to resurrect the Berlin of the Weimar Republic with its desirable bohemian ways. Ponsold shared their enterprise.

Ponsold was in her early twenties when she embarked on her adventure, still in progress, with the artistic life of New York. She set out for America, characteristically, by freighter and arrived in New York with enough money for a three-week sojourn. In no time she had found friends—one of her great gifts—and prolonged her visit. Very soon she decided that New York was her place: "After that, I never left New York without a return ticket." She soon found a cheap apartment on the Lower East Side and, supporting herself with a number of odd jobs including that of governess, set about discovering her new world. In this she was fortunate to have a cicerone of considerable social means, the gregarious poet and anthologist Oscar Williams, who, as she says, knew just about everyone in the art world. I myself had met him two years before and, when I saw Ponsold's photograph of him, had to smile. She caught the very quality that most described him: his rather innocent, even boyish pride in his own works. That cluttered and typical bohemian studio of the 1950s and Oscar brandishing his latest opus were very much a part of our youth. In fact, I had met Williams because he was brought to my place by Stanley Kunitz who smilingly stood back while Oscar presented me with his most recent book—an anthology that I believe was his most successful work. The other photograph of her first year in New York—that of Julio de Diego—also tells of her young pleasure in the more flamboyant aspects of New York's art world. Julio was everyone's favorite actor, and while few of us took his art seriously, we all relished his self-dramatic presence.

By the time Ponsold landed a job at the very heart of the art world, the Museum of Modern Art, she was well acquainted with many of the intersecting smaller groupings within the realm of the arts. At first she worked in the museum's technical section, but soon she was upstairs working as a photographer, watching as well-known artists and their admirers gathered, making split-second decisions as she snapped. Never a slave to technique and always simply accepting whatever light there happened to be, Ponsold managed to build a body of work that reflects her open nature and her enduring curiosity about what makes artists tick.

After the first few years in New York, one feels, she was no longer the romantic ingenue, but rather, a companion who made her subjects feel at ease and who in some cases knew their ways well enough to transcribe telling details. I think of her shot of Bill de Kooning and his bicycle. Anyone who has known Bill for a while can remember encounters with him as he doggedly made that old bike push on. Then, in the studio, Ponsold studied the place, the light, and, above all, the mood of her sitter, catching de Kooning in a remarkably characteristic gesture, head slightly to one side in profile, listening, participating, but inwardly shrinking at the same time. Her shot of the two painters Philip Guston and de Kooning, in intense conversation, states what I myself know to be the case: that these two men could talk for hours about painting, totally indifferent to where they were, what they consumed, or who listened. It is a tribute to the photographer that she could understand the true importance of this exchange between painters.

Although most of Ponsold's photographs are not the result of first encounters, many of them do express her feeling that the first encounter, the "first hello," is the decisive moment. There is one photograph here that is quite literally the first hello—the photograph of the painter Hedda Sterne opening the portal of her magnificent East Hampton studio. Anyone who has ever been greeted by this extraordinary woman will rejoice in the way Ponsold has fixed for all time the spontaneous welcoming gesture.

Although Ponsold insists on the groping character of her work, pointing out that she never positions her subjects, nor does she attempt to find the perfect illumination, she sometimes knows from the first encounter the nature of her model. I think of the poet Robert Lowell, a man of conflict and tides of overwhelming emotion for whom the world was often too much. How poignant is this image of the poet, up against the wall, so to speak, and bravely peering out into the world as symbolized by the lens of the camera. Something of a similar spirit lingers in her portrait of the playwright Edward Albee, although Albee's determination to meet the world on its own hard terms is also apparent.

Ponsold has not neglected the difficult question of context. The expression on a face is often not enough to "express" the individual. Body language, gesture, apparel, objects, or attributes—all contribute to how an "other" reads the meanings of a face. In common parlance, a photograph freezes a moment. A good photographer struggles against his medium to go beyond the freeze, or else to exaggerate it to a point where the viewer is coerced into a moment of supreme attention—an act that initiates once again the fabulous function of photography. Ponsold has caught (caught is the right word) the body language in several instances with notable alacrity. There is the artist Saul Steinberg flinging up his hands in a typical gesture of half refusal to emerge from his solitude. There is the artist Stamos, always fierce of demeanor, also half refusing but in a more aggressive posture. There are Gabriella Drudi and her husband Toti Scialoja in a beguiling portrait, each responding in his or her special way to some conversational gambit—Scialoja laughing up his sleeve, Drudi thoughtful as always. Apparel and attributes are also rendered eloquent in certain of these portraits. Sculptor Carl Andre in his overalls and with his Cézanne-like stance is a latter-day harlequin. Art critic Harold Rosenberg in his checked shirt—I never saw him in any other kind—ensconced in his Faustian study, considering, no doubt, his riposte to a visitor, is very much the man of letters that he was. And sculptor George Segal, emerging from his crowd of plaster human effigies, is also very much the man he is.

Do these photographs sum up a particular culture? I rather think they do if by culture we accept Sartre's broadened definition. Ponsold's desultory chronicle, for all its impromptu character, does describe an artistic milieu that goes beyond both local and national boundaries. Each of these visages represents a spirit that has contributed some incalculable minim to the general texture of our time. In one sense, this book is about one individual's perception of the time. In another, it is about a charming and affectionate individual who has taken her means—the photograph—and turned it into a way of life, or perhaps a way of commemoration of life. Ponsold has gone out into the world as Henri Cartier-Bresson recommended, using photography as a means of understanding. In his words she finds her confirmation:

> "Manufactured" or staged photography does not concern me. And if I make a judgment, it can only be on a *psychological* or sociological level. . . . For me, the camera is a *sketch book*, an instrument of *intuition* and *spontaneity*, the master of the instant which—in visual terms—questions and decides simultaneously. . . . One must always take photos with the greatest *respect for the subject* and for oneself.

The italics in this quotation were made by Ponsold herself and serve as a shorthand summary of all the things she values in her life and art. It is not surprising that a woman of her temperament met and married a painter who all his life pursued these same values, Robert Motherwell. And it is not surprising, either, that she has made of her sketchbook an ensemble in which, finally, the whole is greater than the parts.

EYE TO EYE
THE CAMERA REMEMBERS

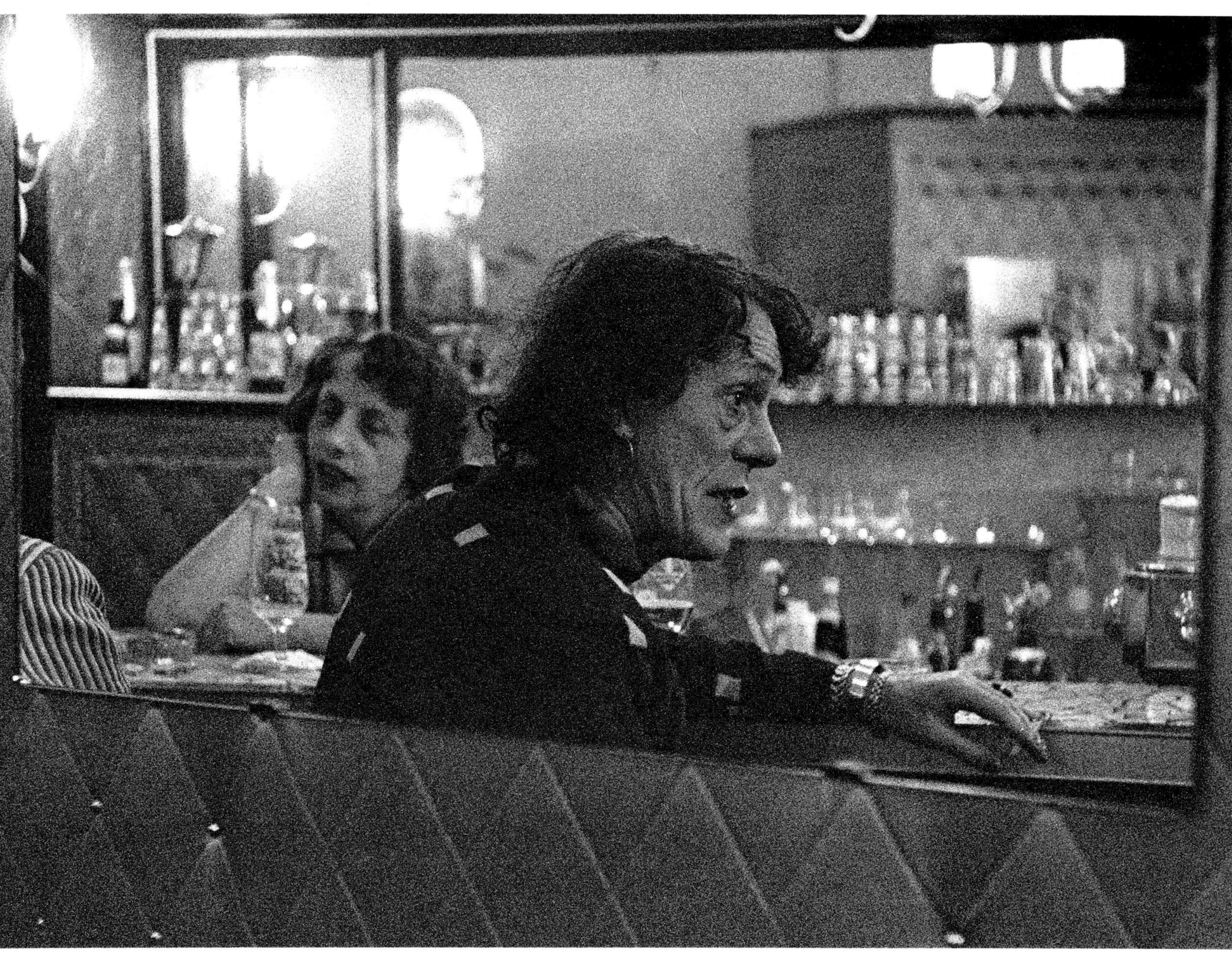

Wilma (Stauber)   1958

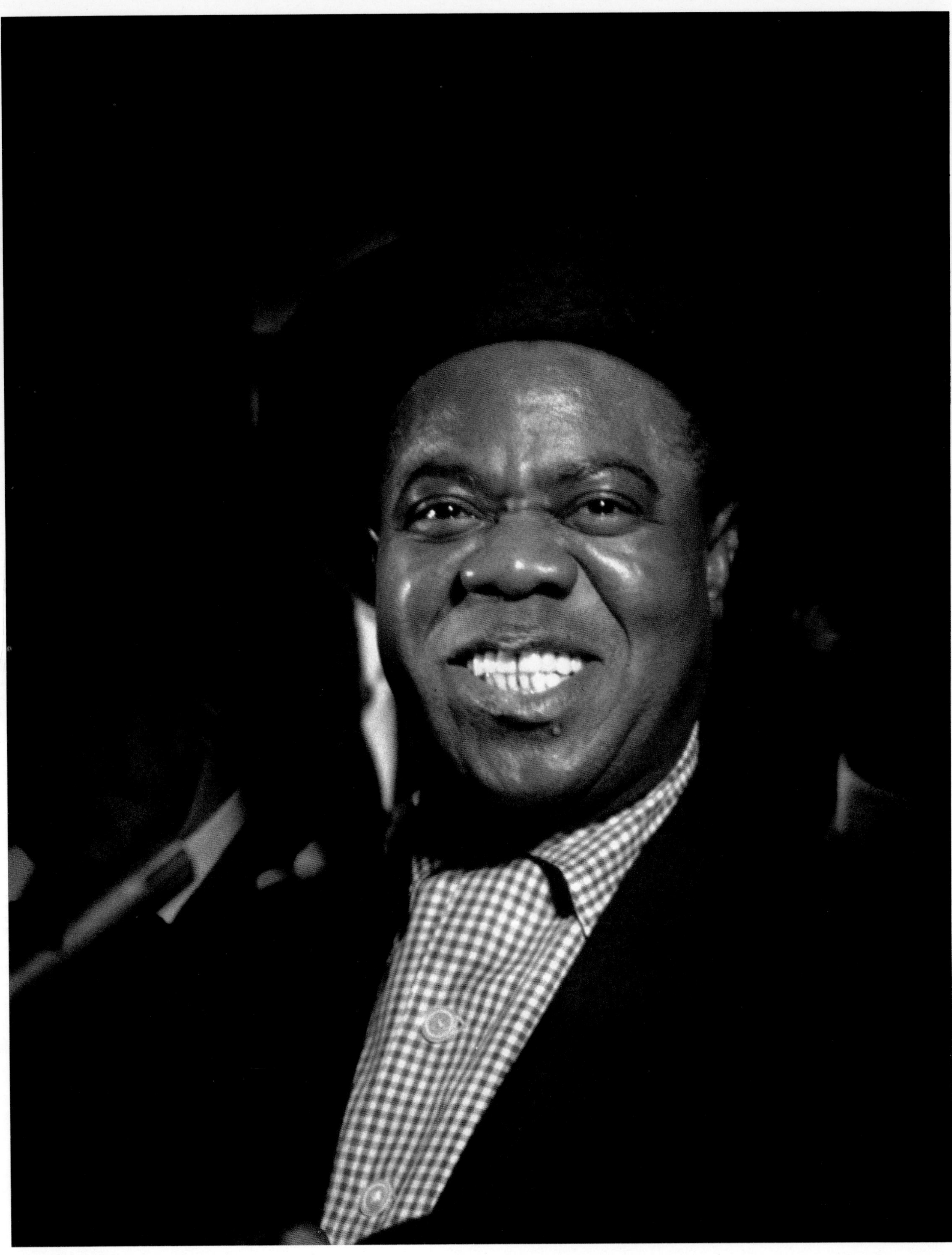

Louis Armstrong   1958

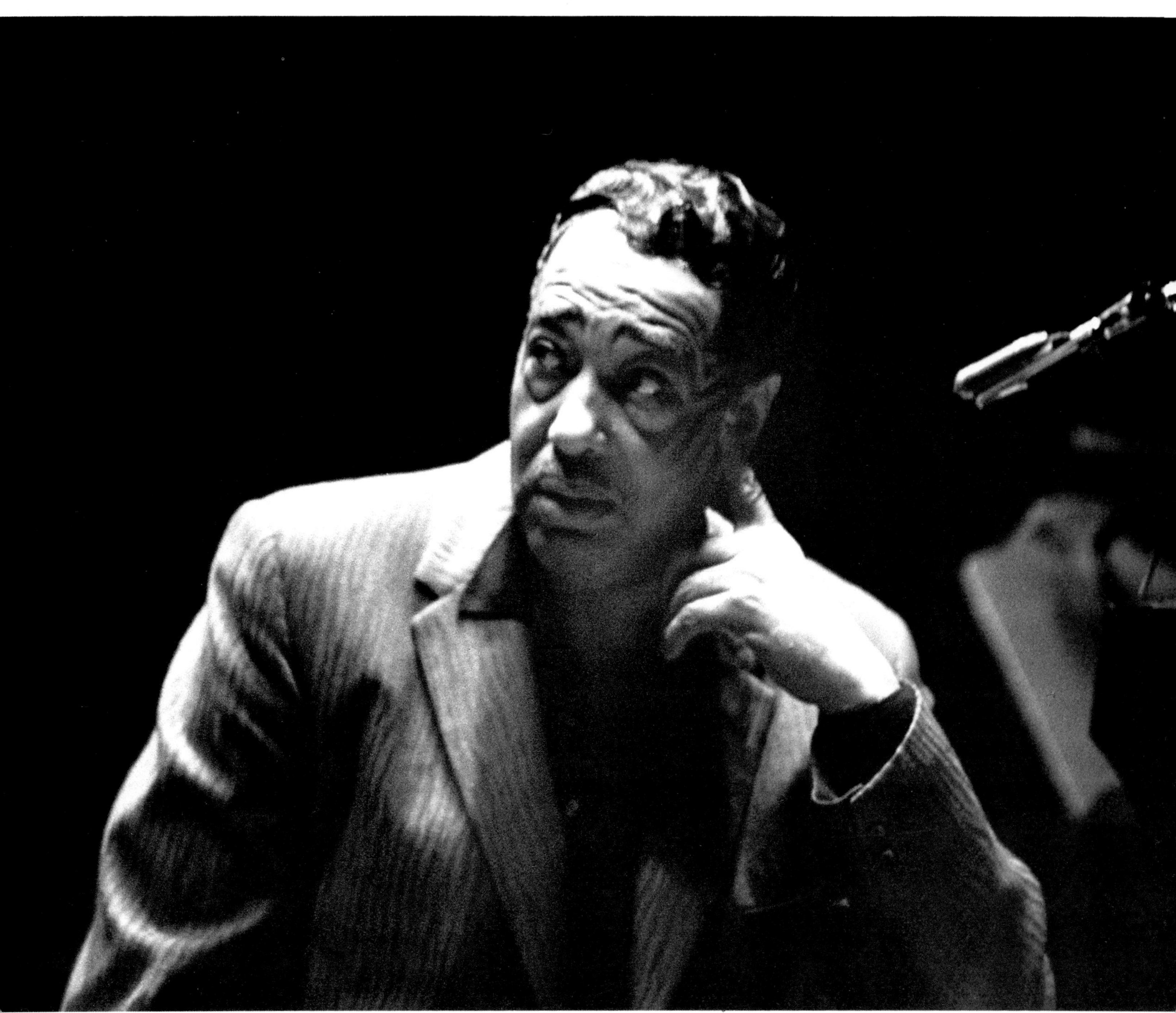

Duke Ellington   1960

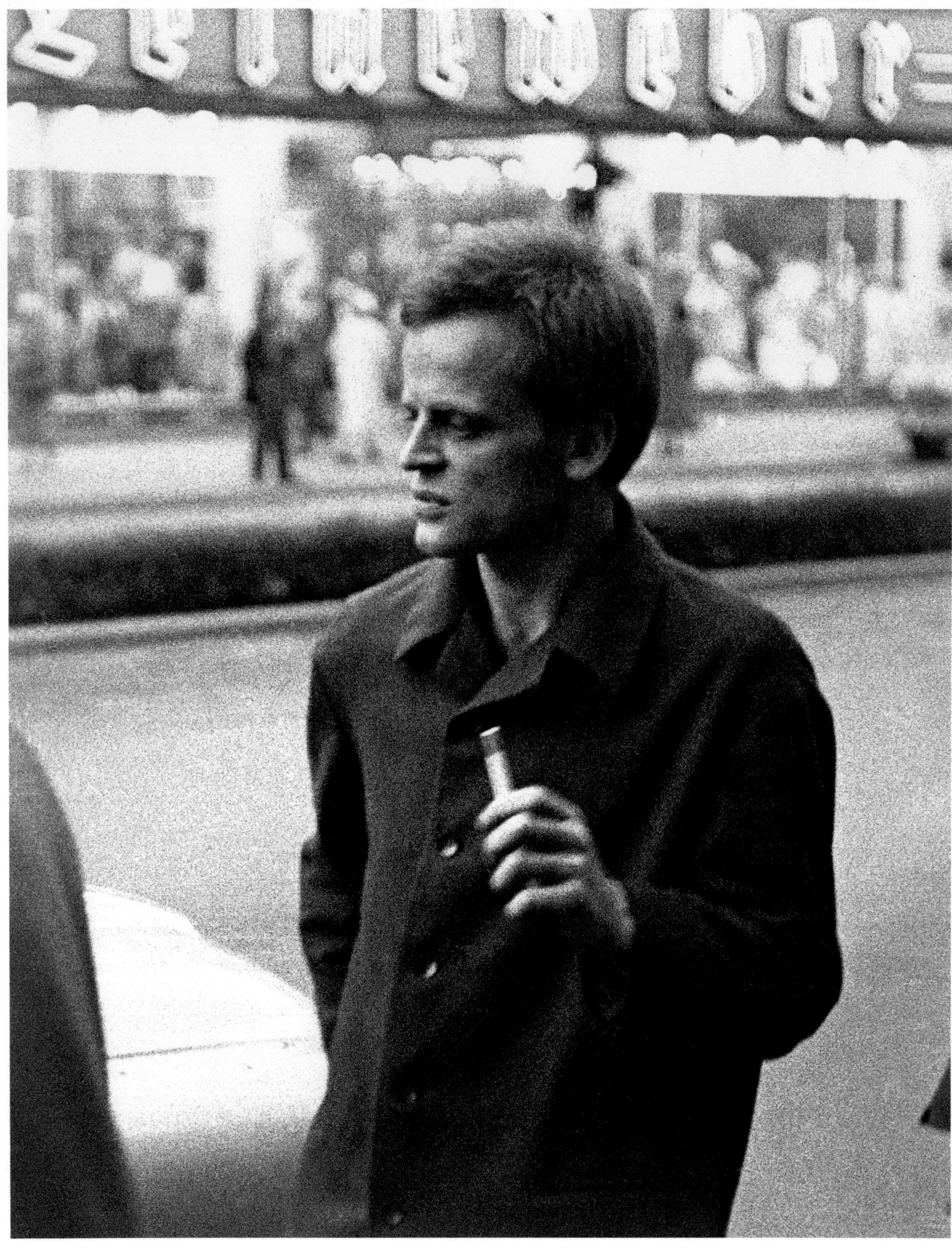

Klaus Kinski   1958

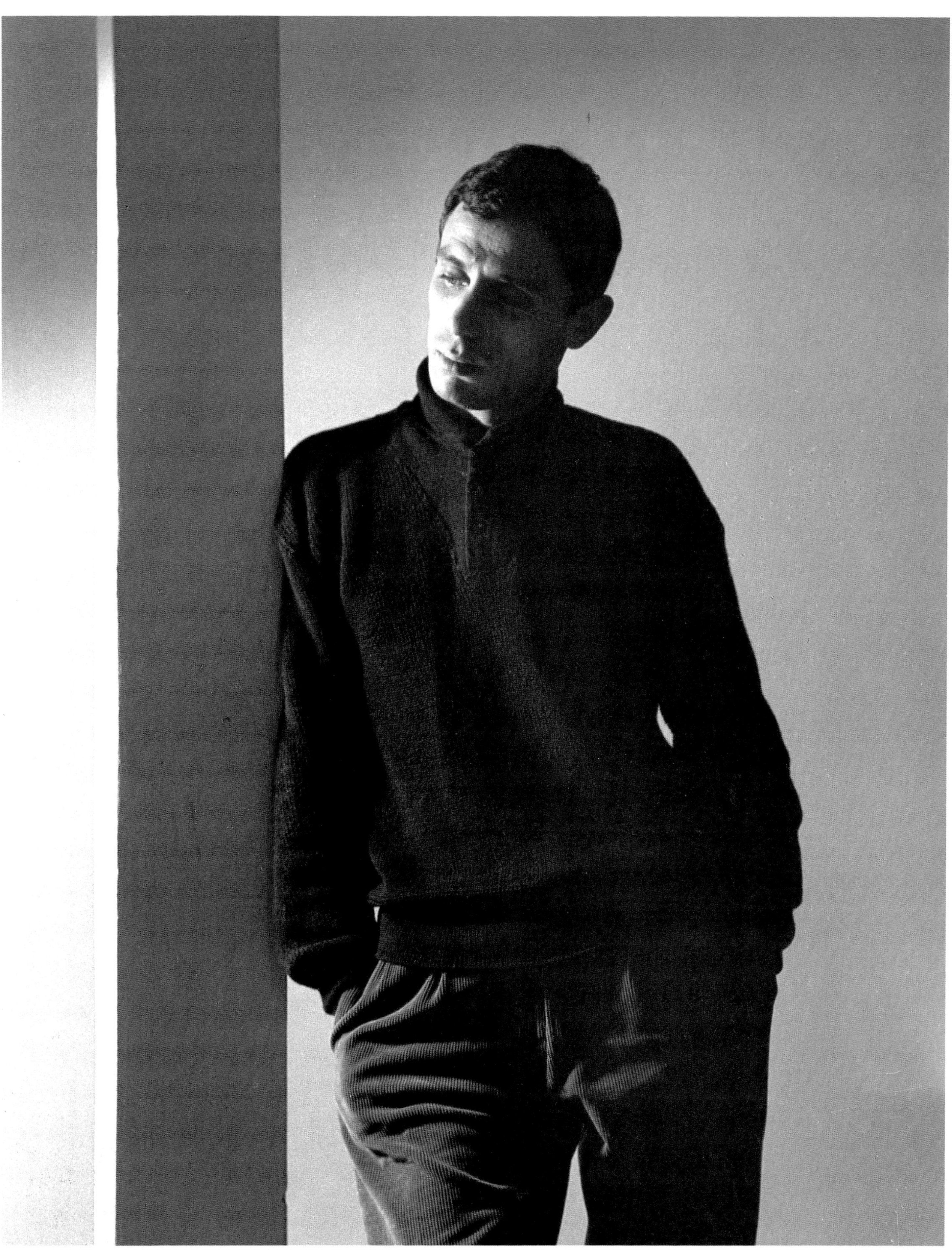

Gaetano Pompa   1958

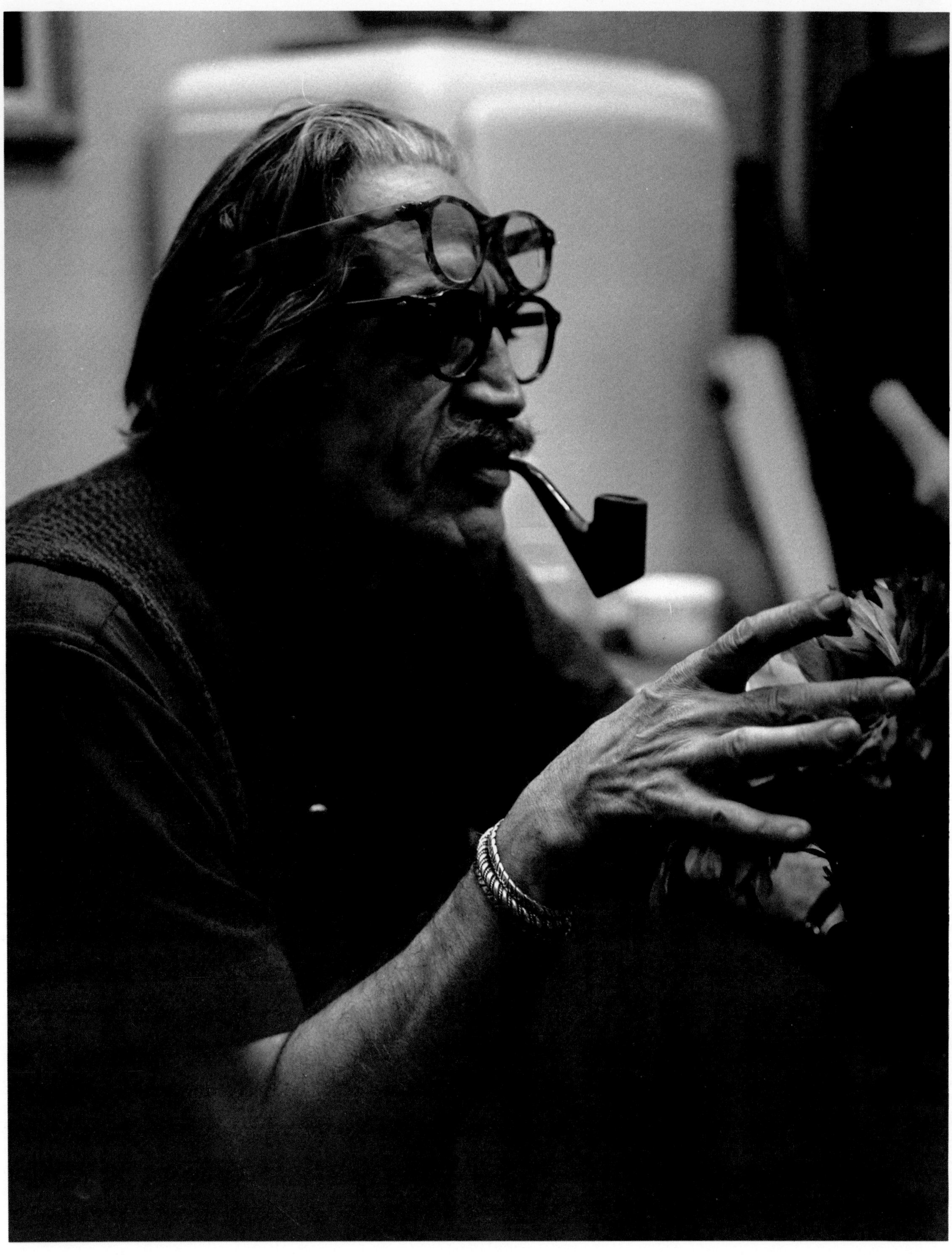

Julio de Diego   1960

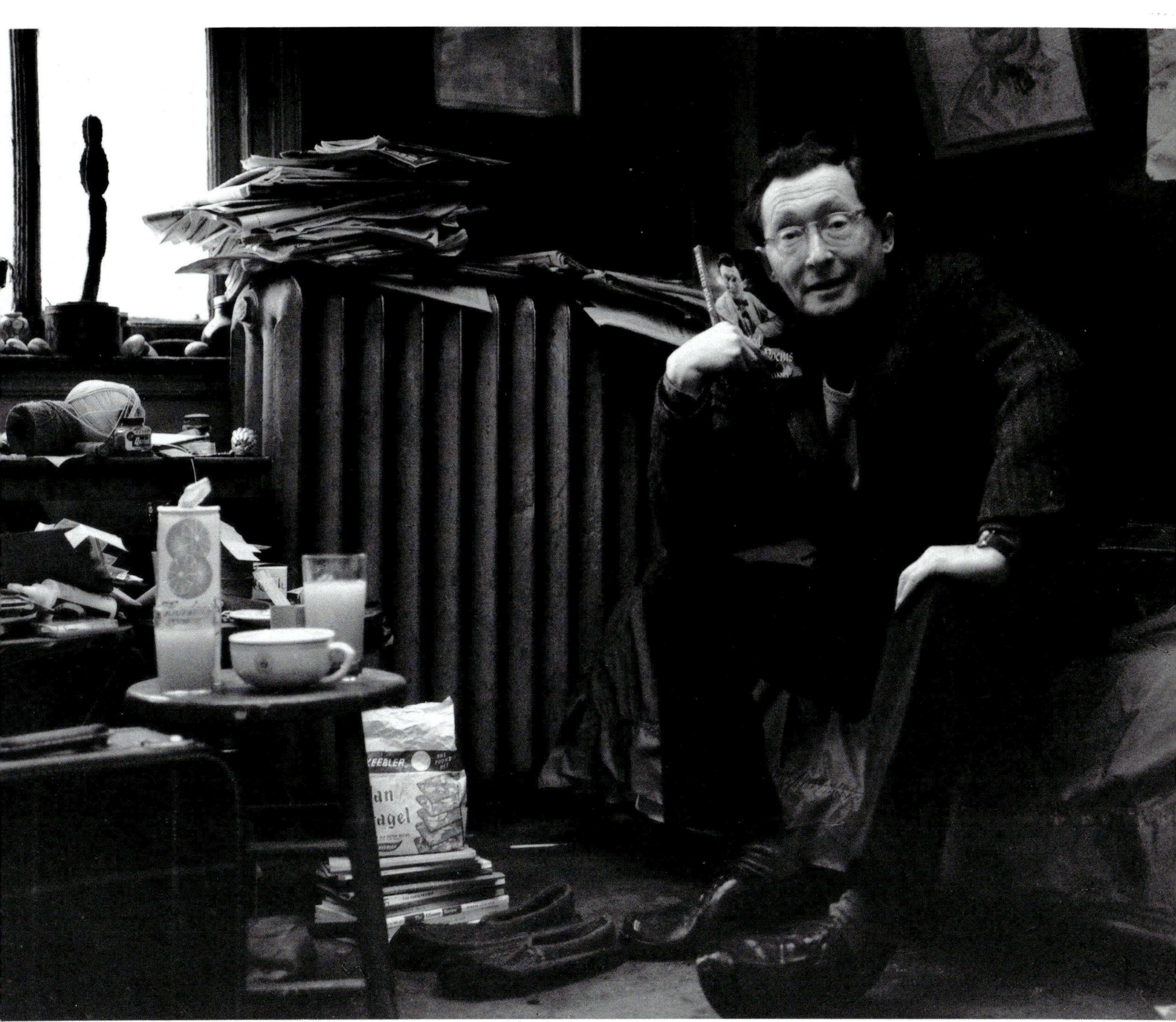

Oscar Williams   1961

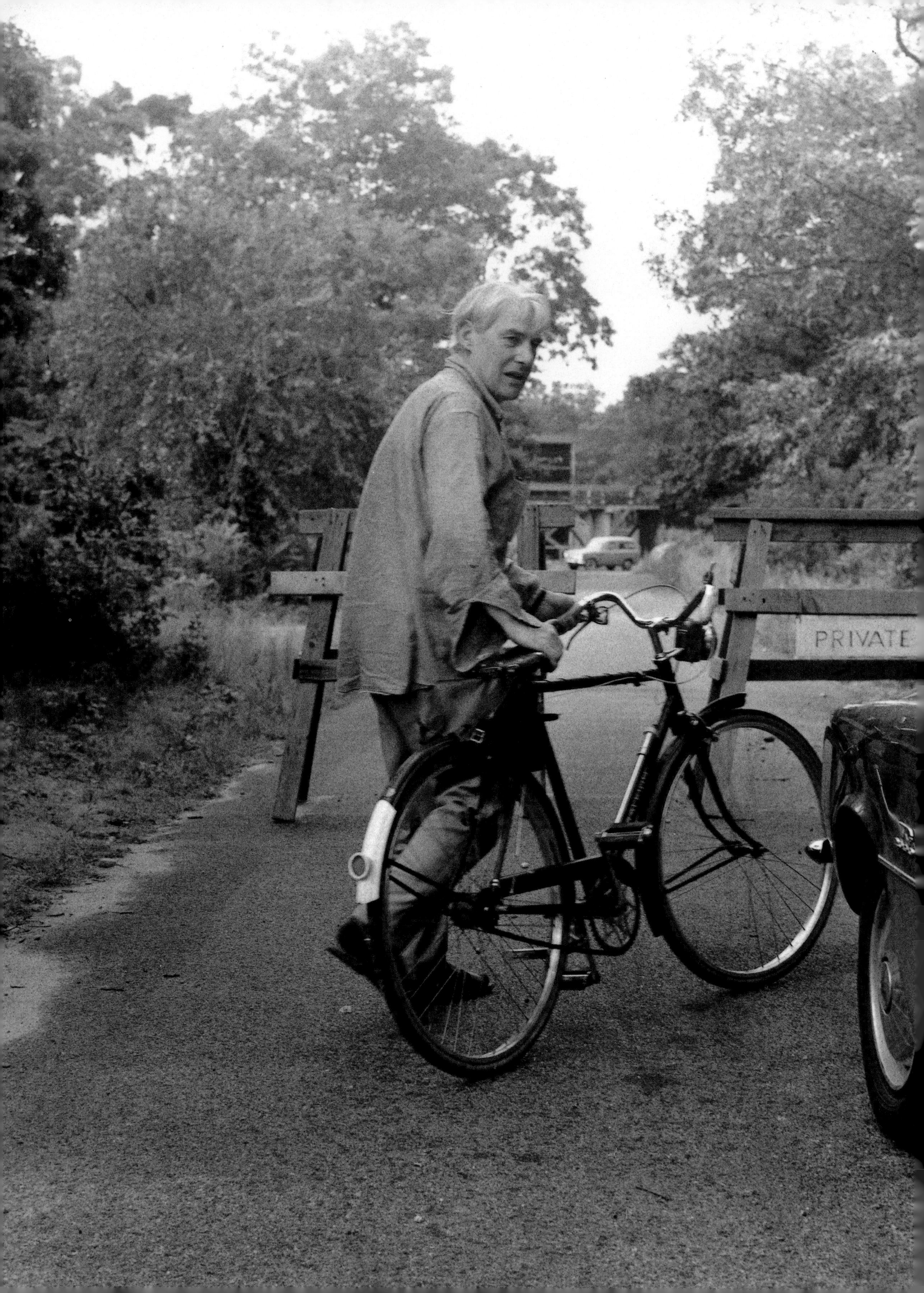

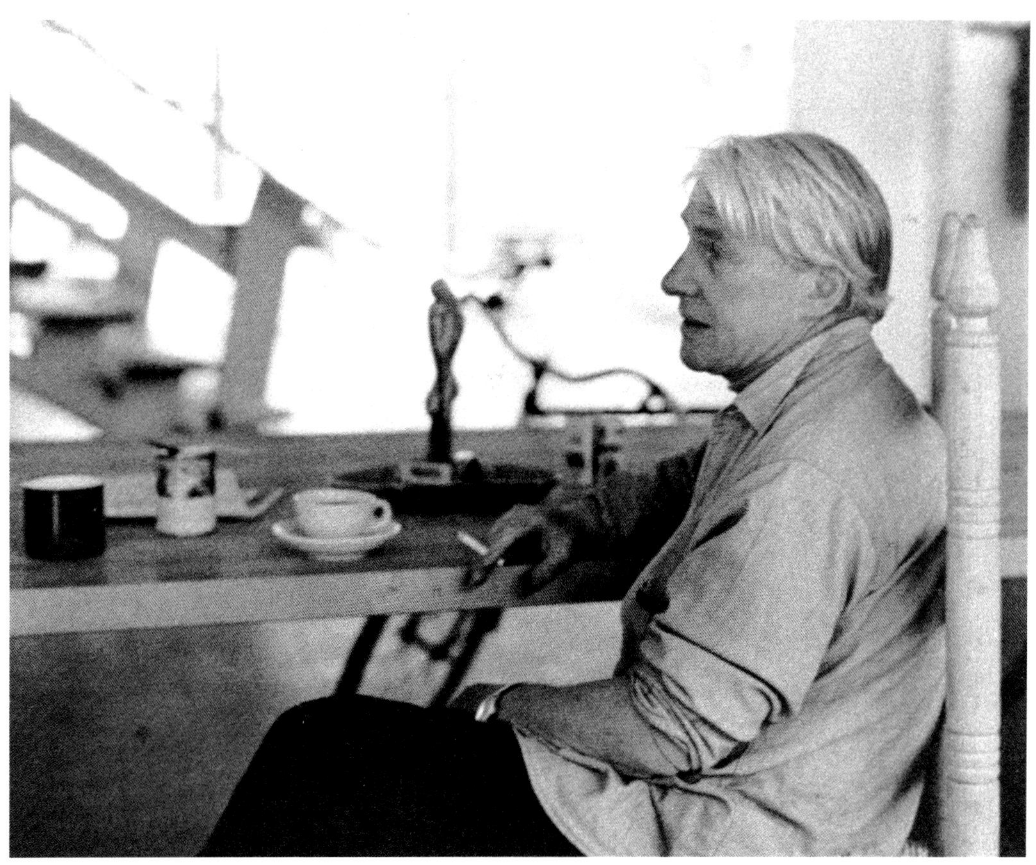

Willem de Kooning   1965

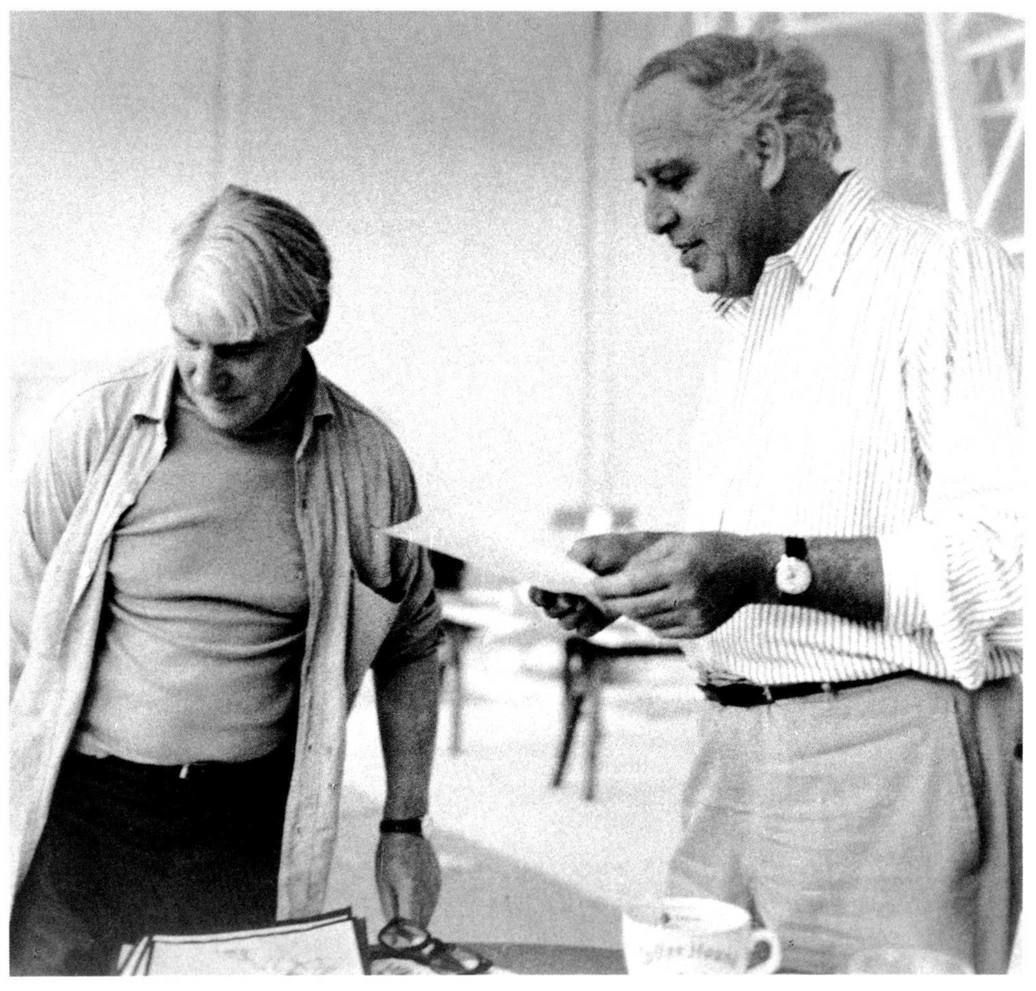

Willem de Kooning with Philip Guston   1965

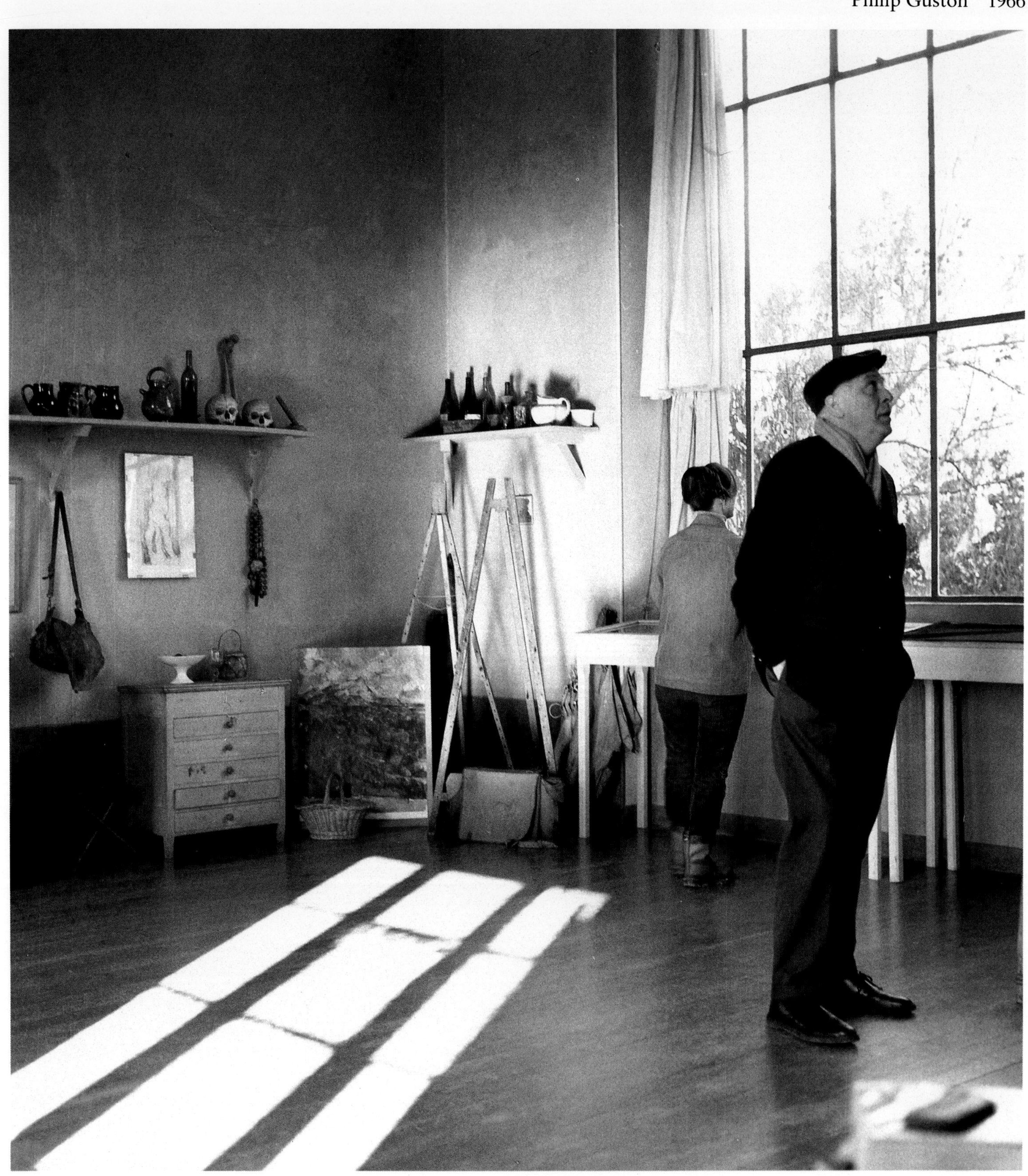

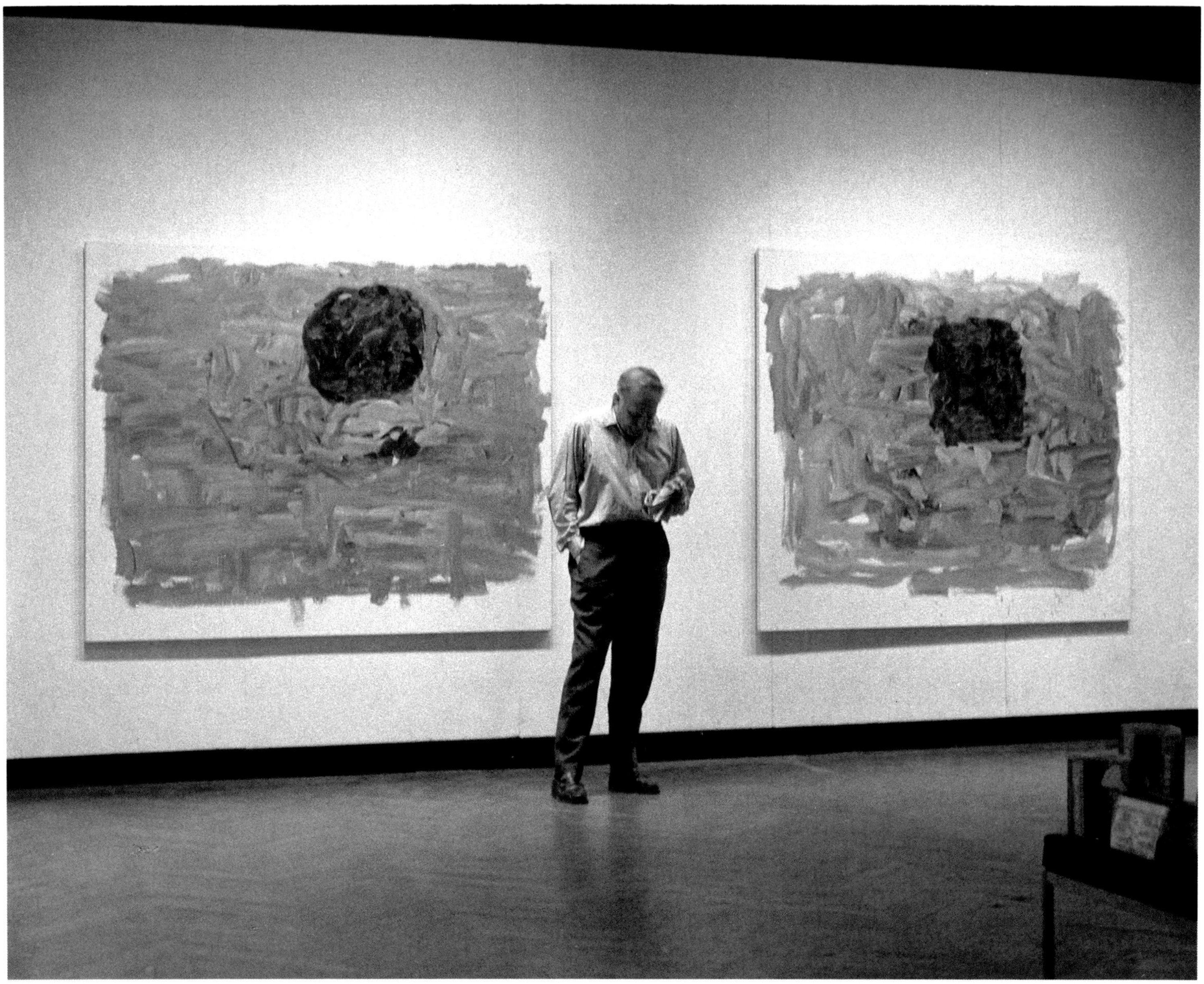

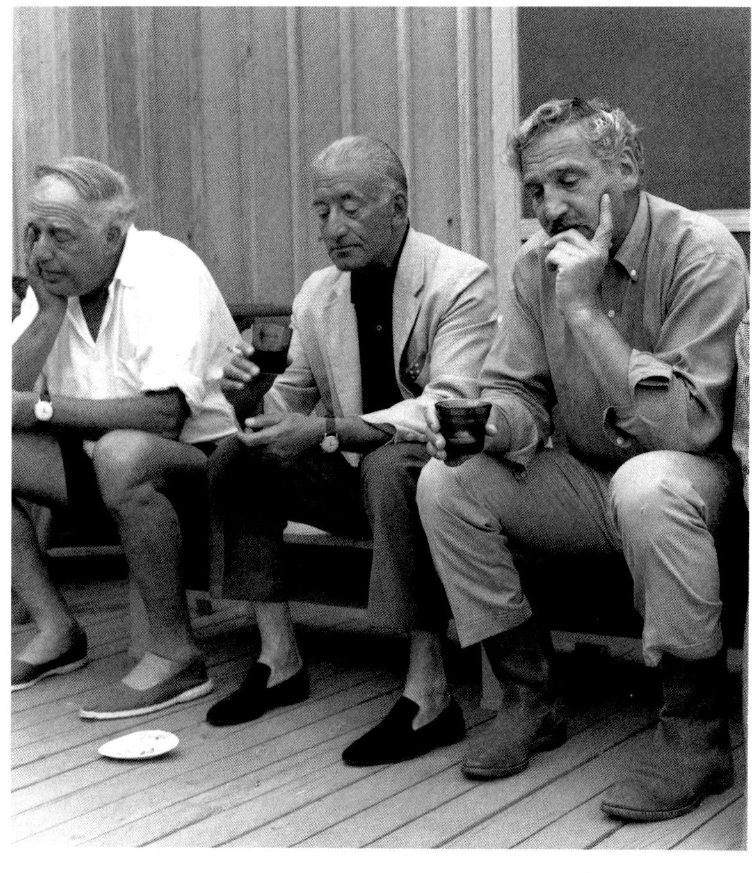

Philip Guston, Adolph Gottlieb, Syd Solomon   1965

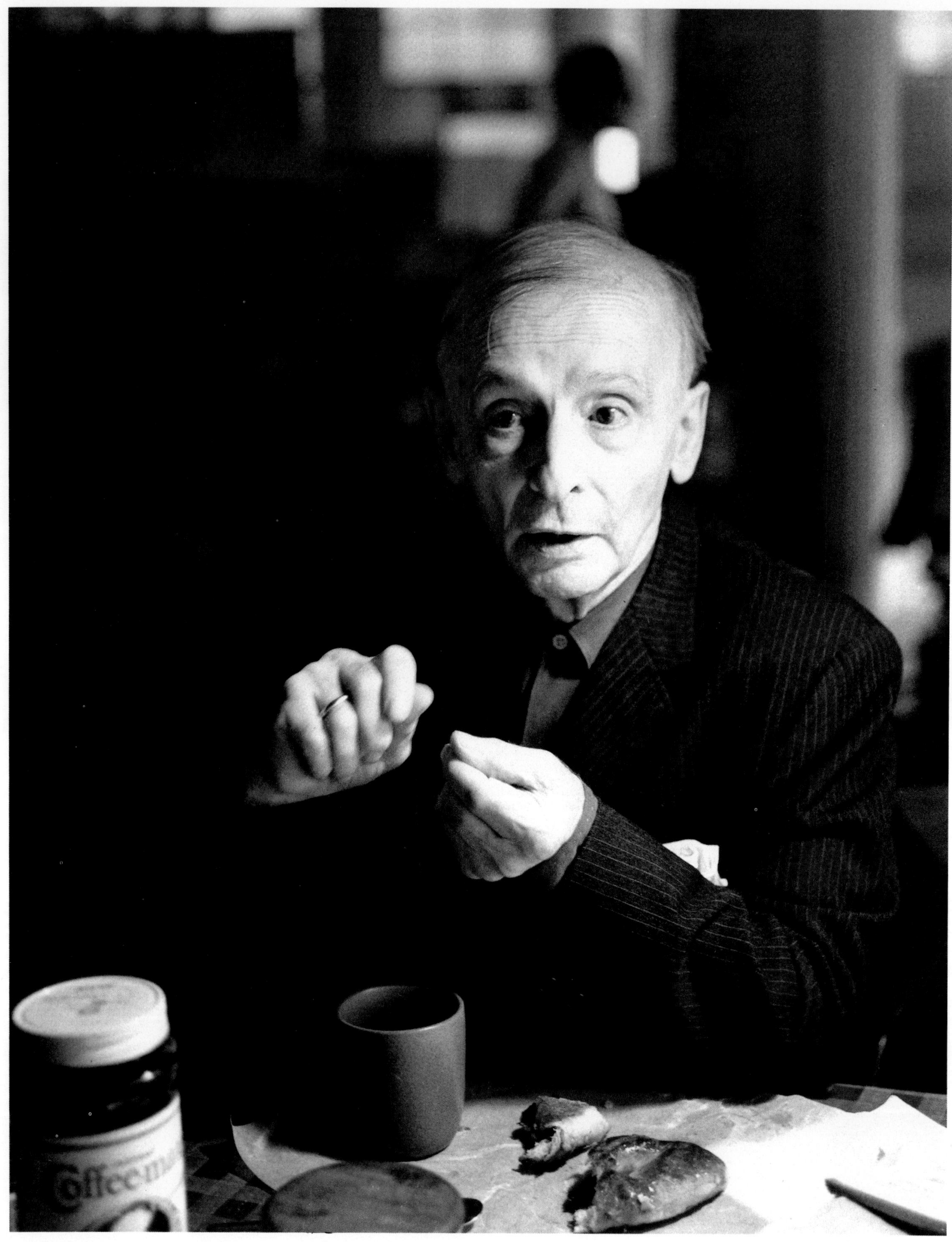

Frederick Kiesler   1965

Marisol   1965

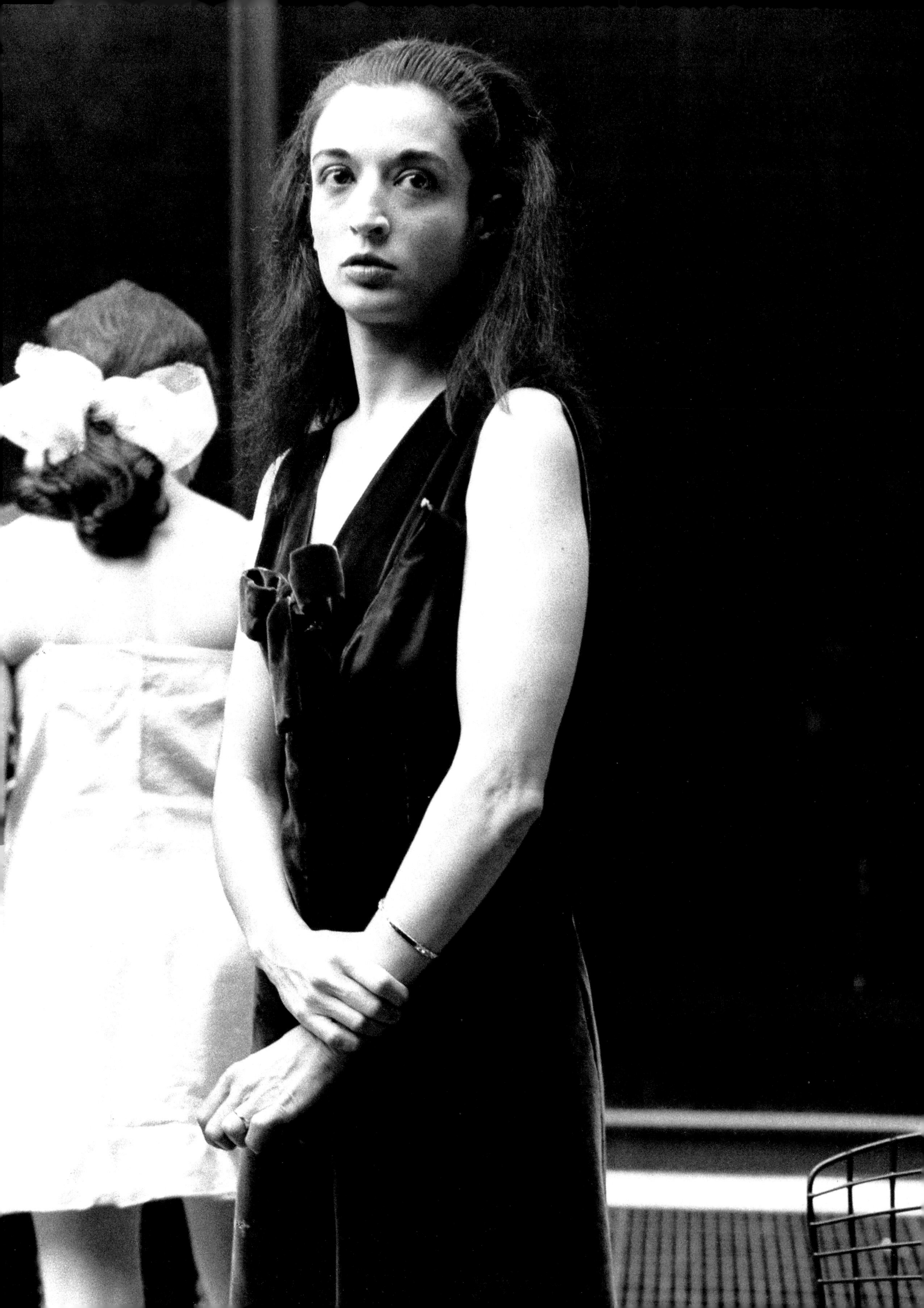

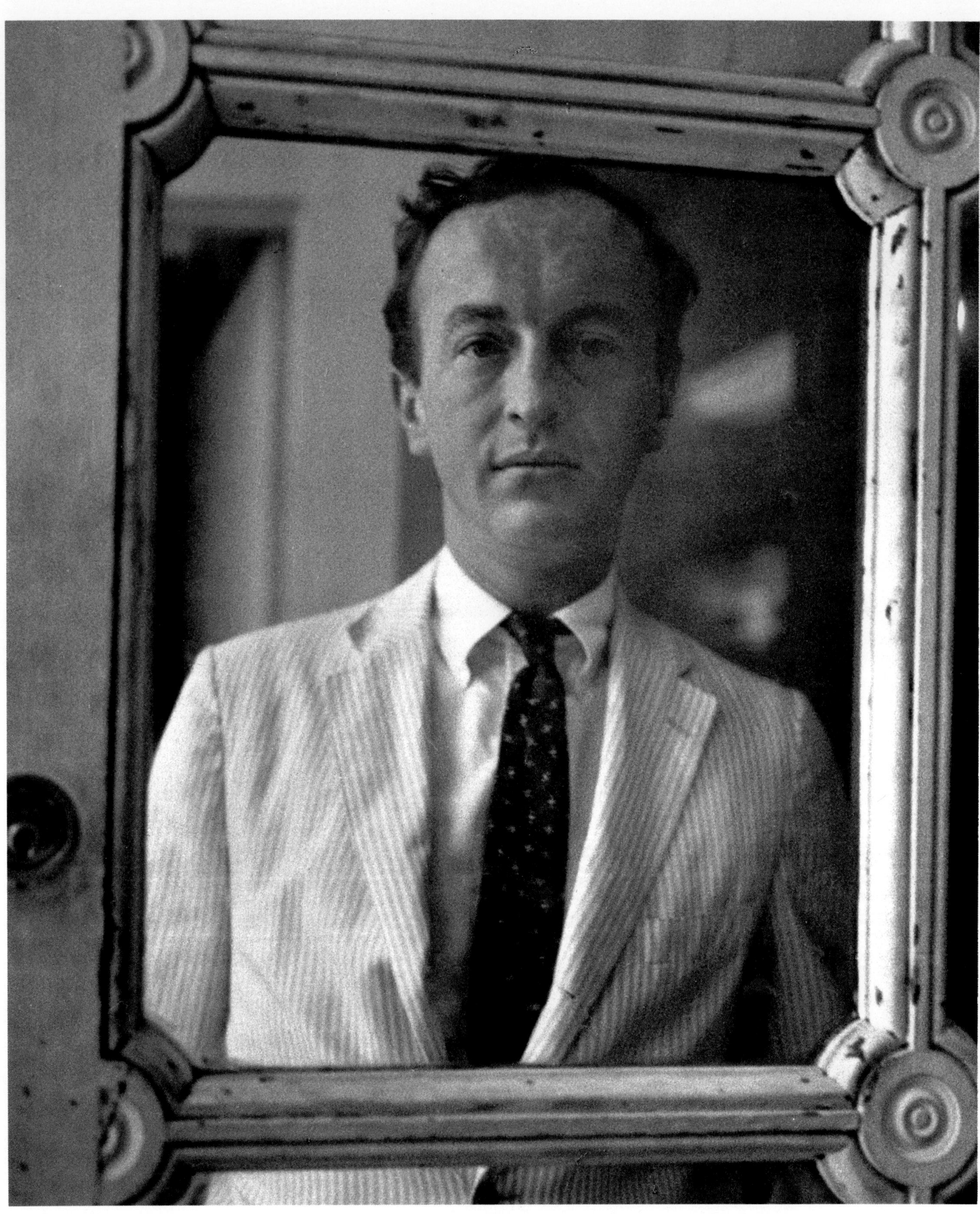

Frank O'Hara   1965

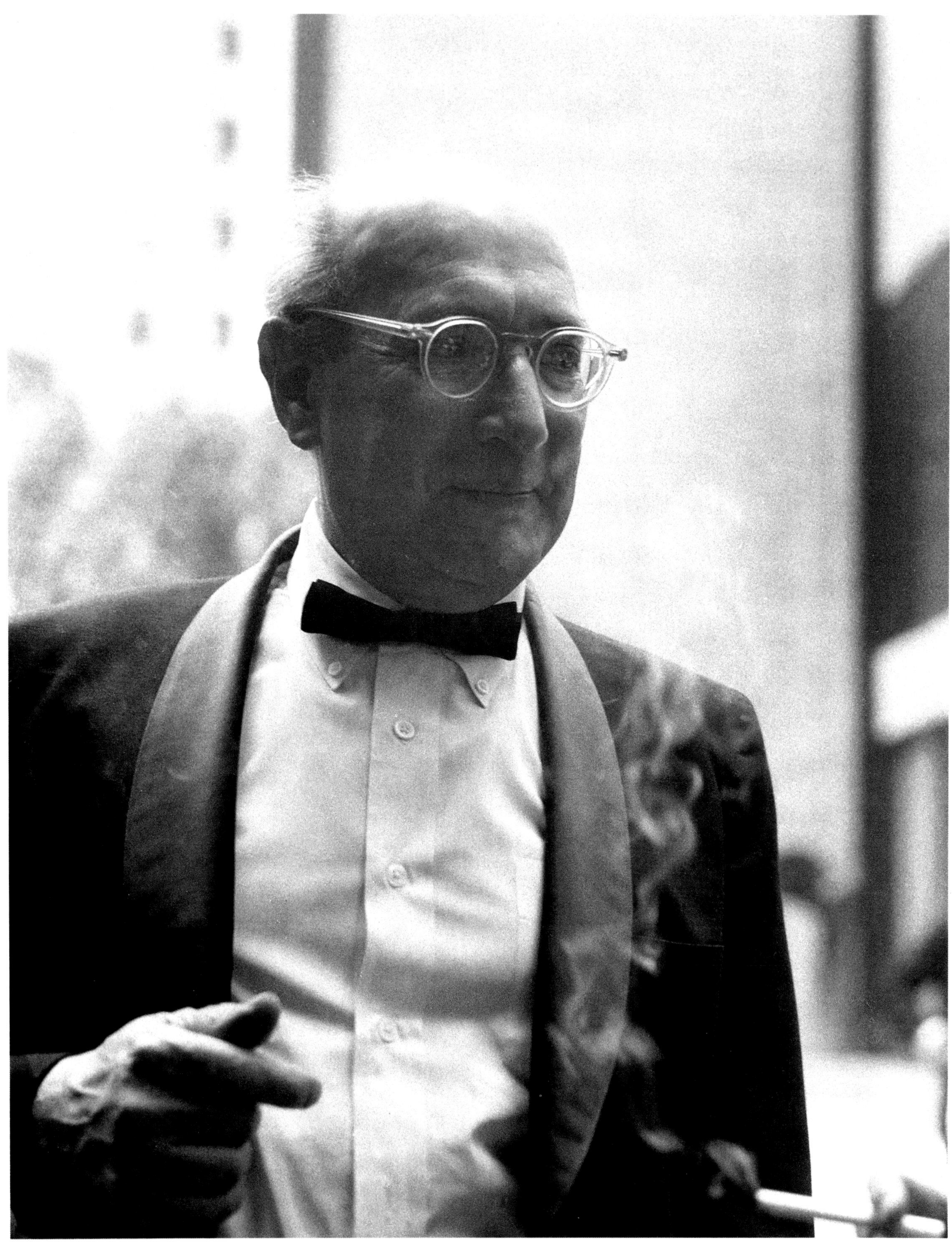

Mark Rothko   1965

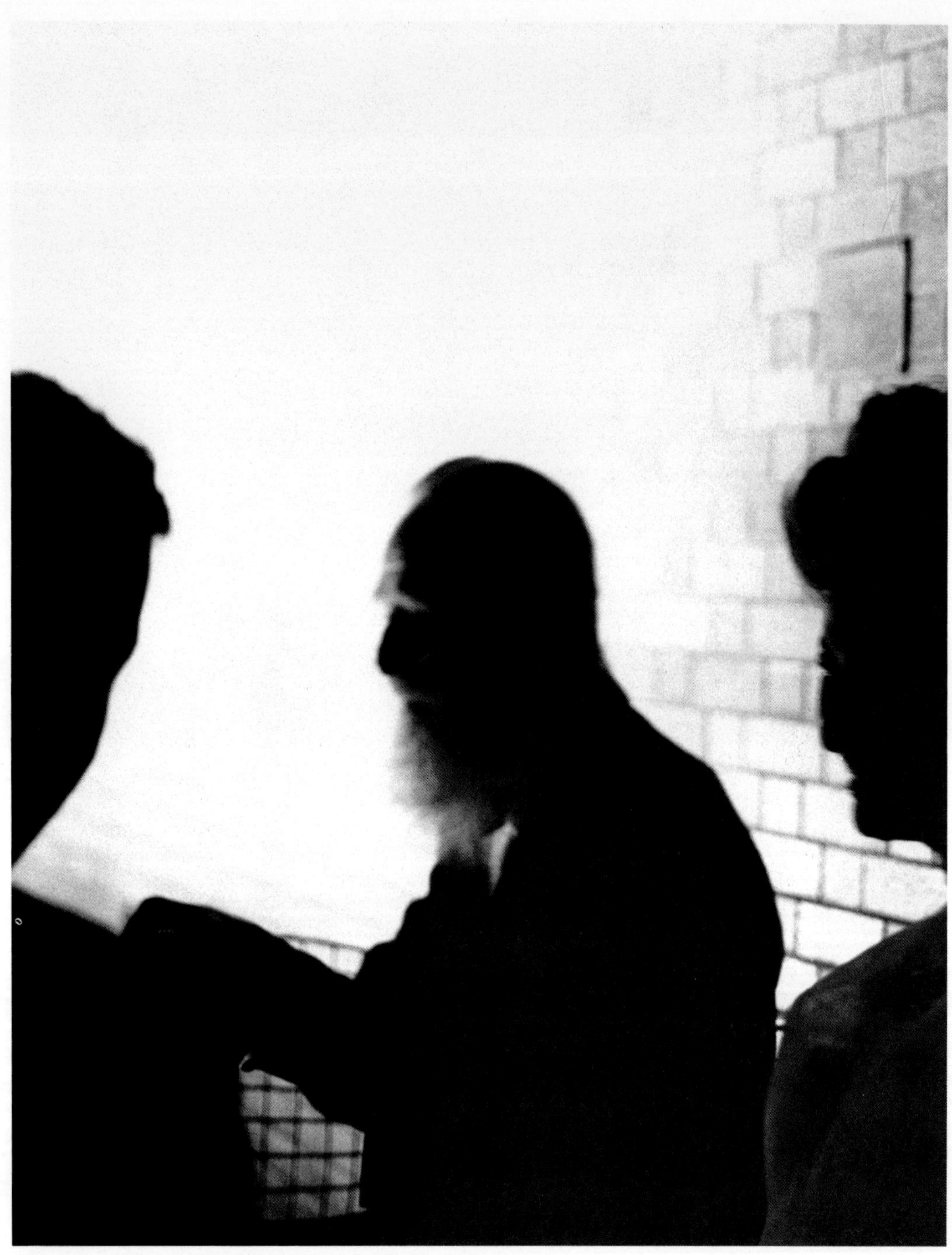

Edward Steichen   1965

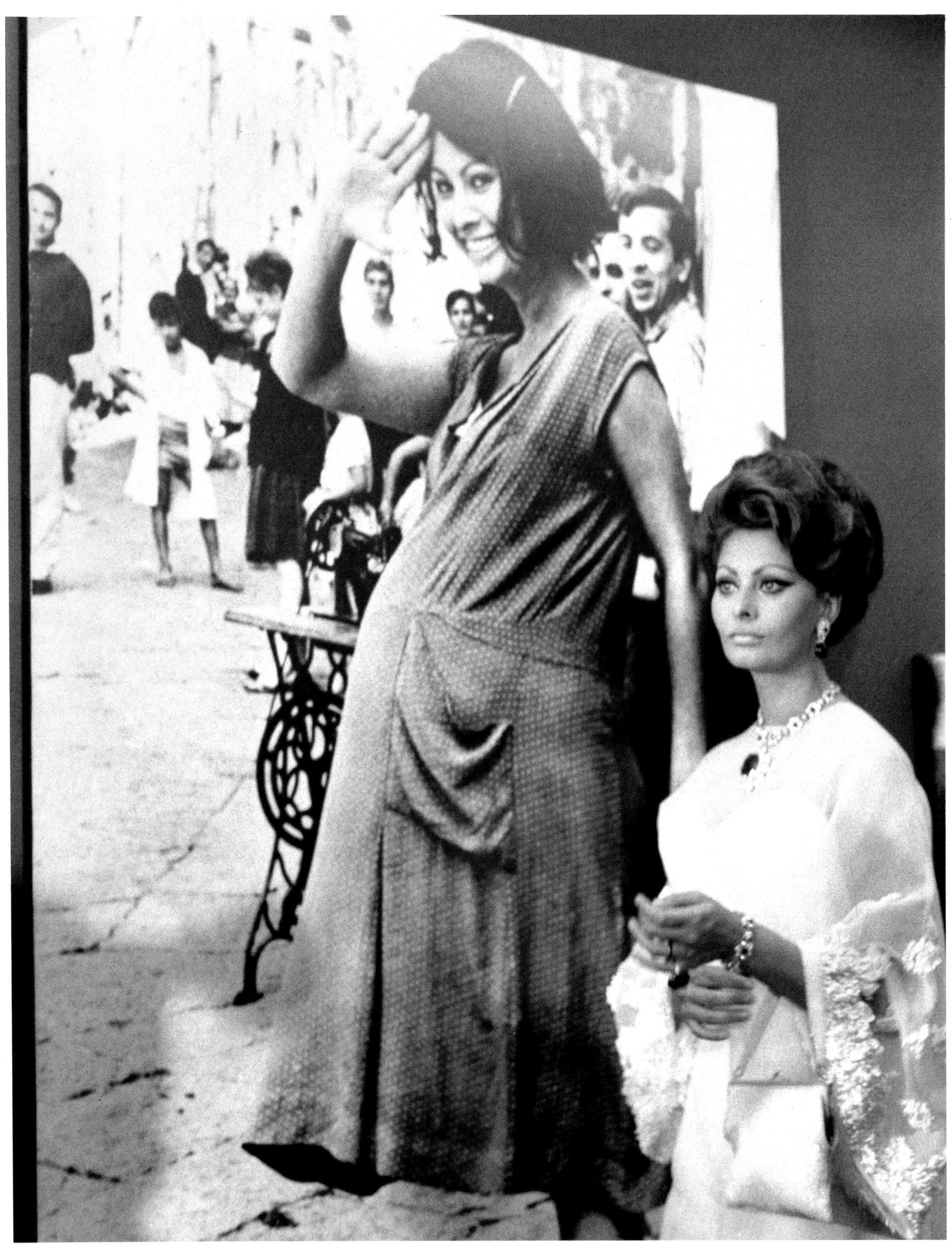

Sophia Loren   1965

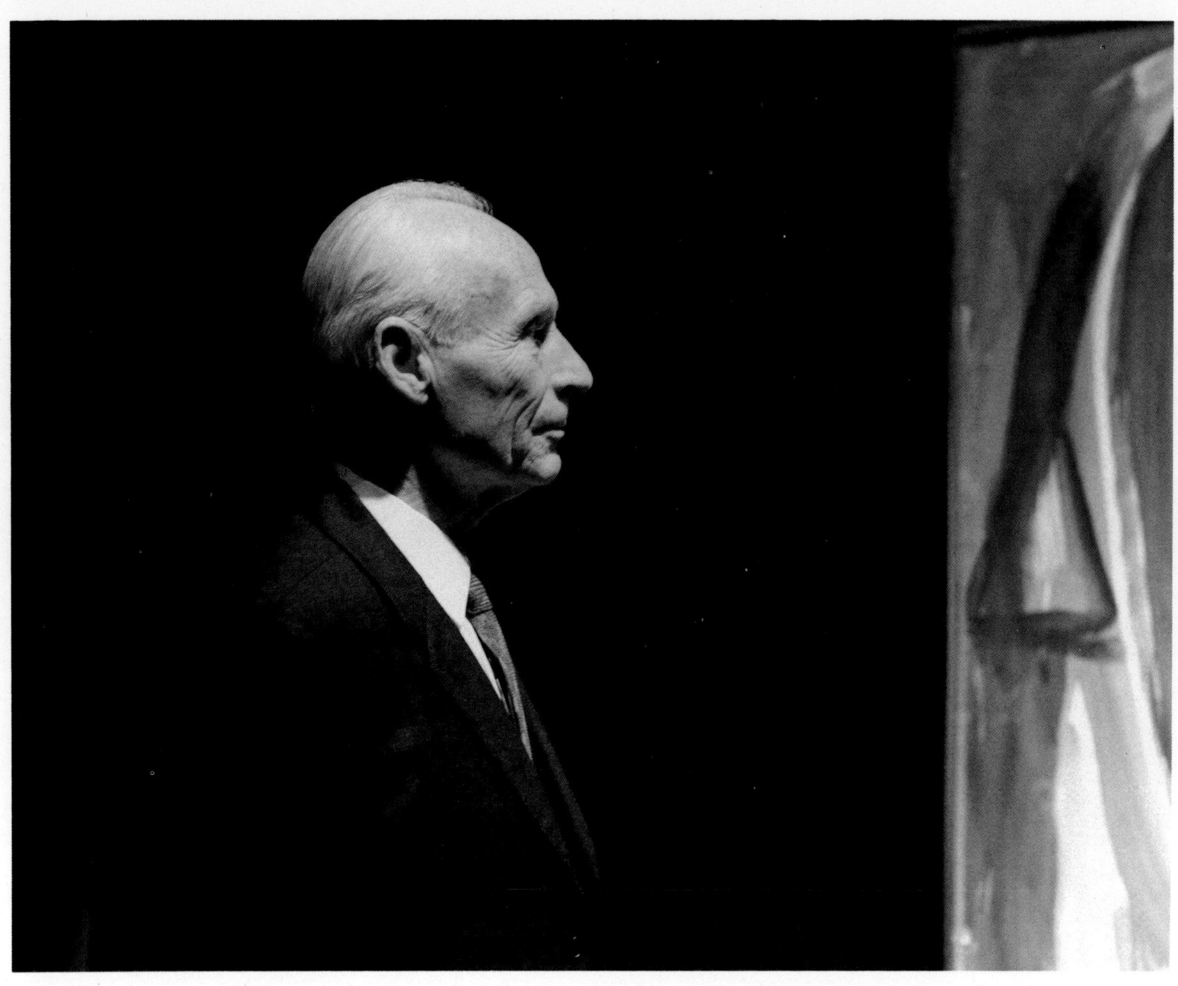

Bram van Velde   1968

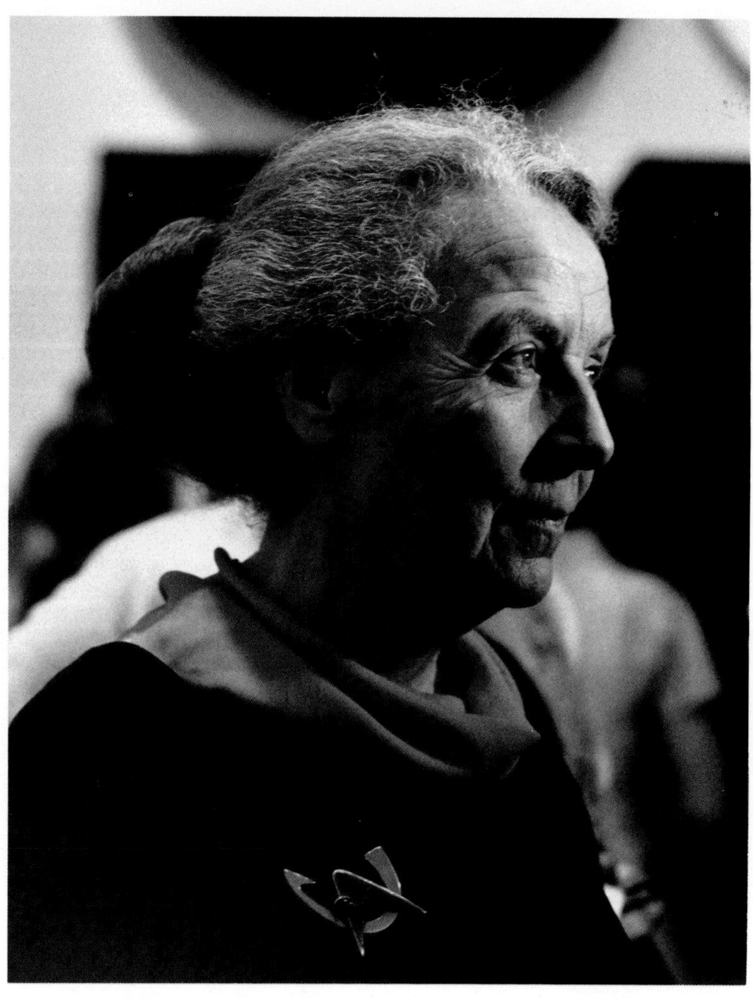

Sybil Moholy-Nagy   1968

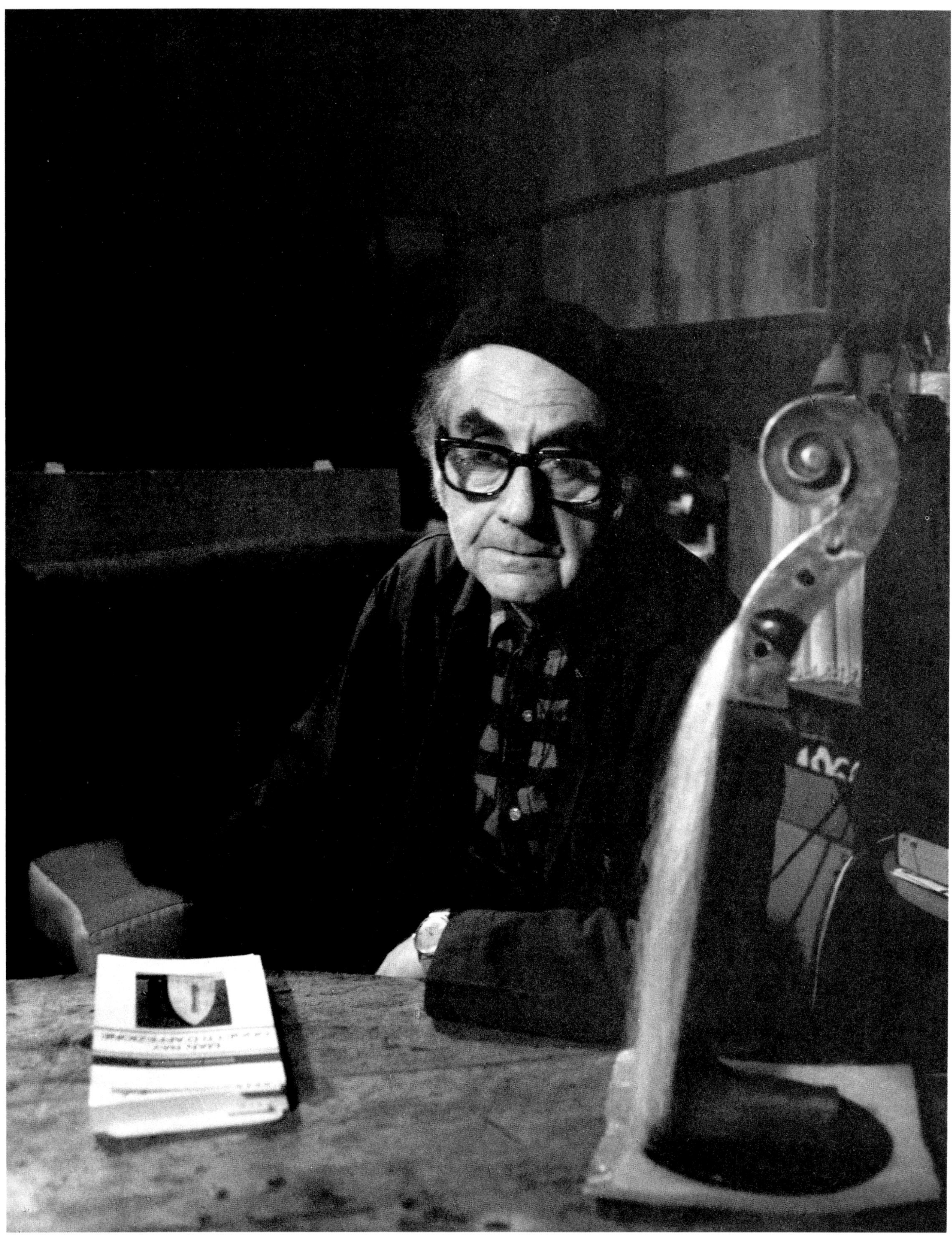

Man Ray   1970

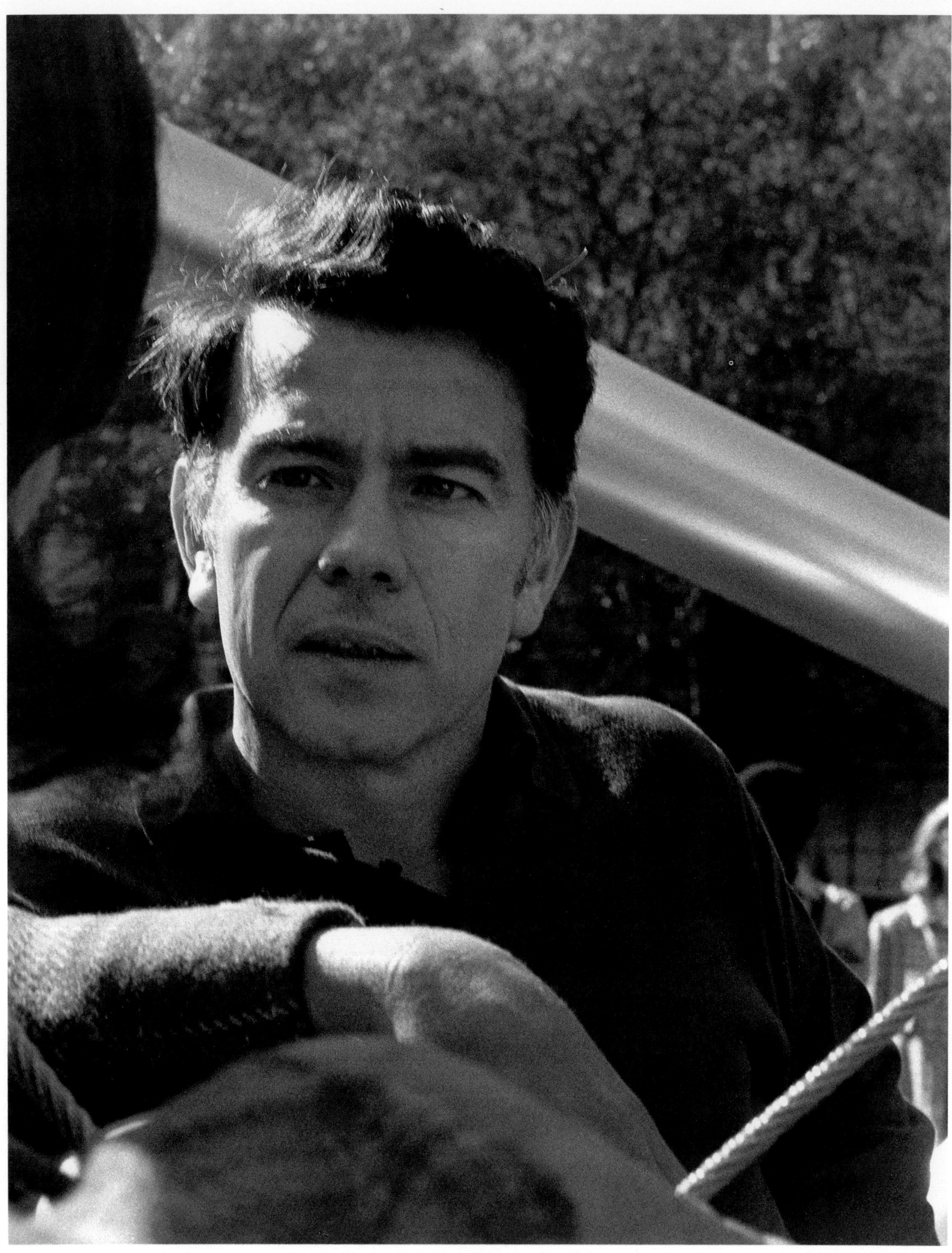

Kenneth Snelson   1968

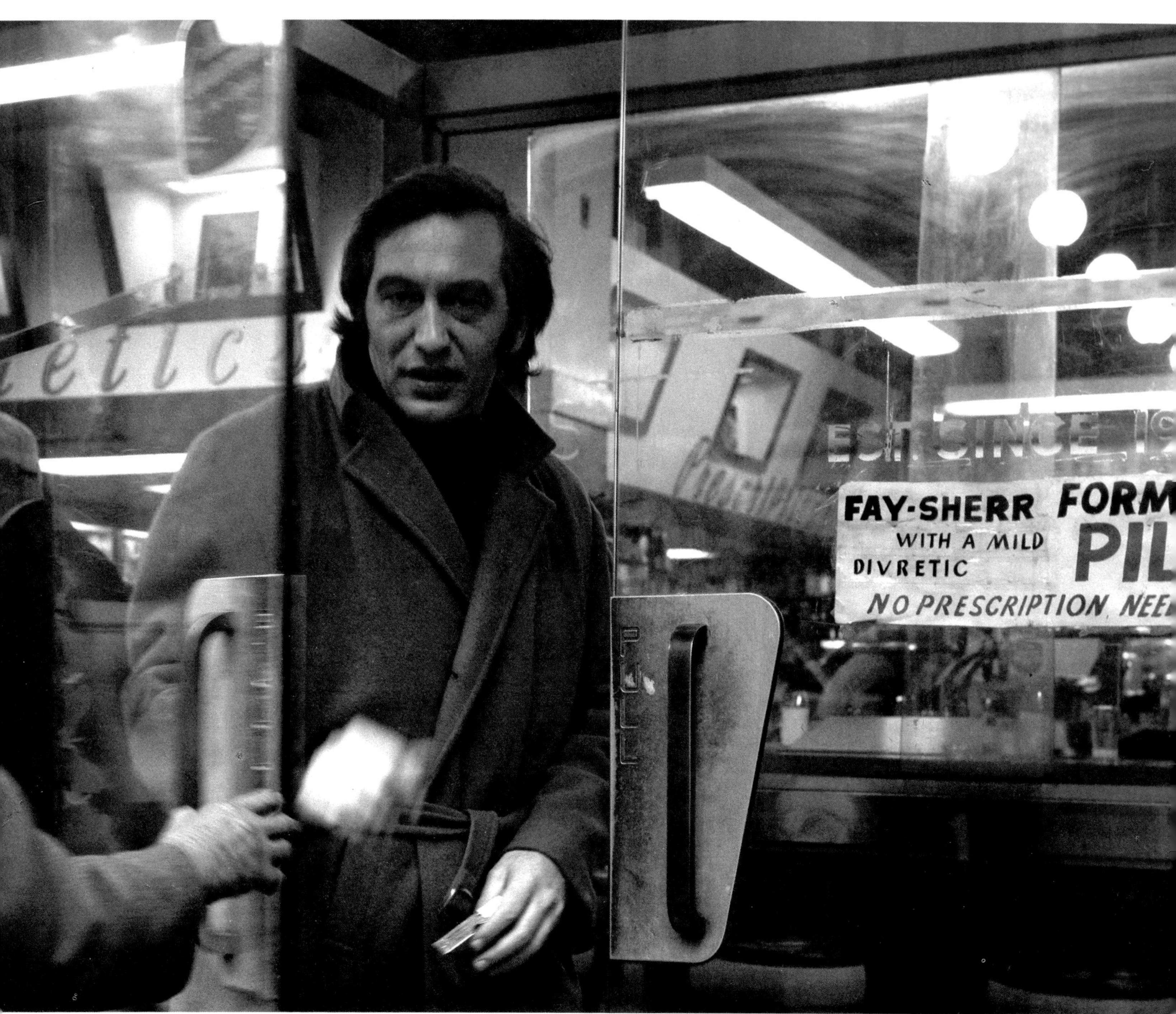

Allan d'Arcangelo   1969

W. H. Auden   1969

James Baldwin   1970

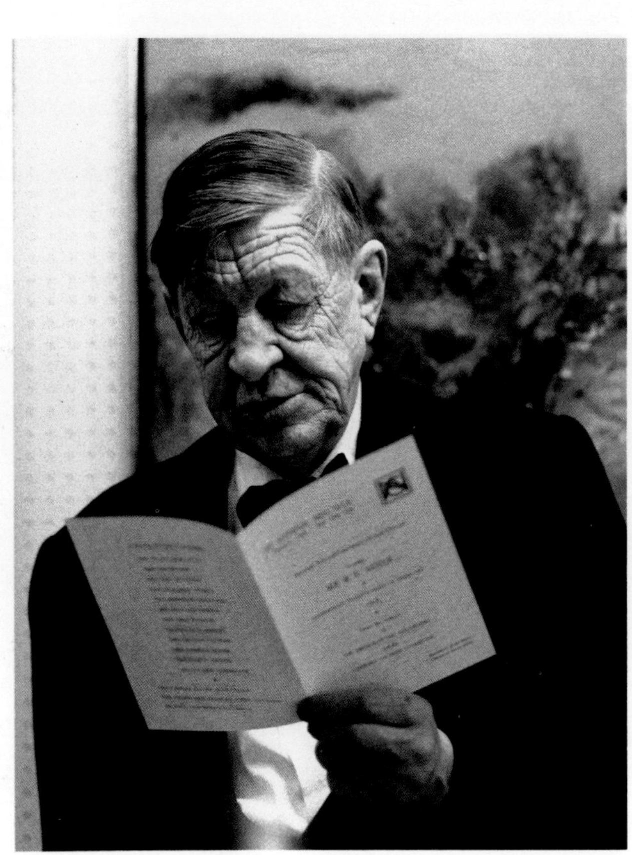

Thornton Wilder   1970

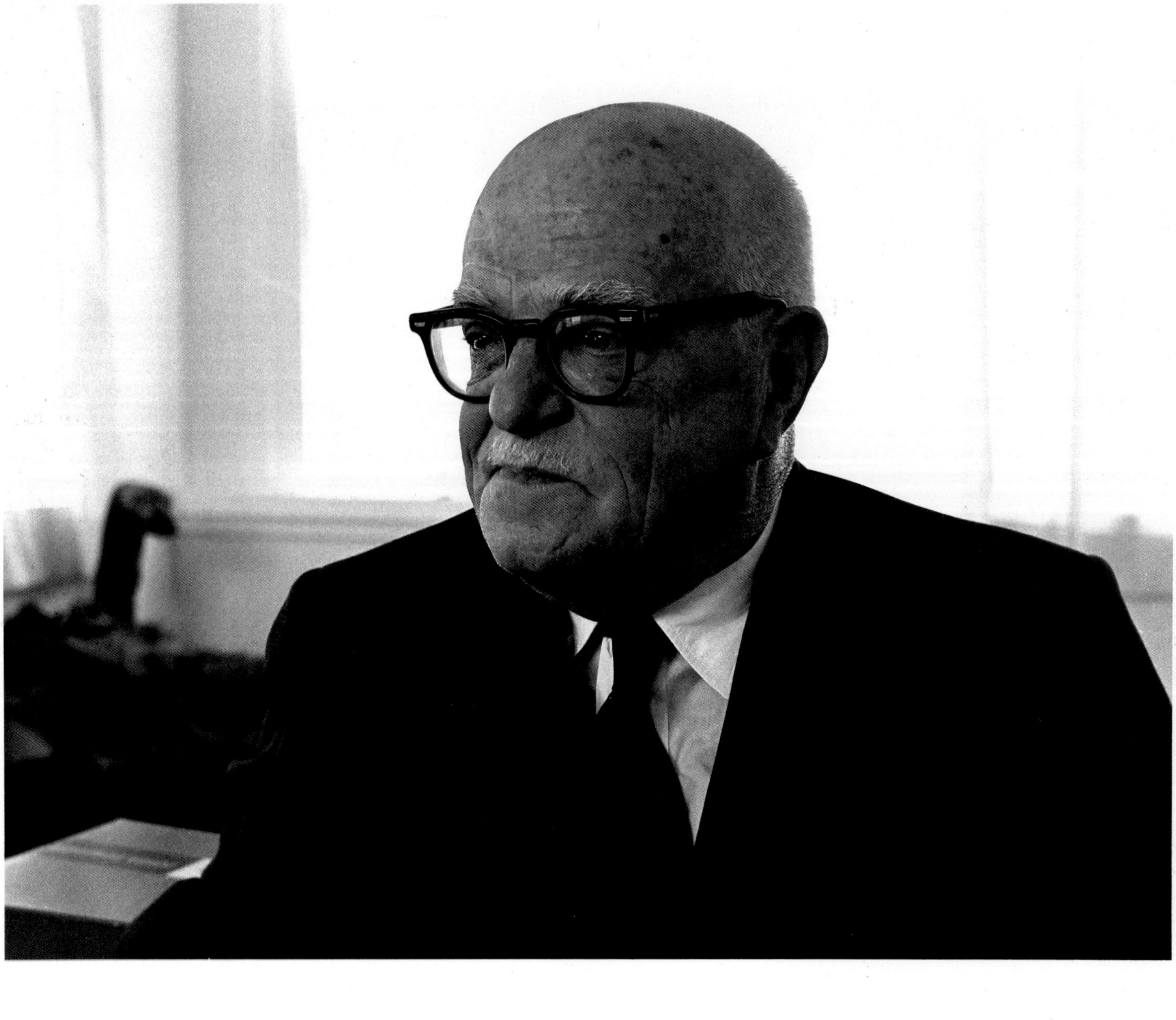

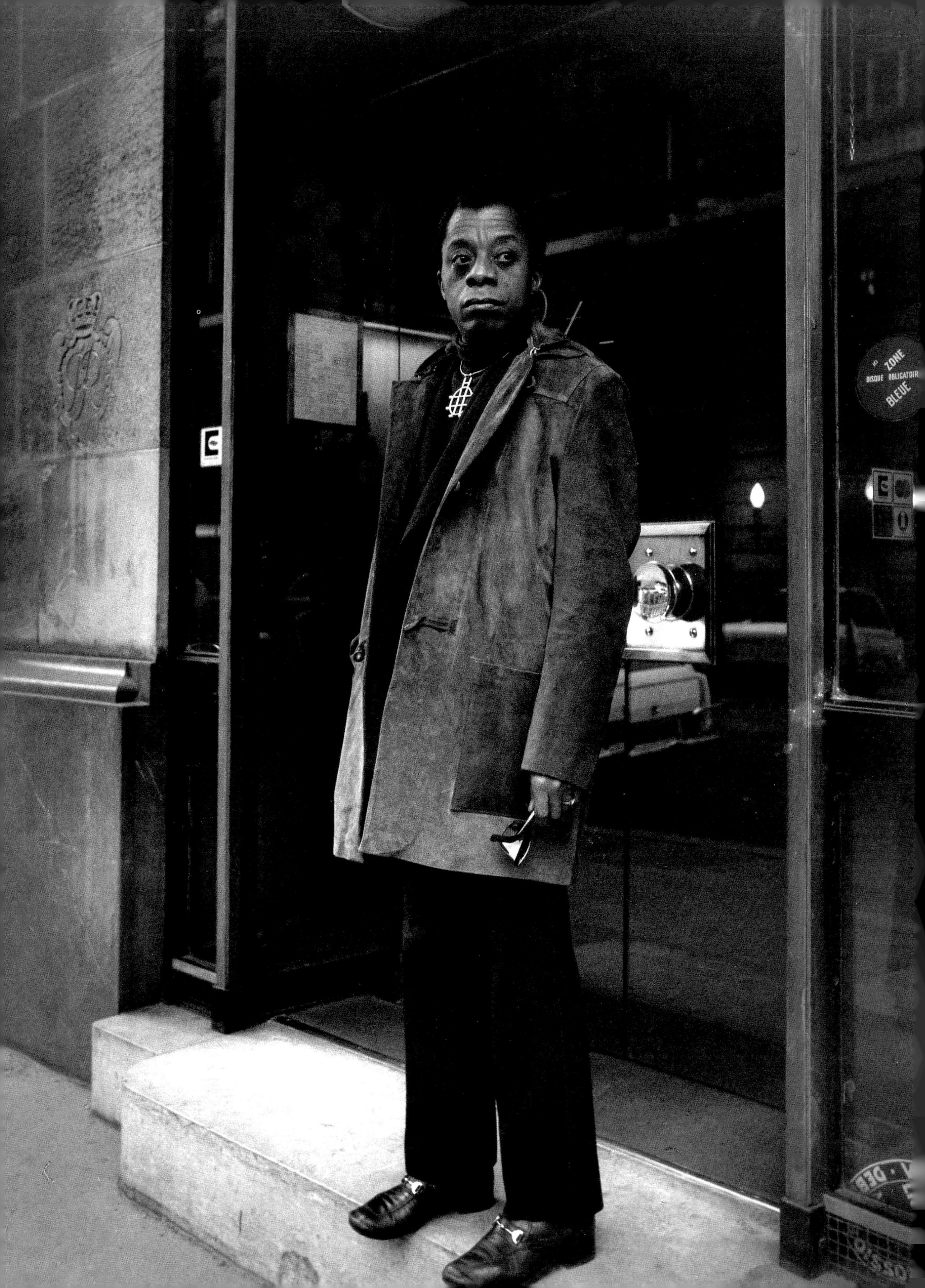

ZONE
DISQUE OBLIGATOIR
BLEUE

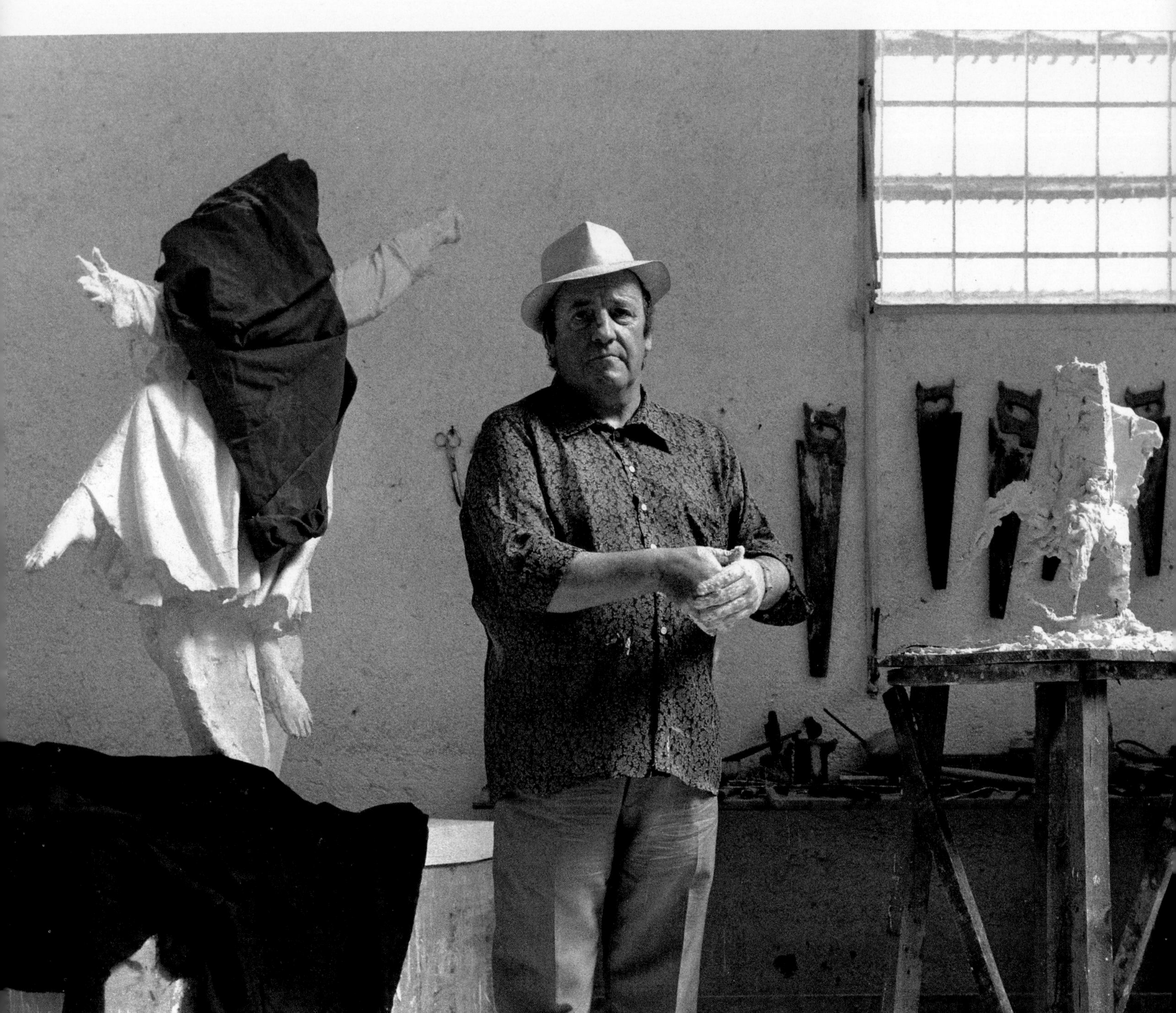

Giacomo Manzù   1969

Emilio Greco   1969

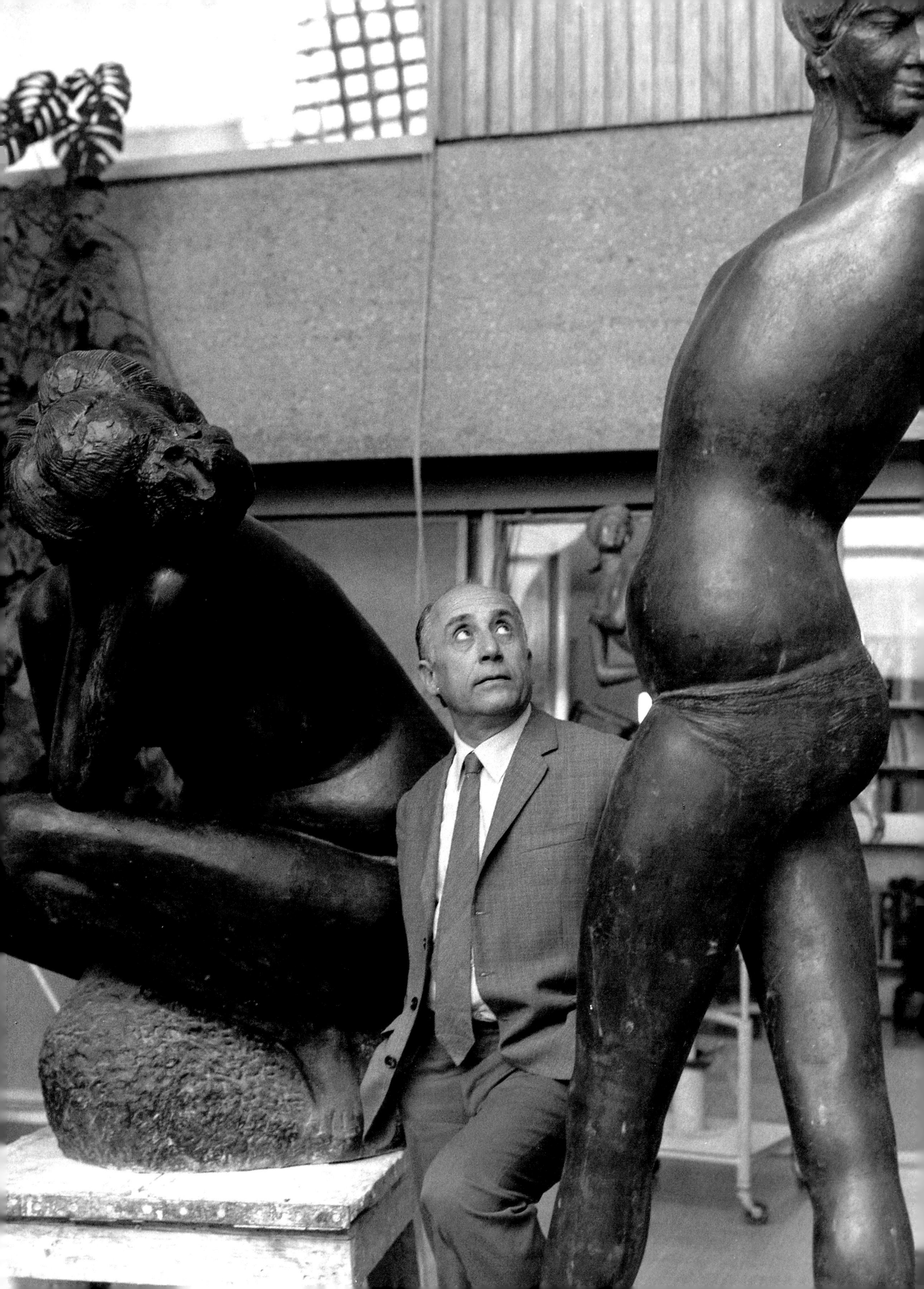

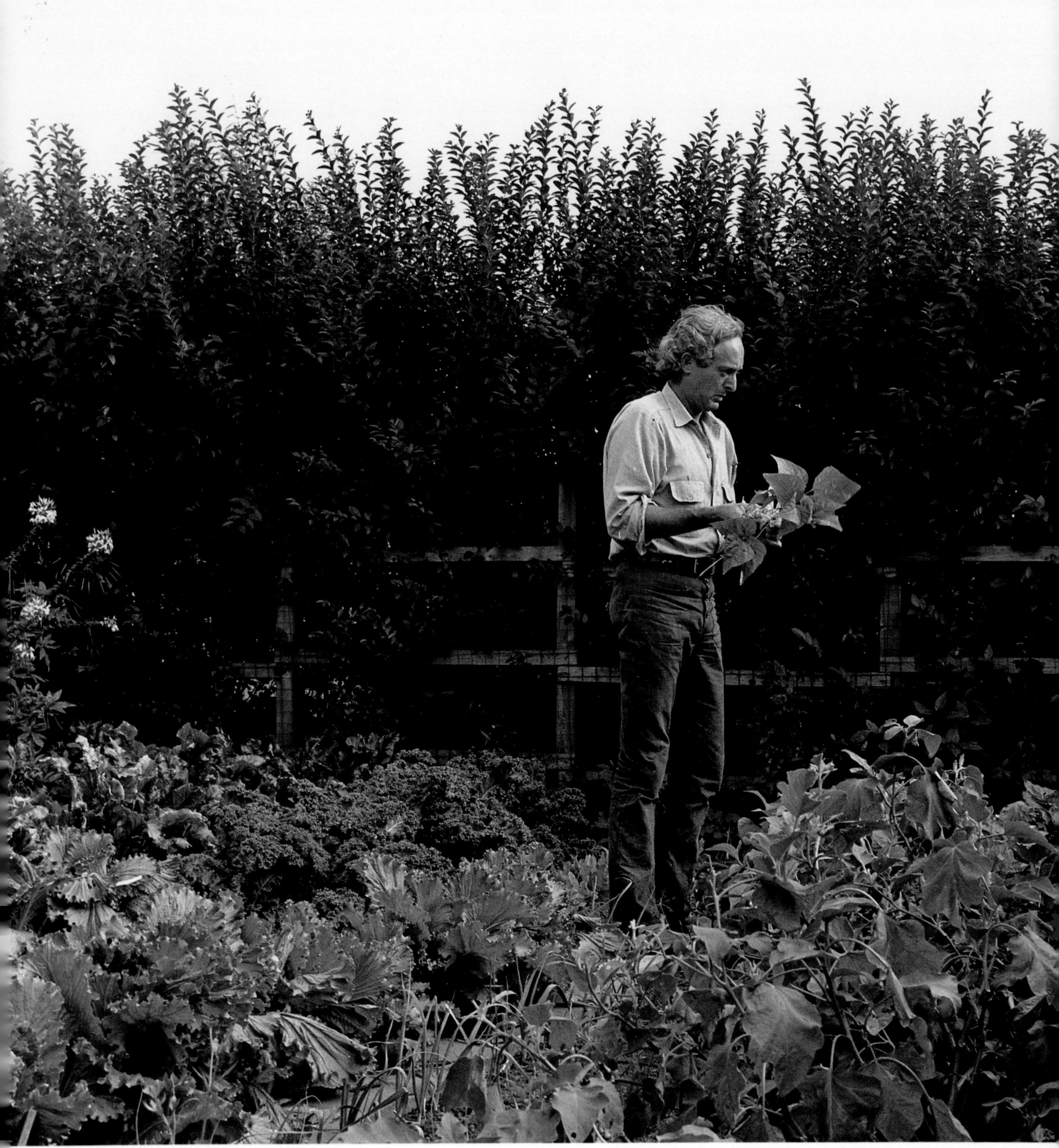

Robert Dash   1971

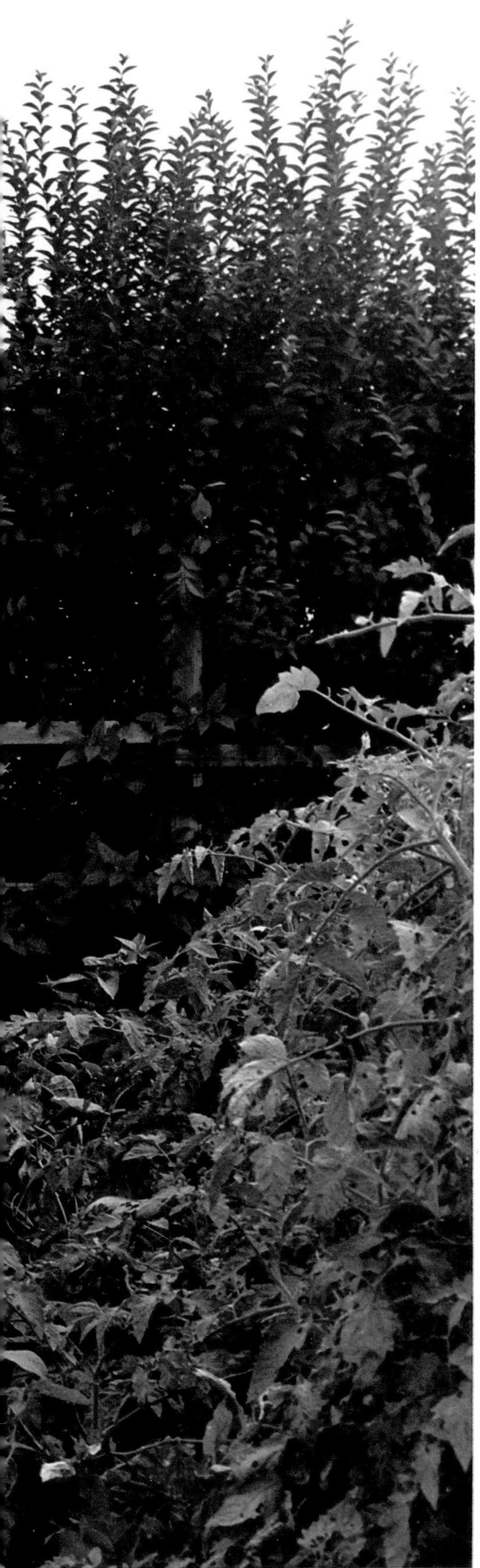

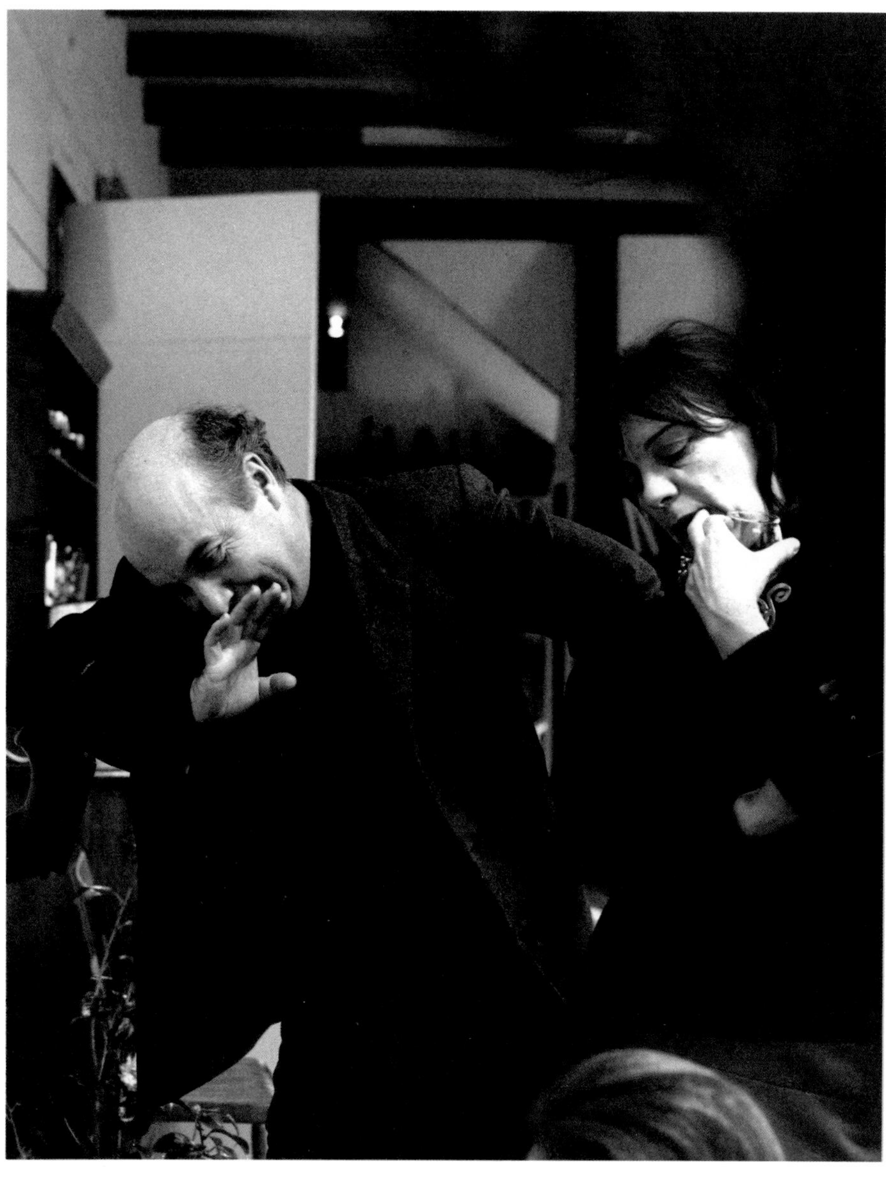

Gabriella Drudi and Toti Scialoja   1972

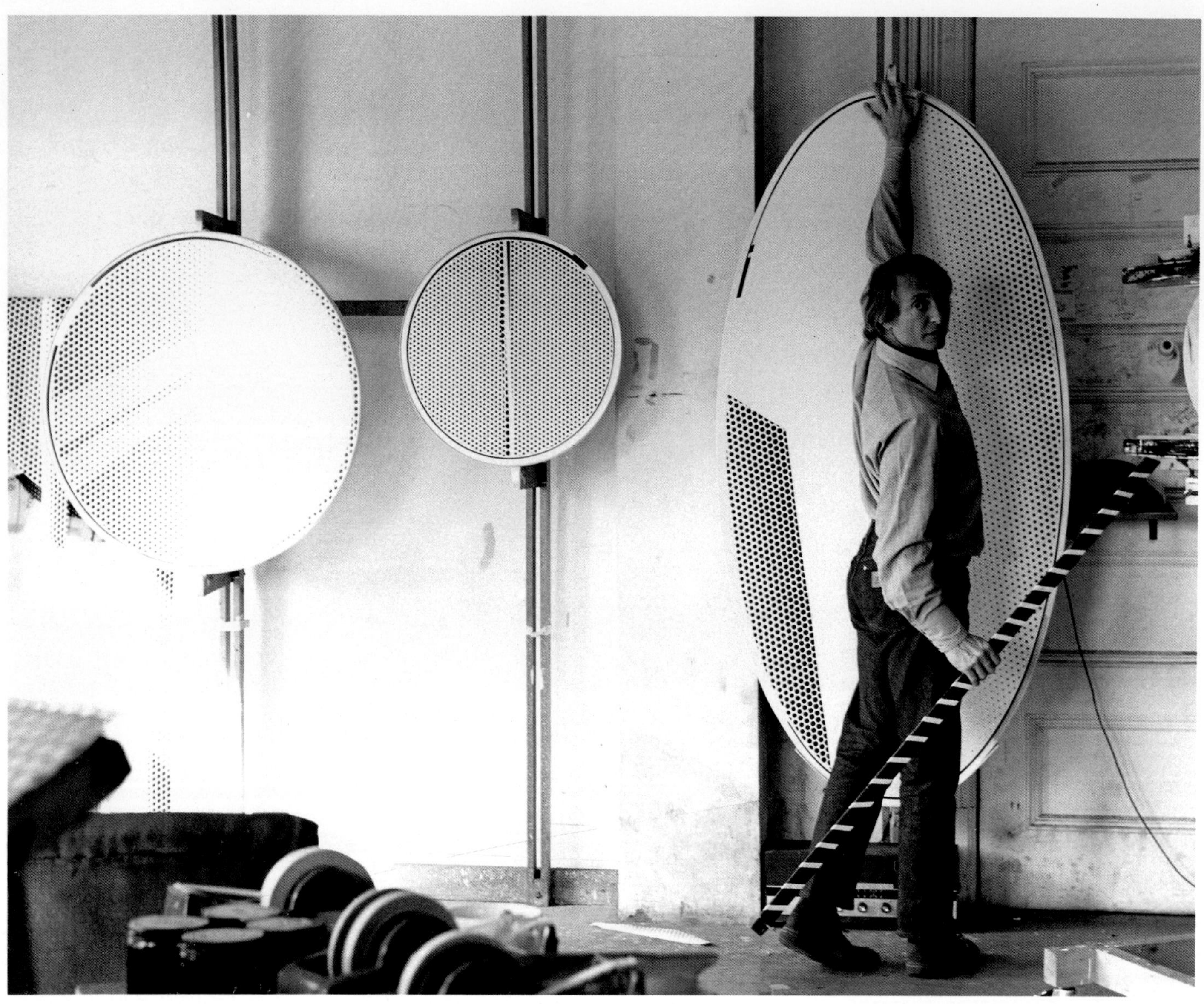

Roy Lichtenstein   1971

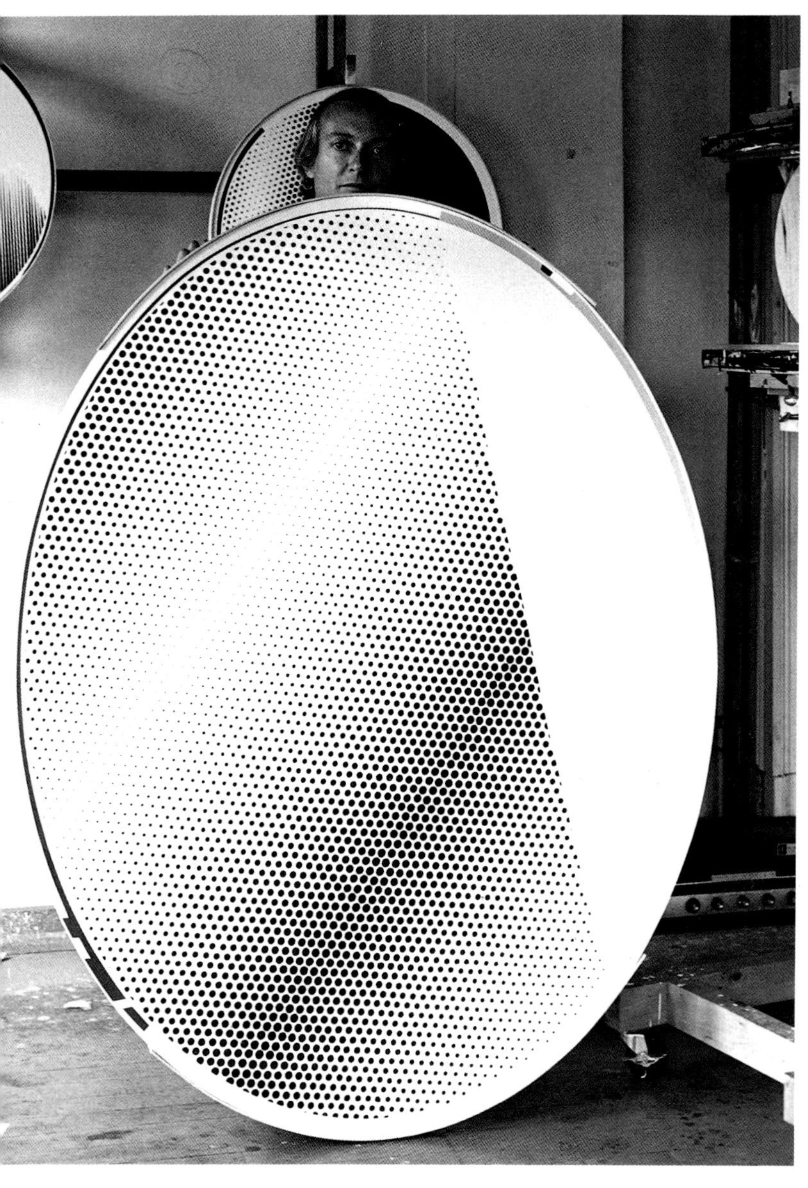
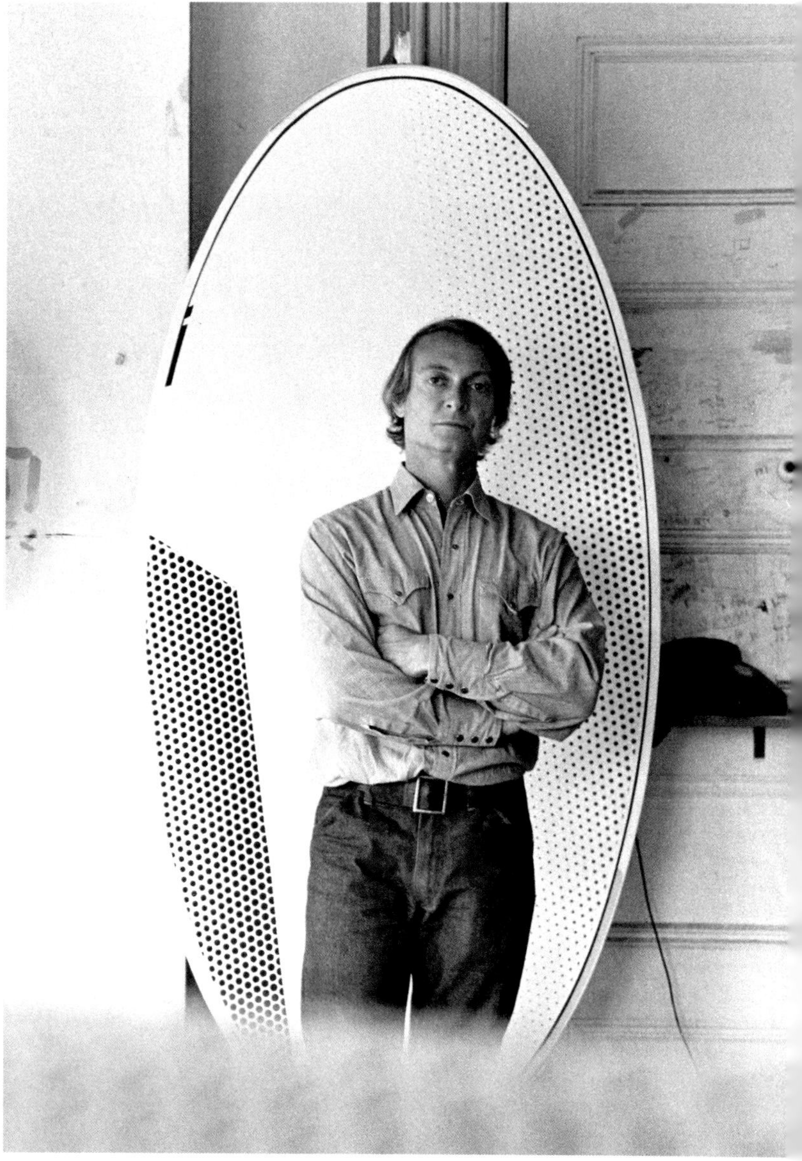

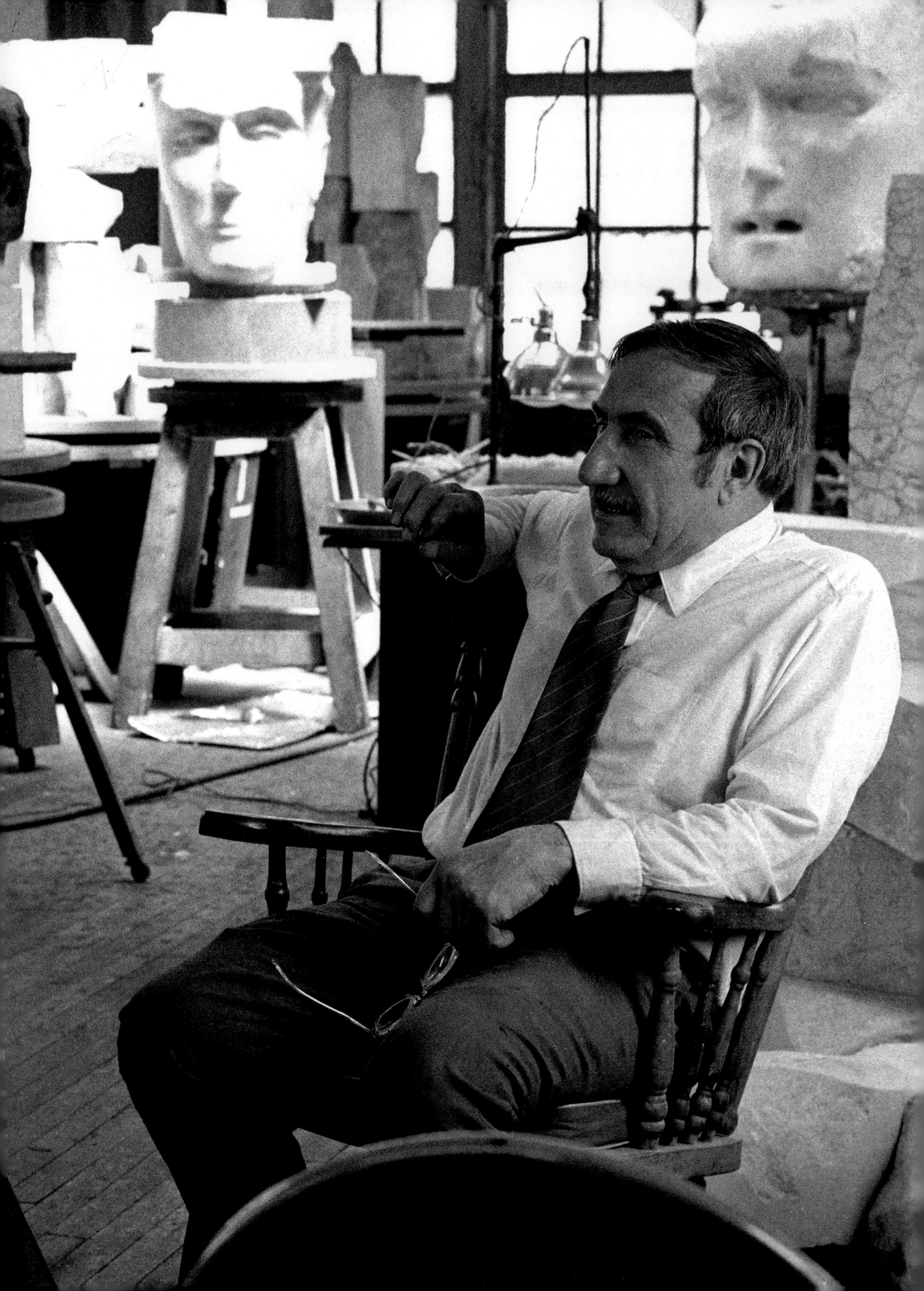

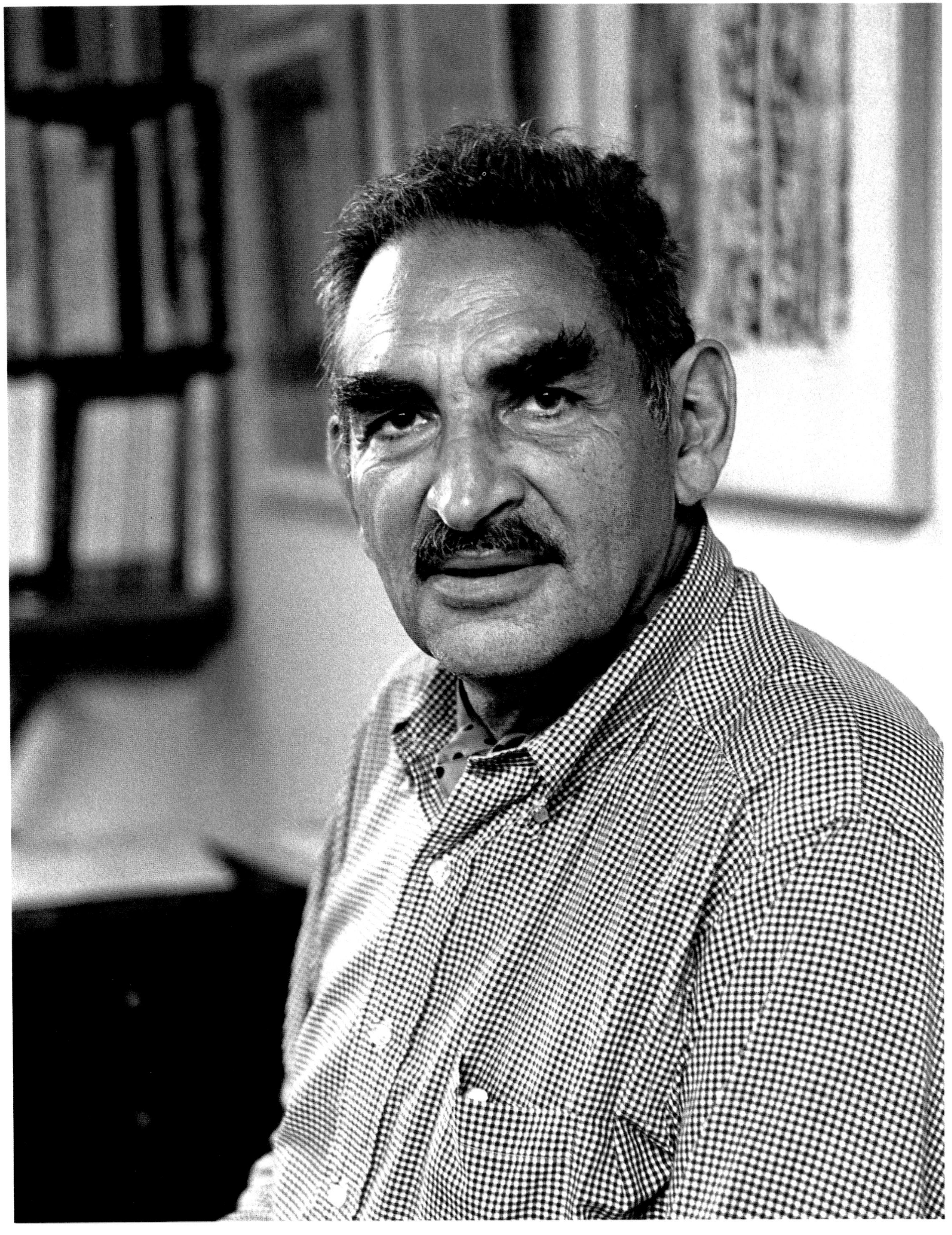

Harold Rosenberg   1971

Philip Pavia   1971

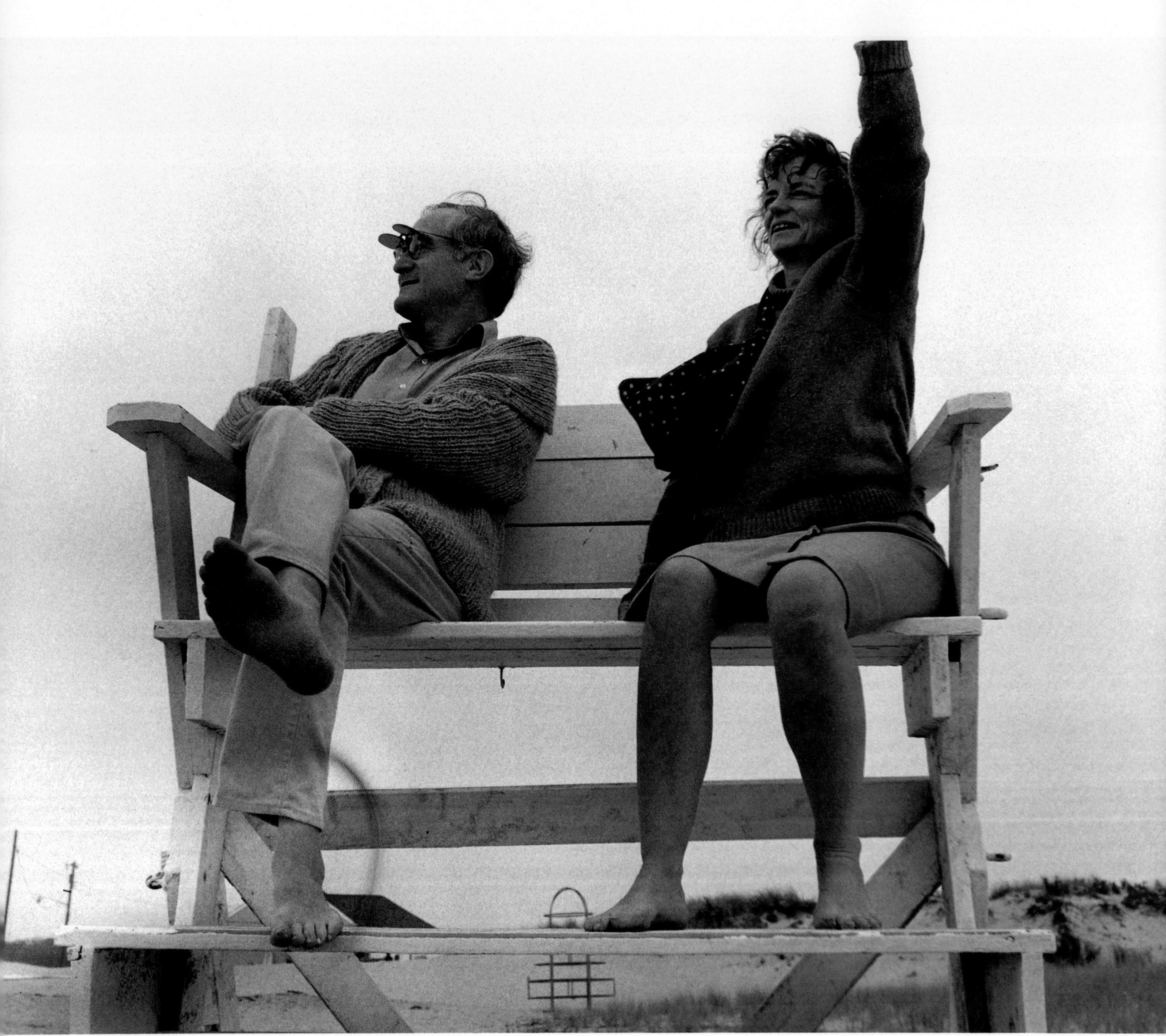

Yvonne Hagen and Bob Fabian   1971

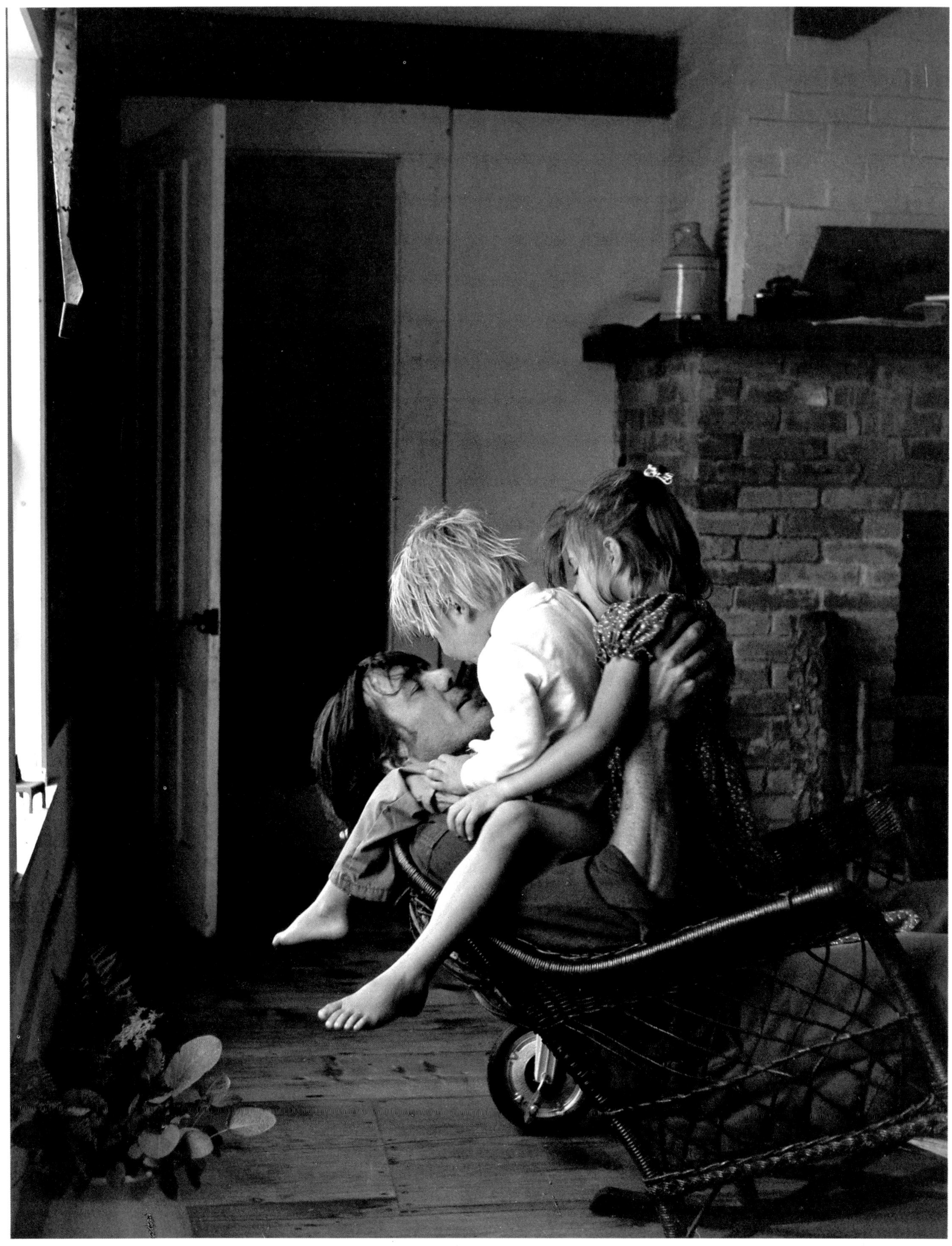

Galway Kinnell   1971

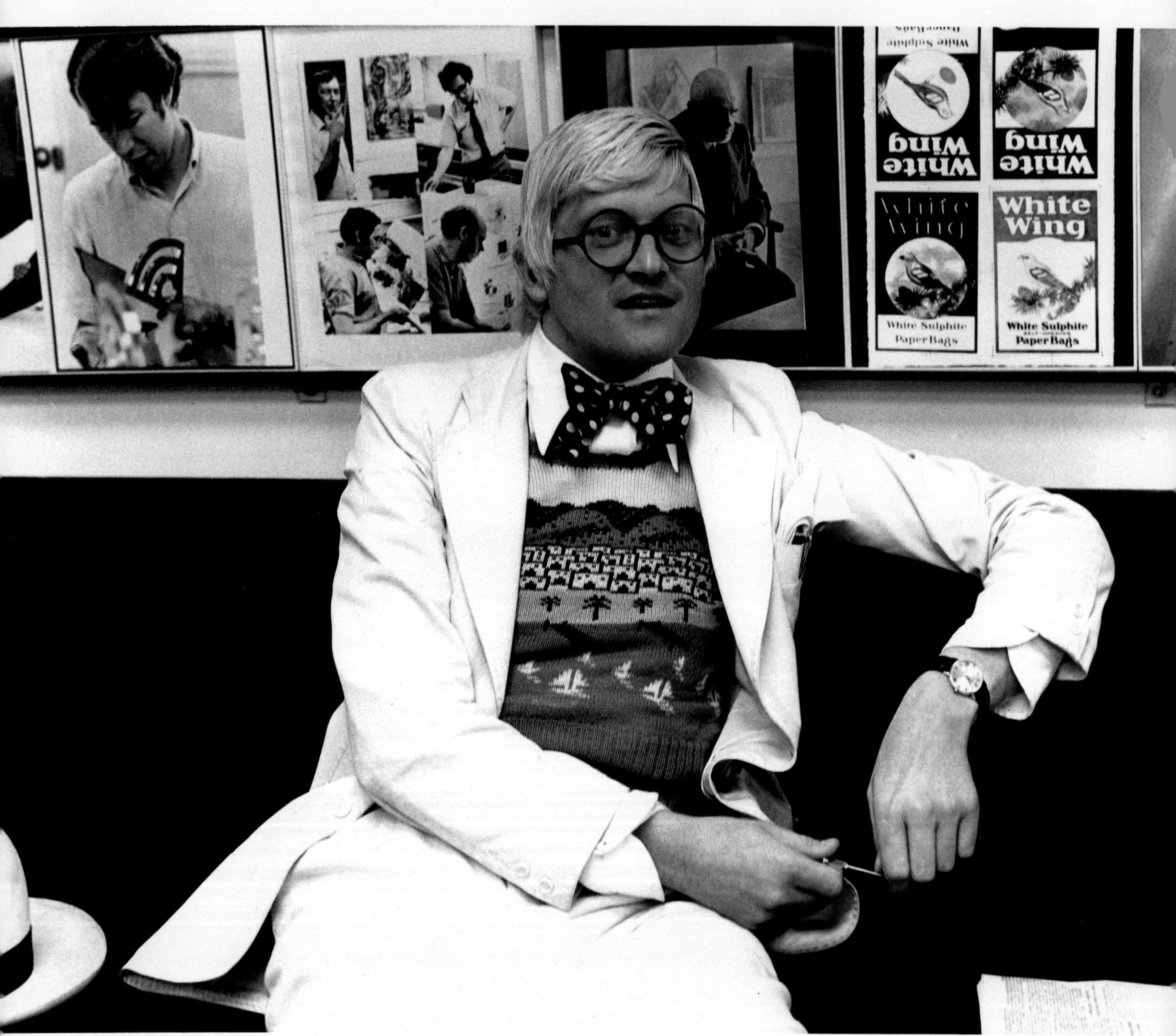

David Hockney   1973

Tony Stubbing   1970

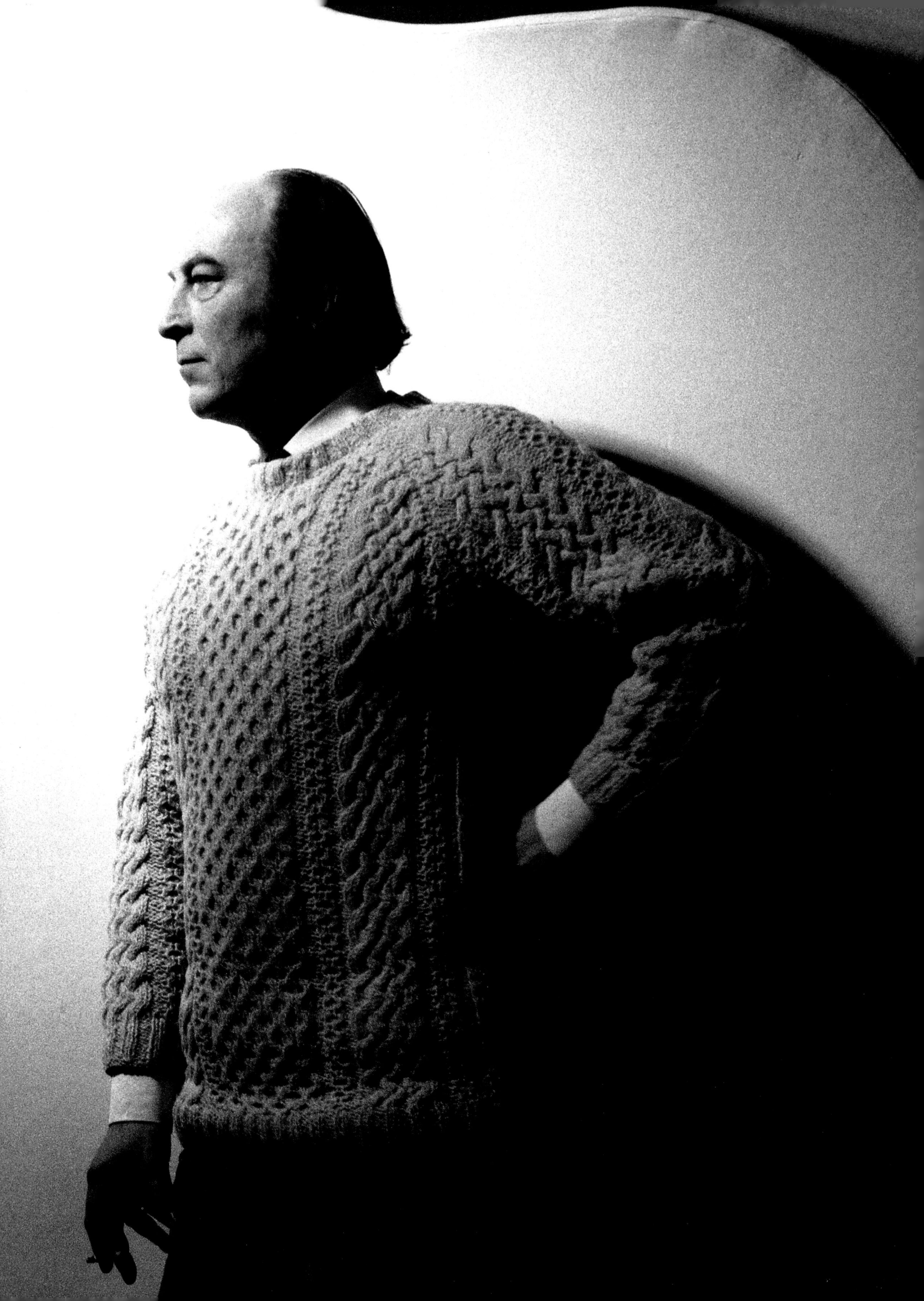

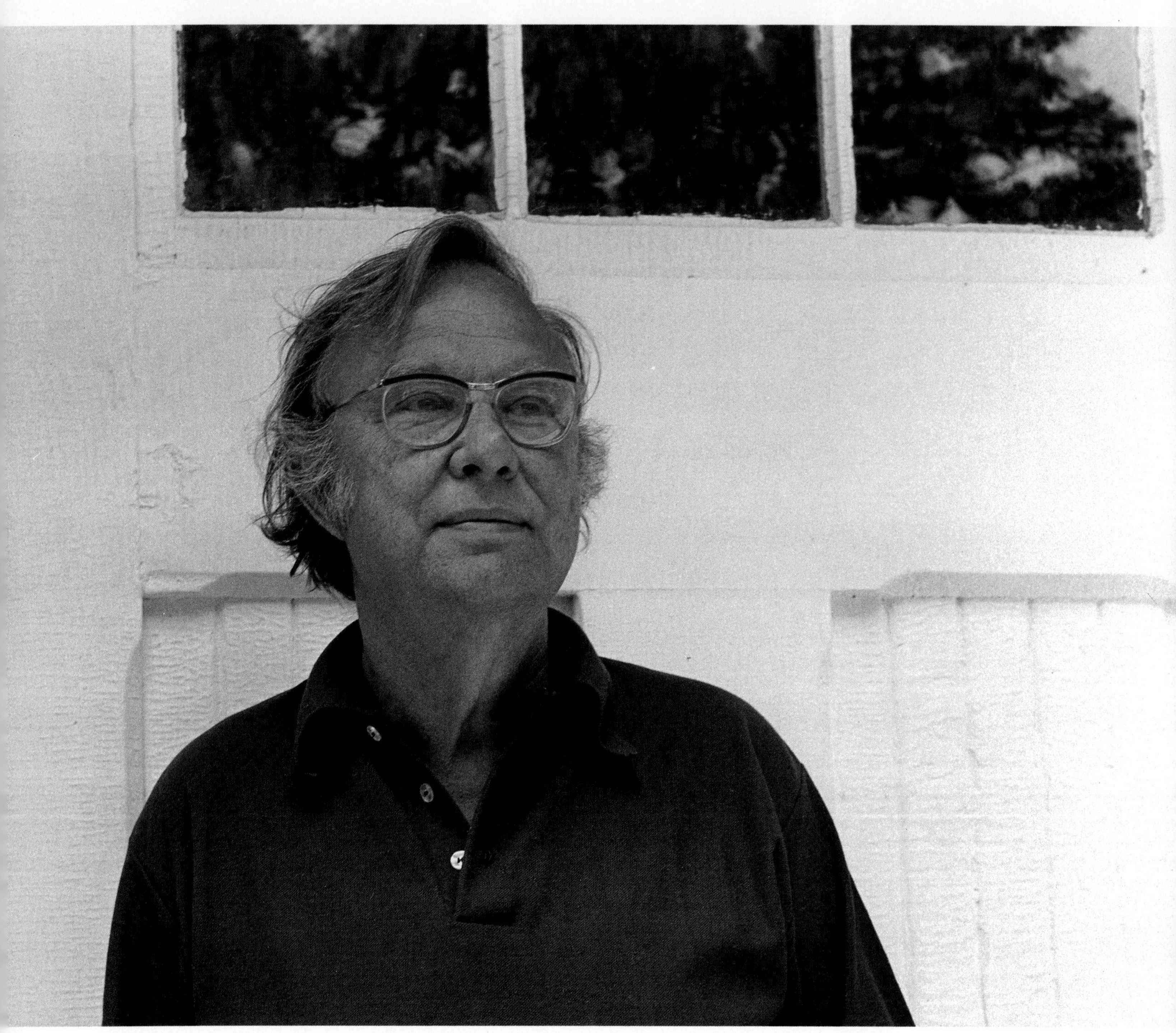

Robert Motherwell   1973

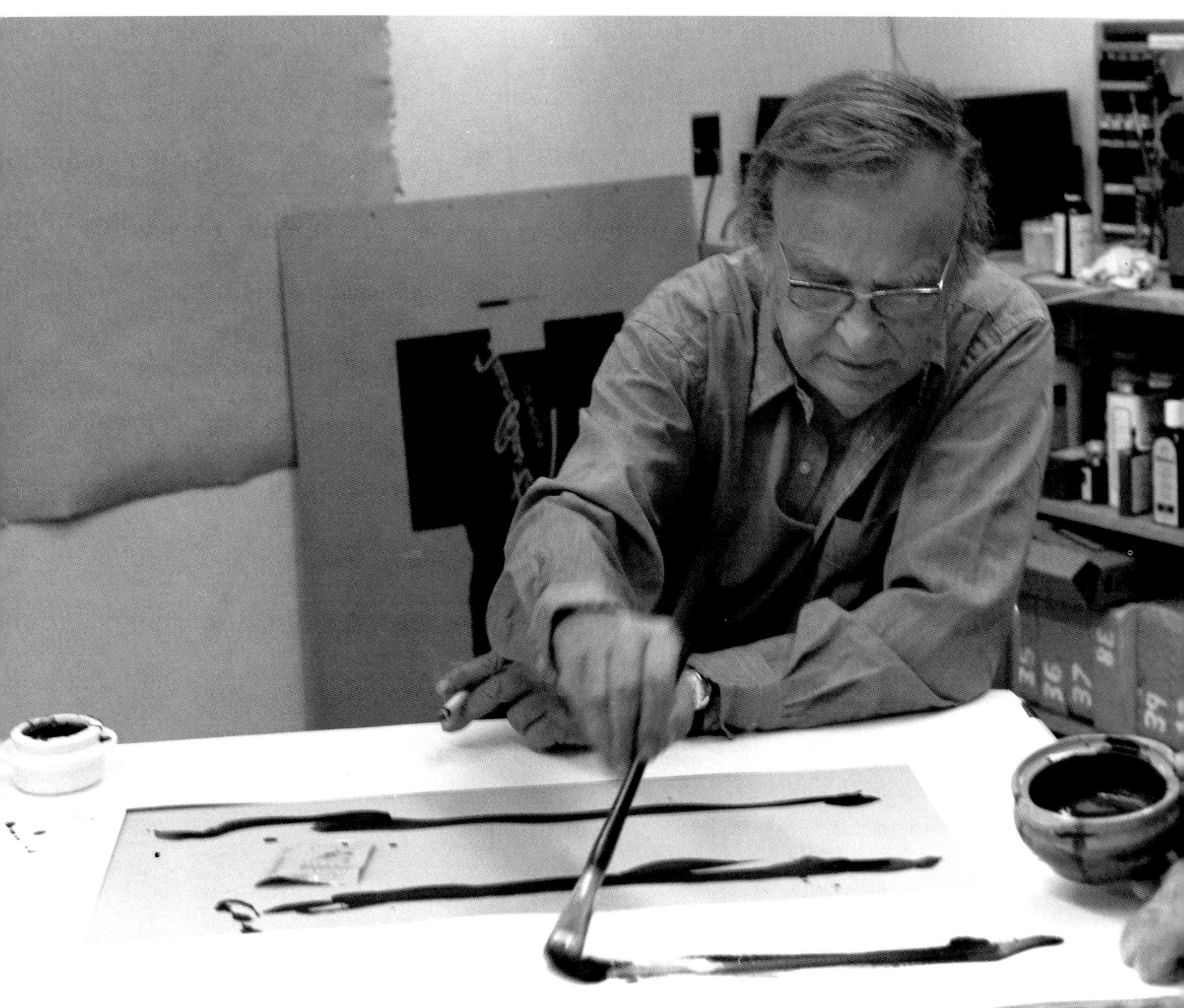

Robert Motherwell   1974

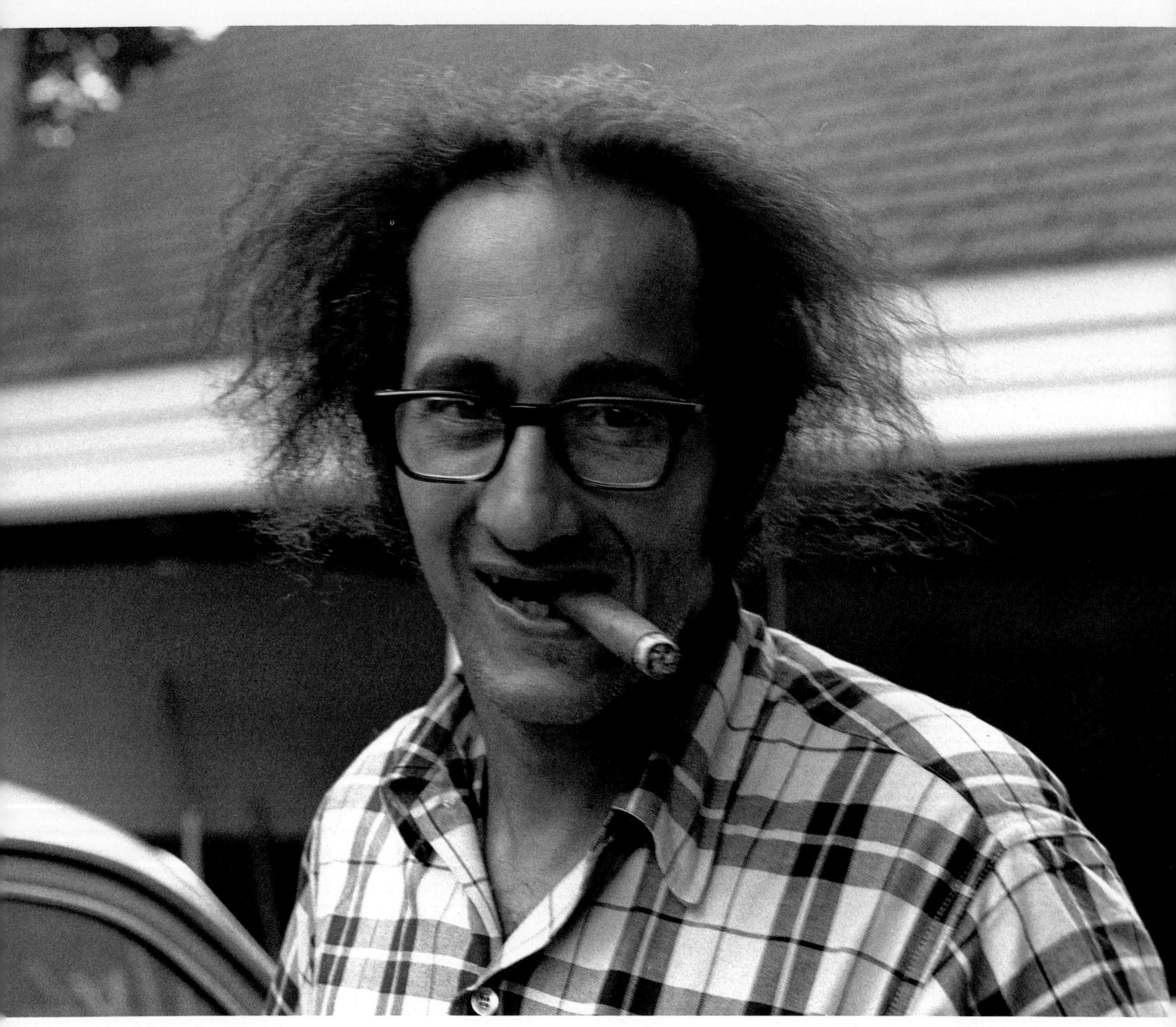

Frank Stella   1974

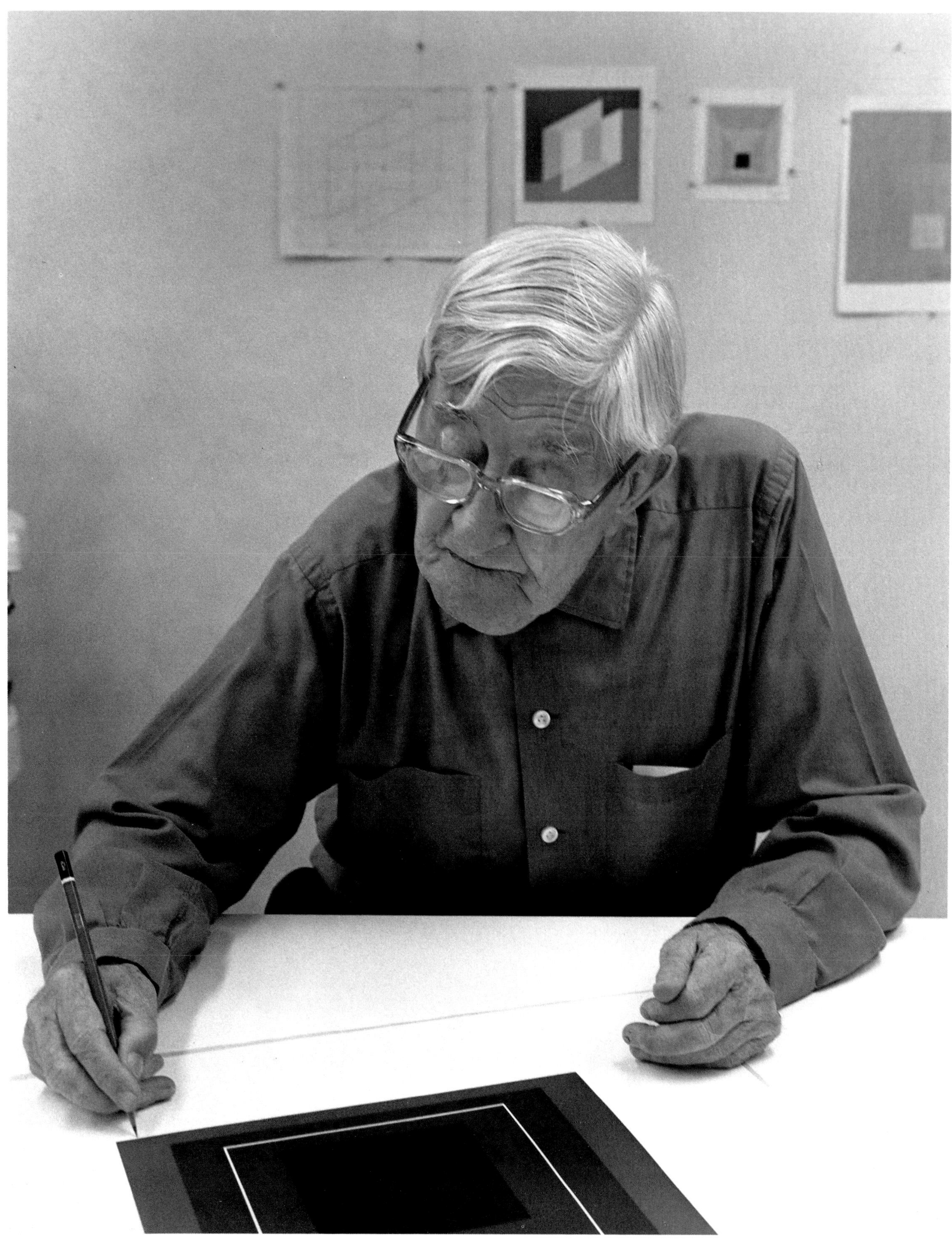

Josef Albers   1974

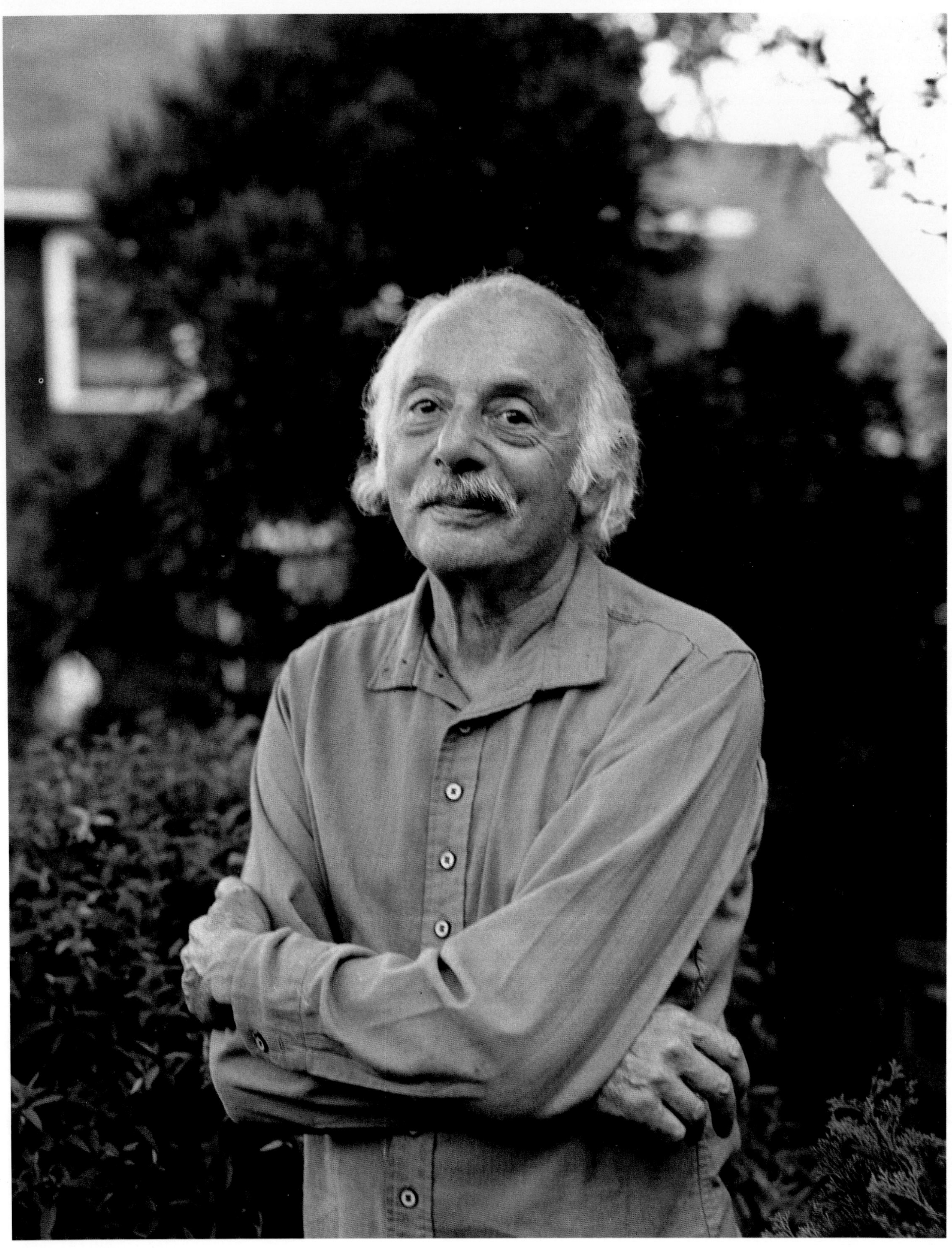

Stanley Kunitz   1974

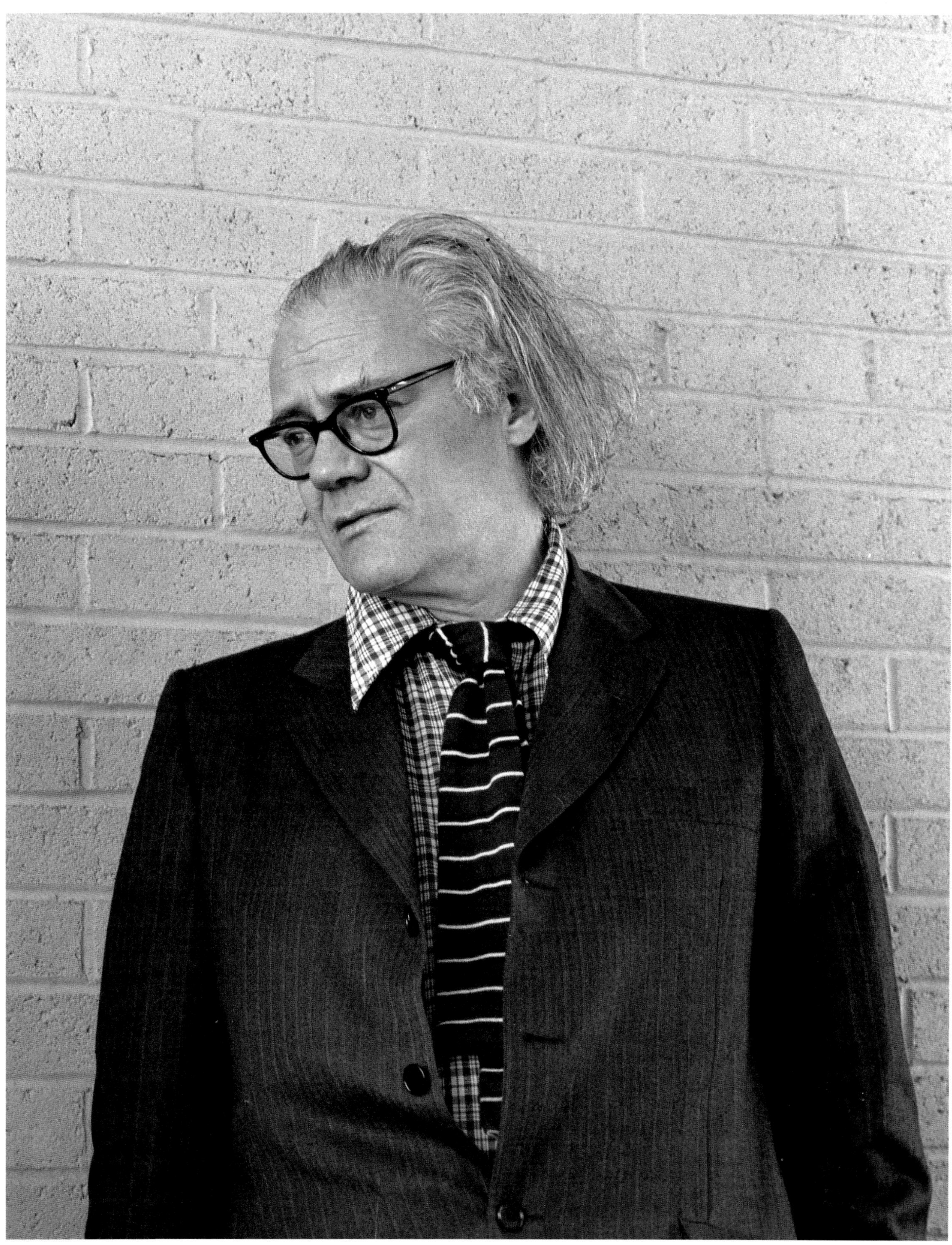

Robert Lowell   1974

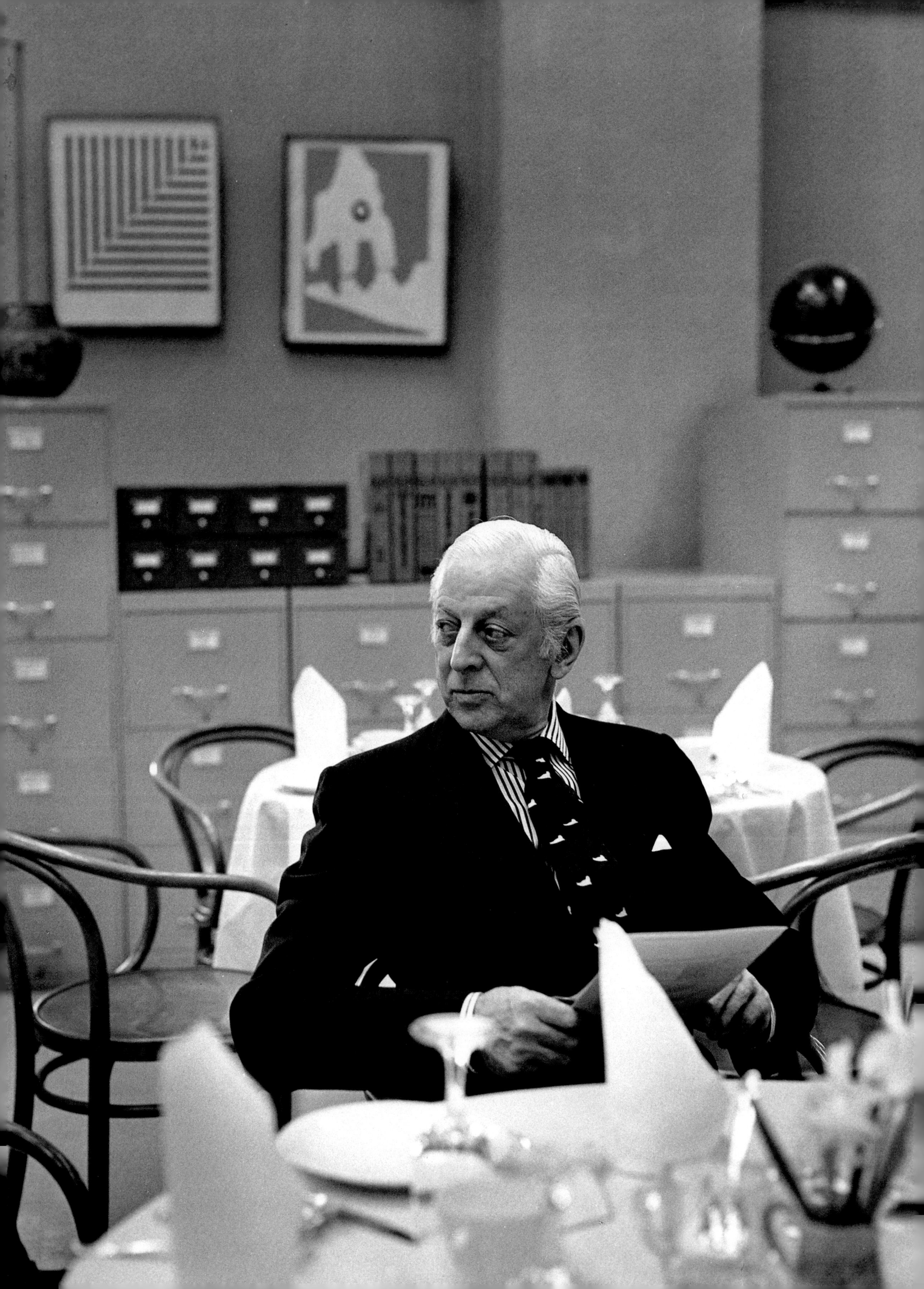

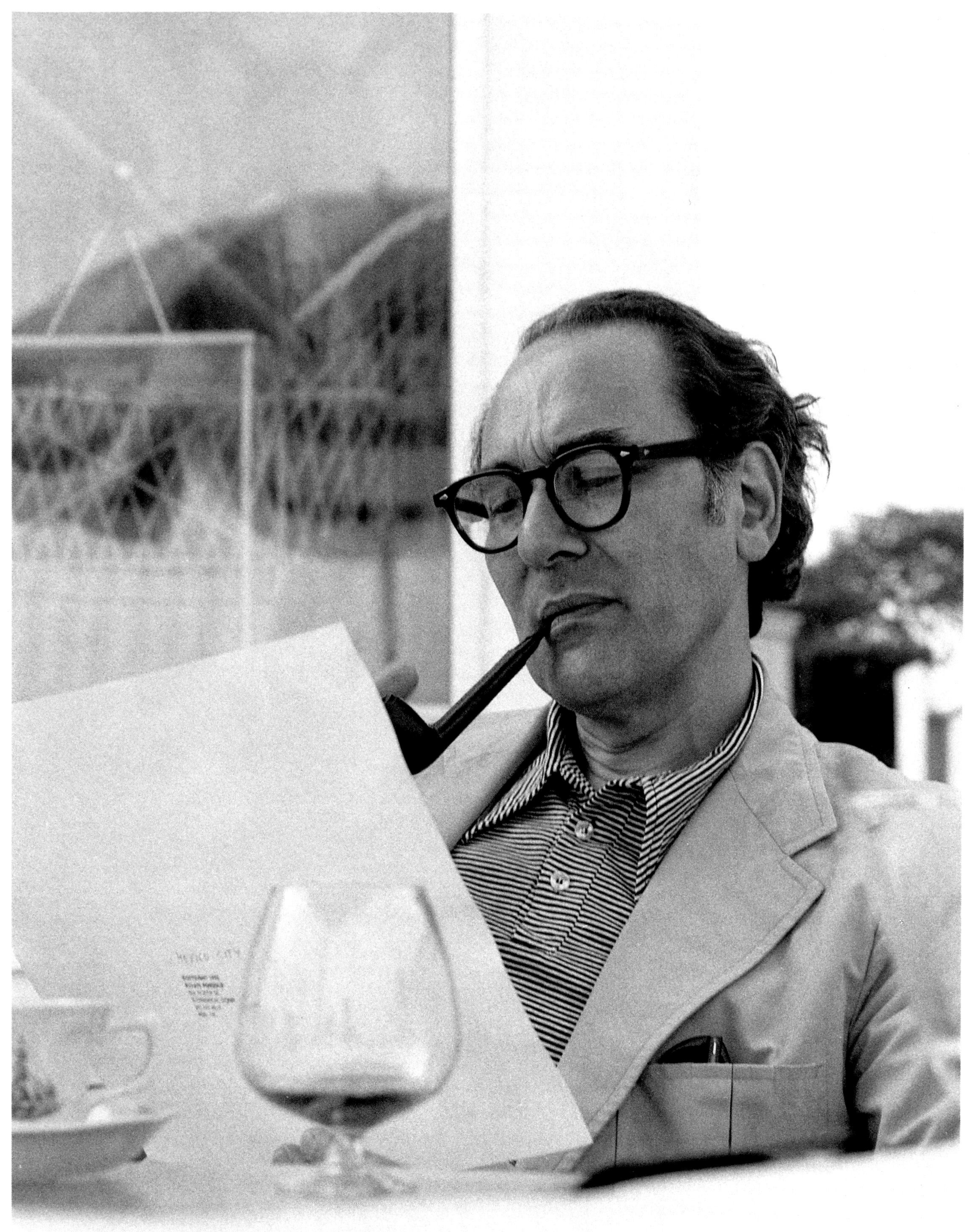

Alistair Cooke   1974

Hilton Kramer   1976

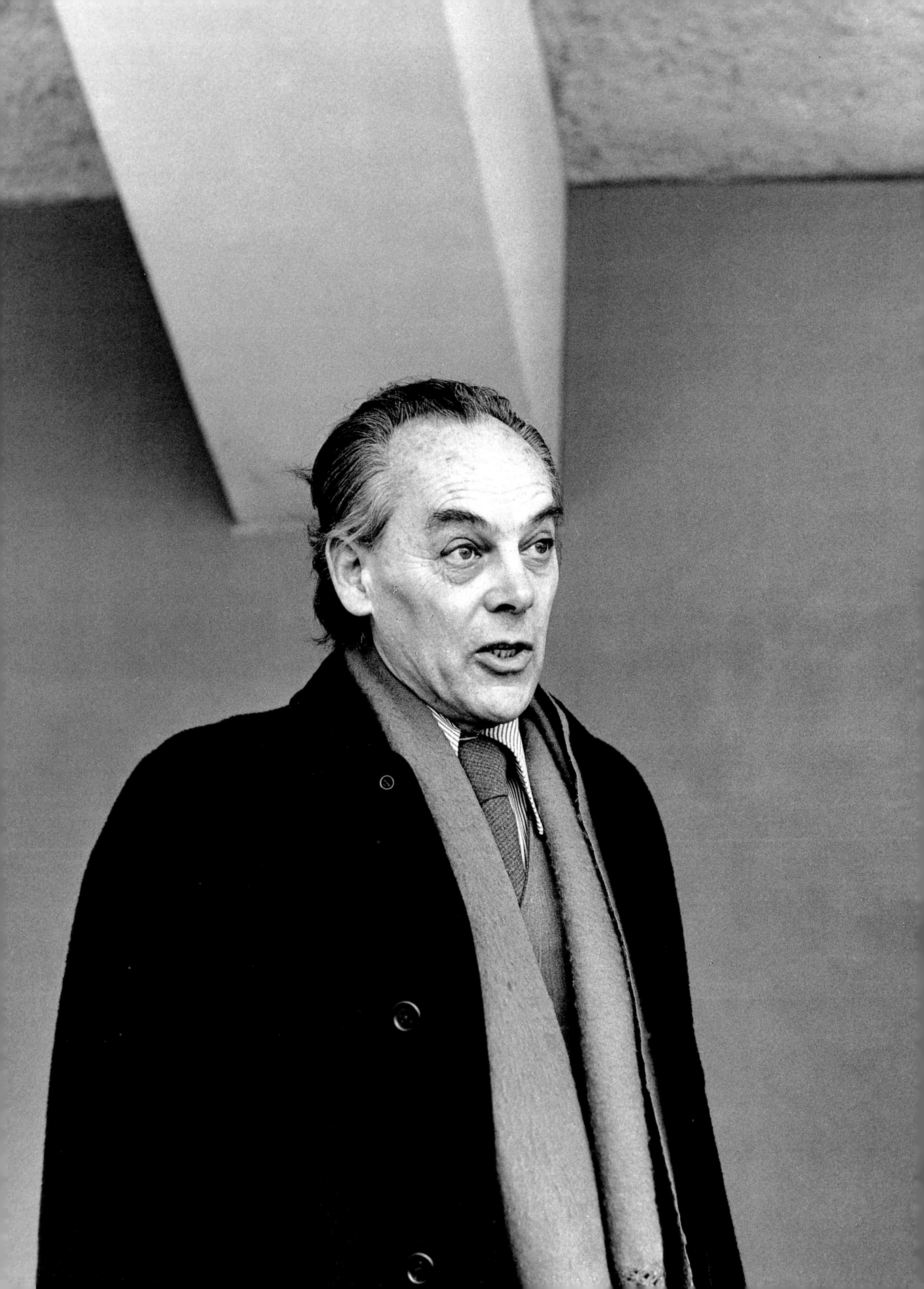

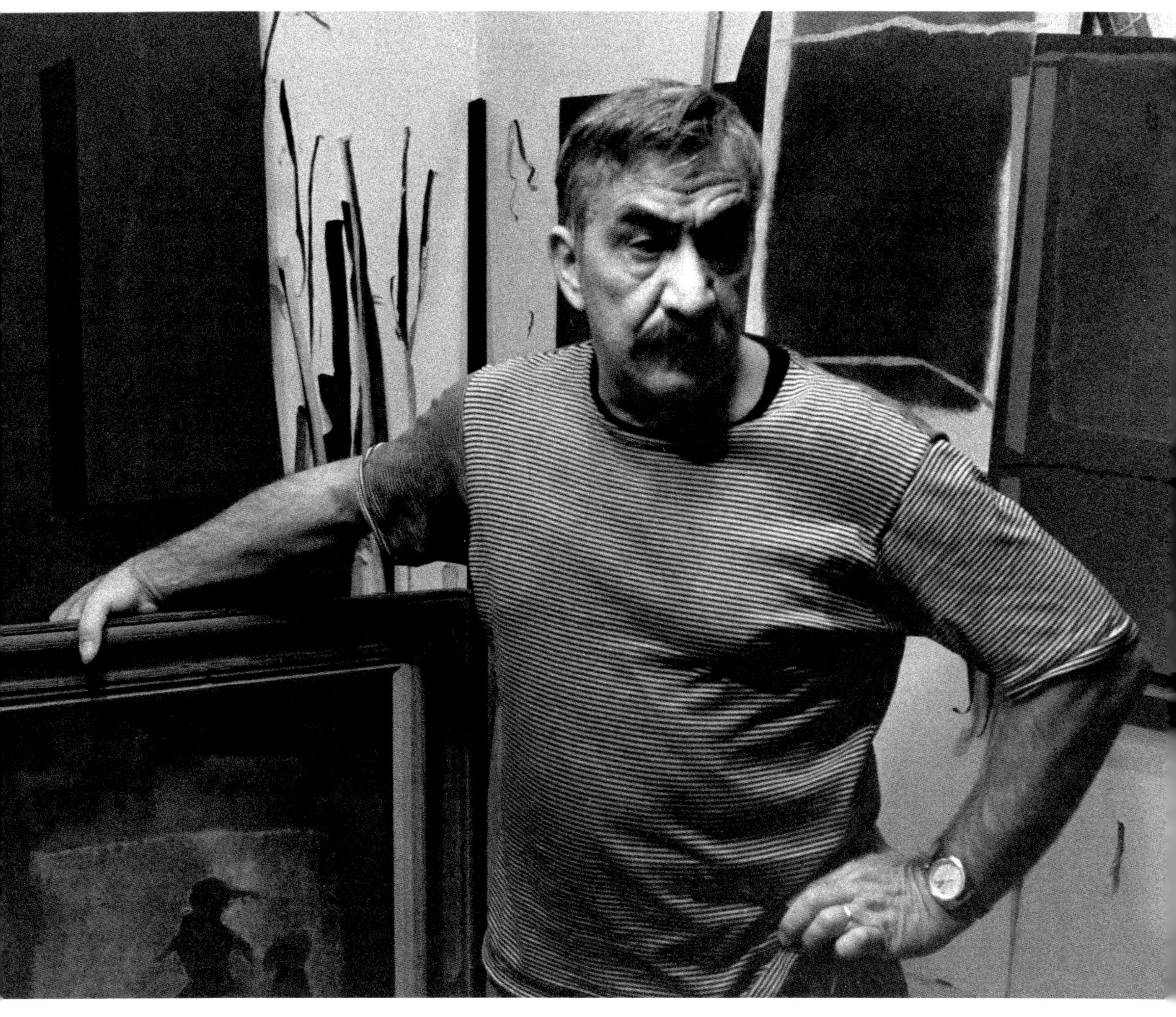

Theodoros Stamos   1975

Gyorgy Kepes   1974

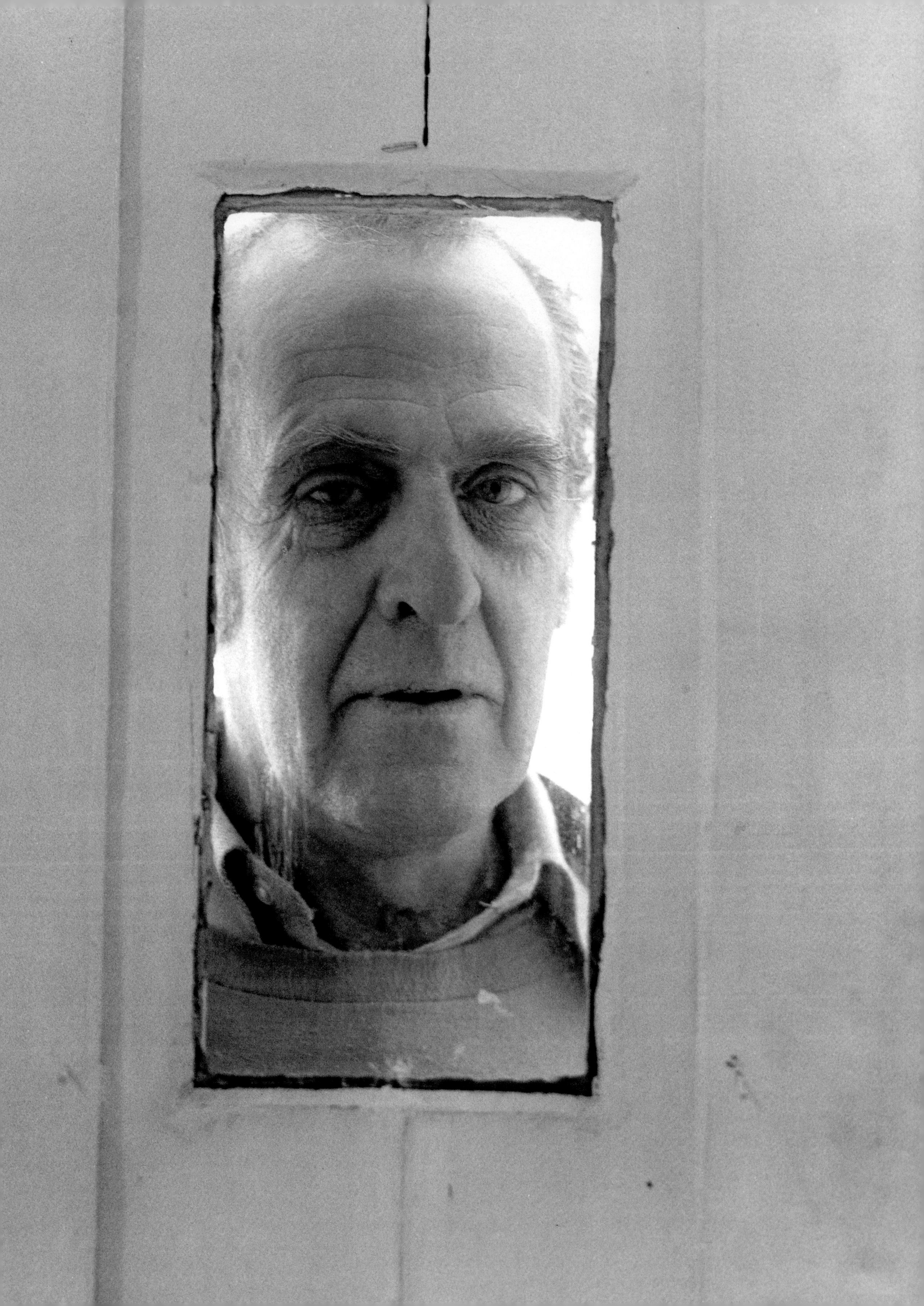

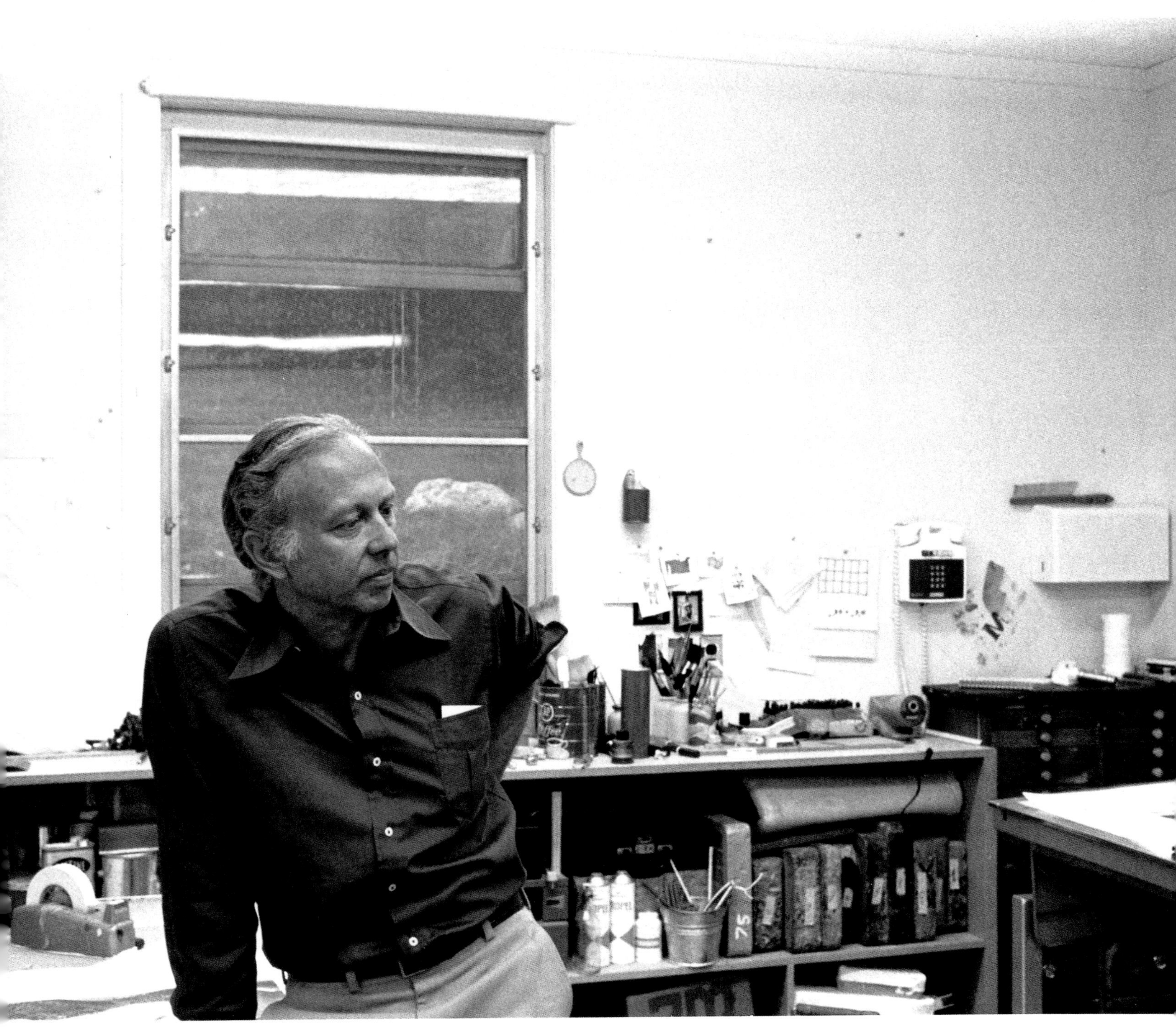

Ellsworth Kelly   1975

Jim Forsberg   1975

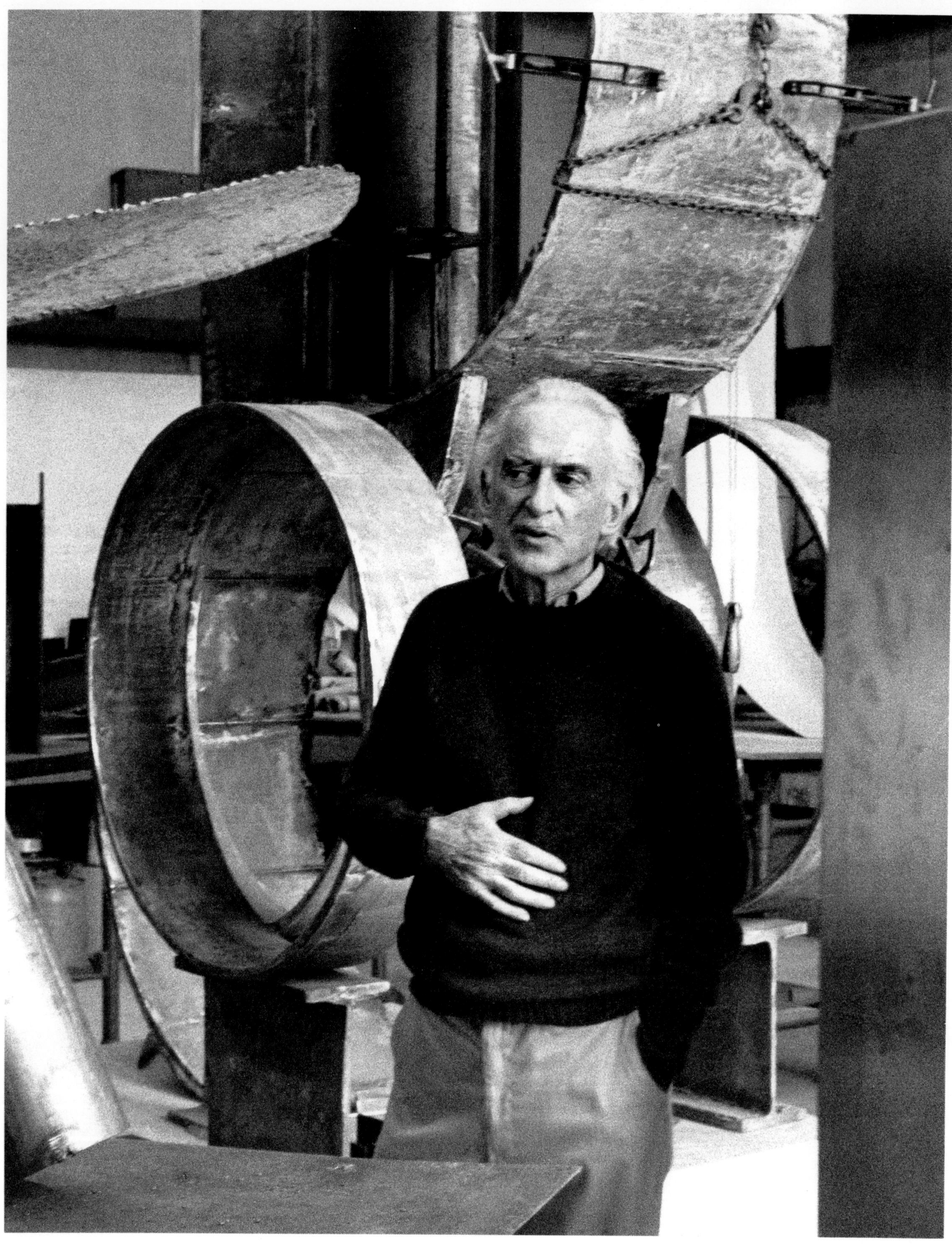

Alexander Liberman　1975

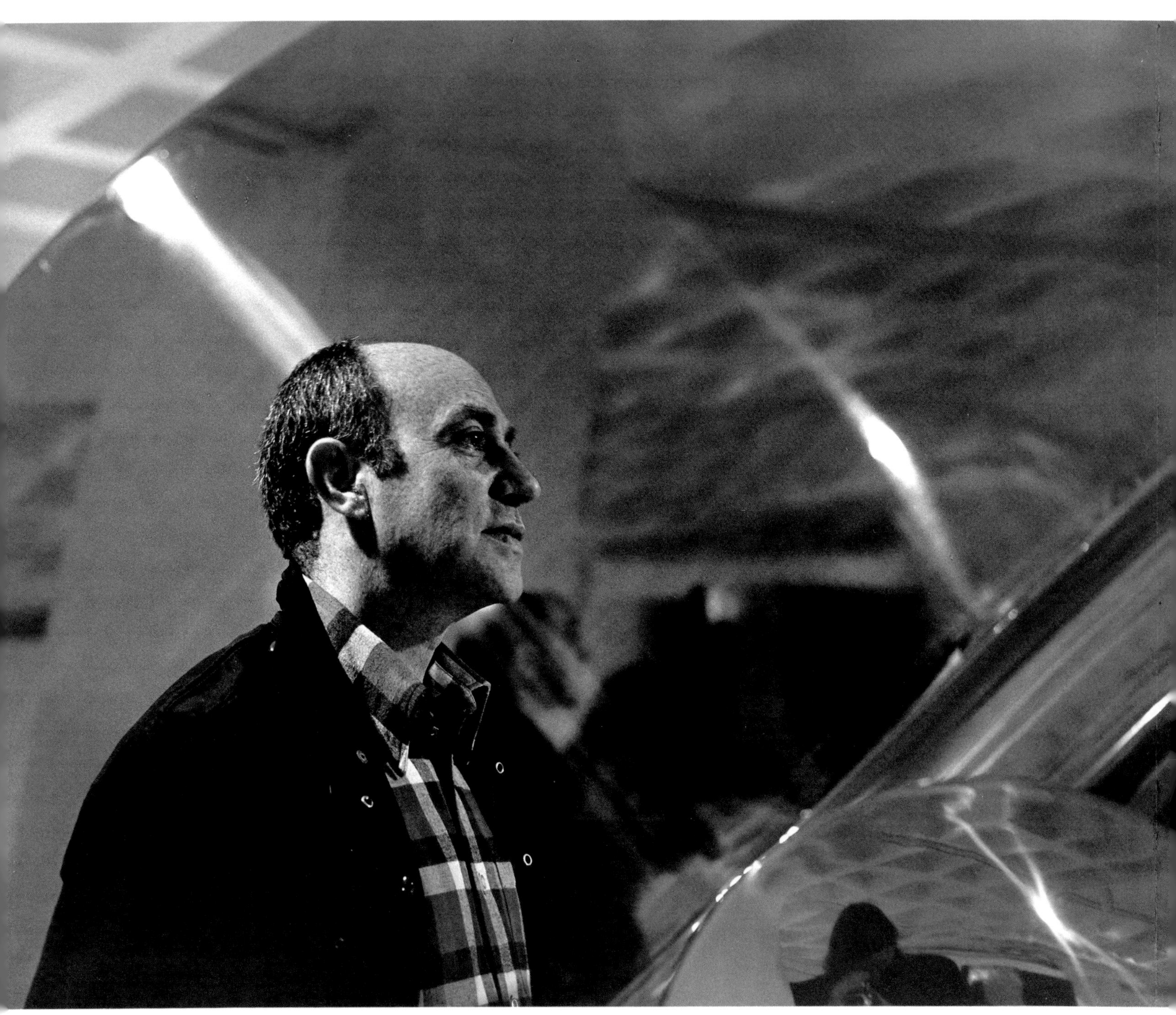

Arnaldo Pomodoro   1976

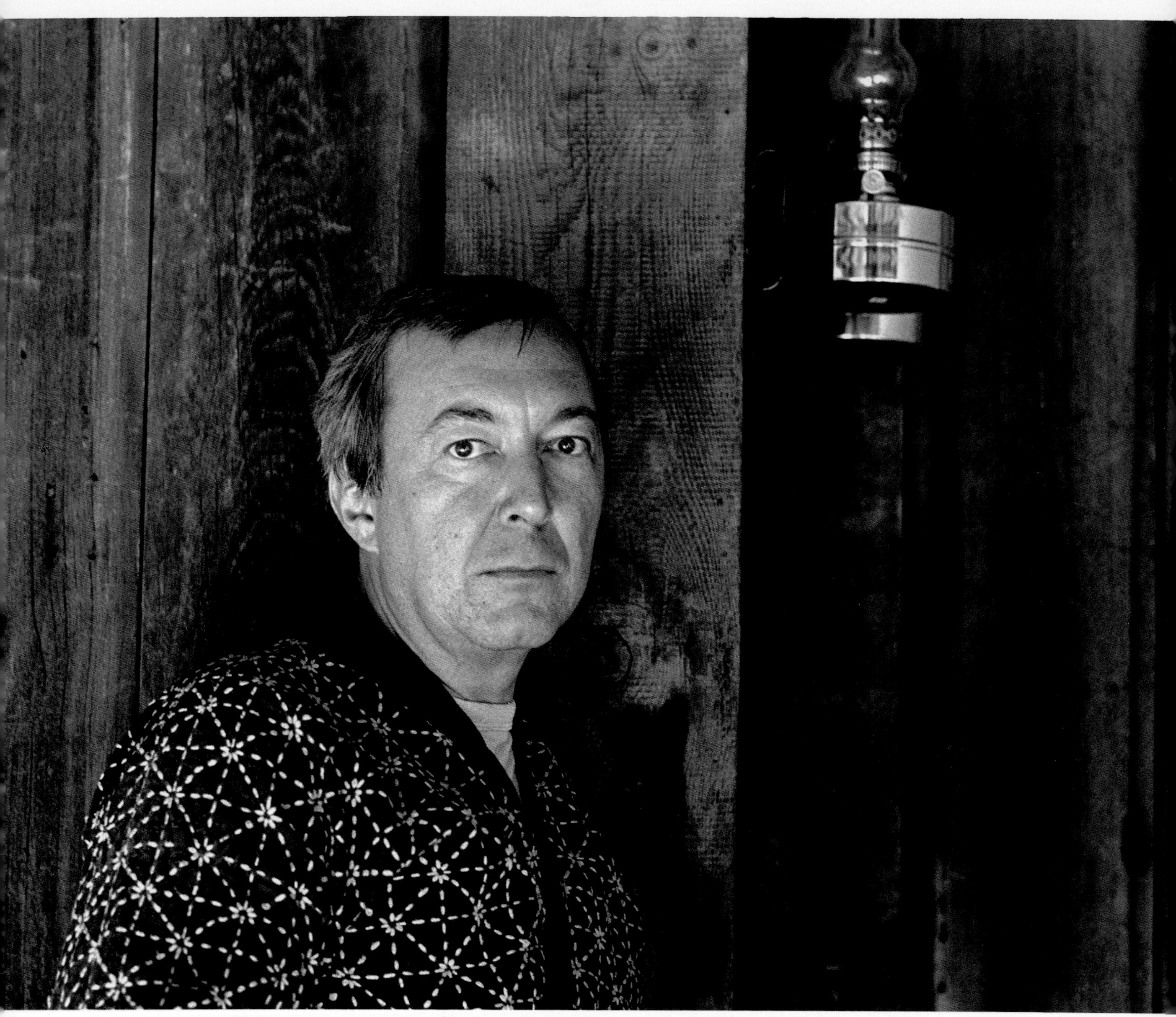

Jasper Johns   1976

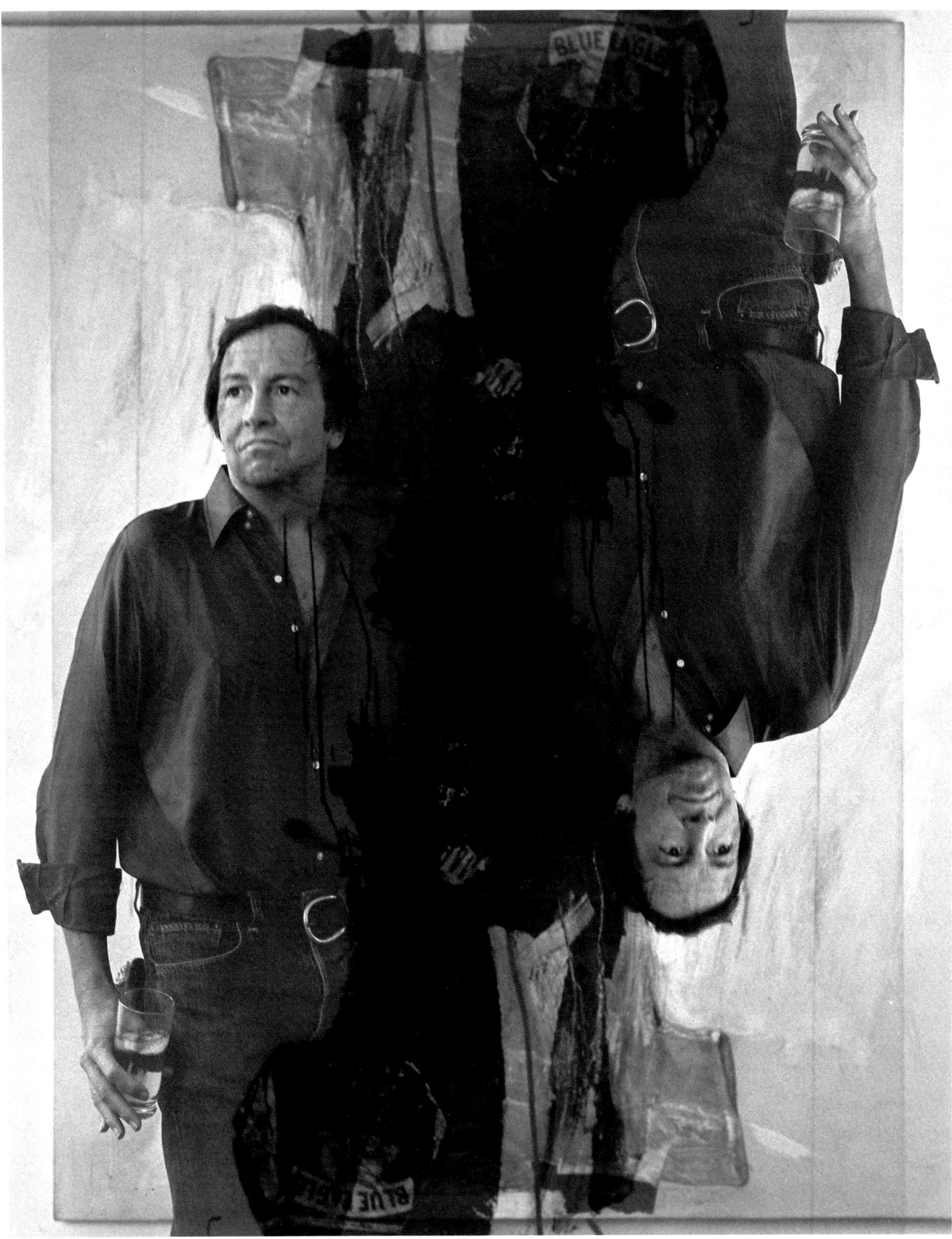

Robert Rauschenberg   1976

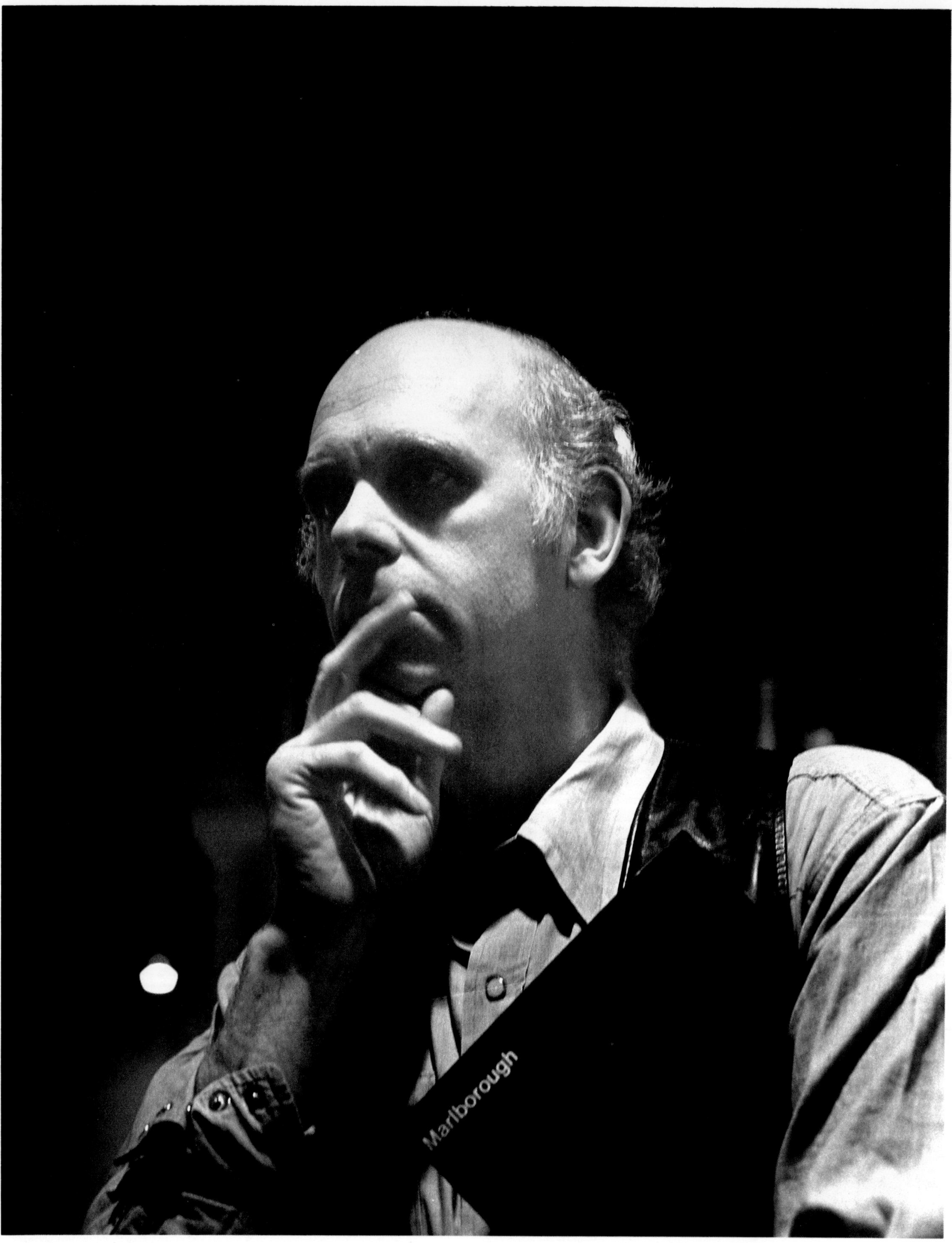

Claes Oldenburg   1976

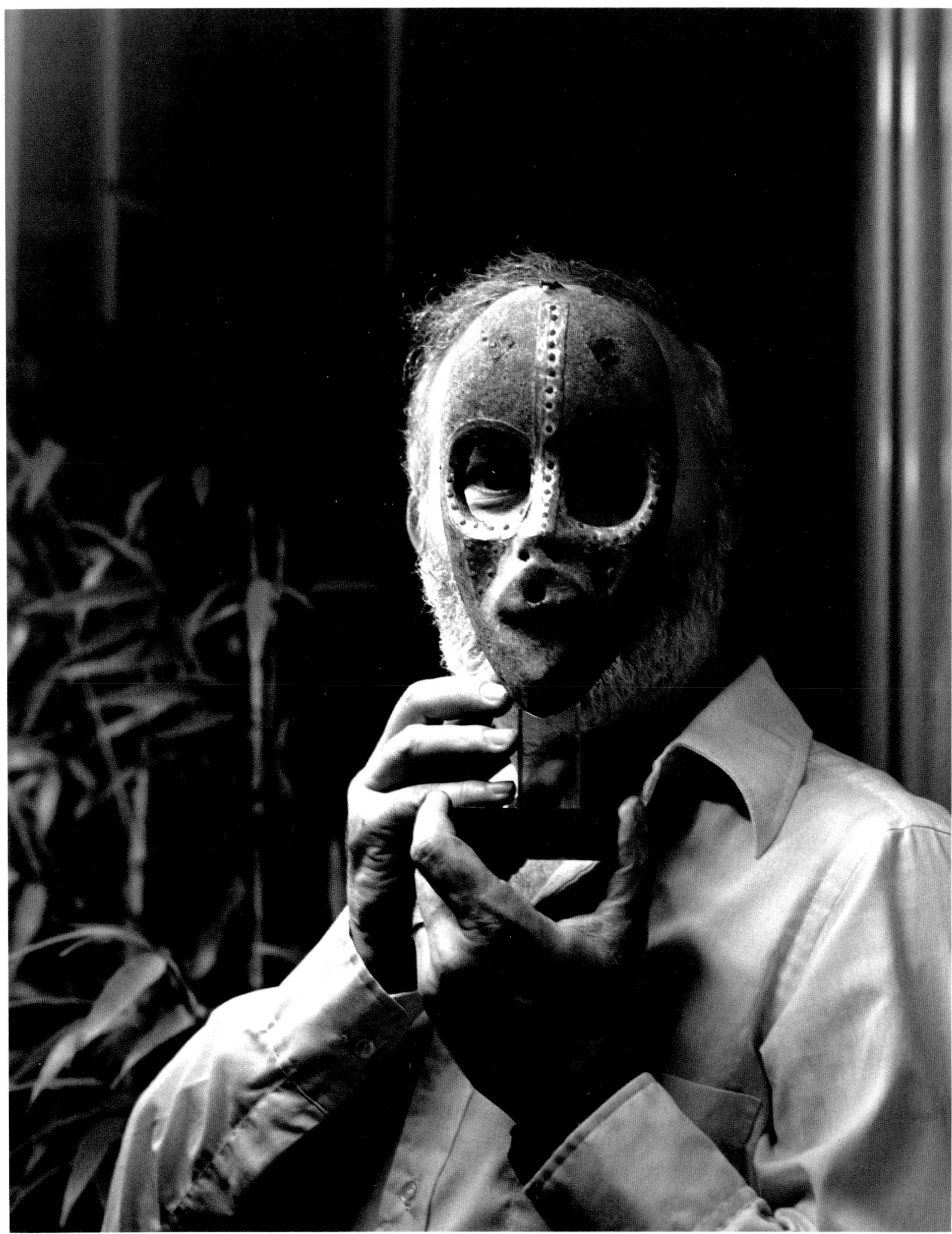

Arman   1977

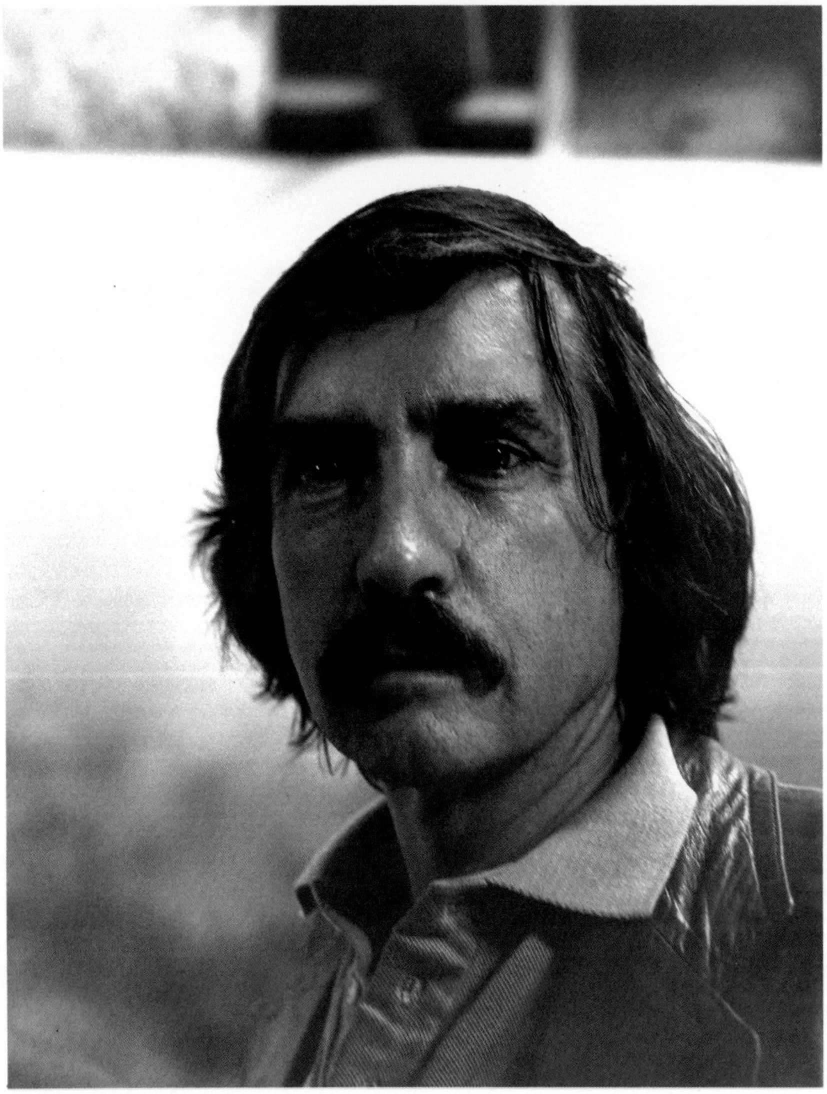

Edward Albee   1977

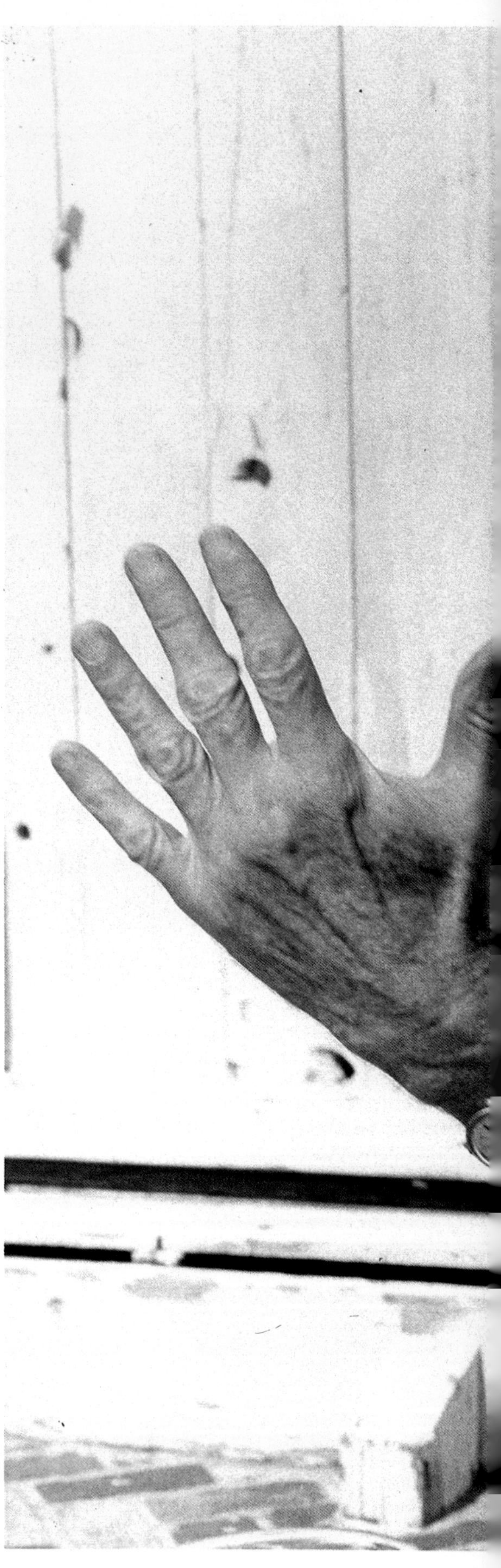

Erick Hawkins   1976

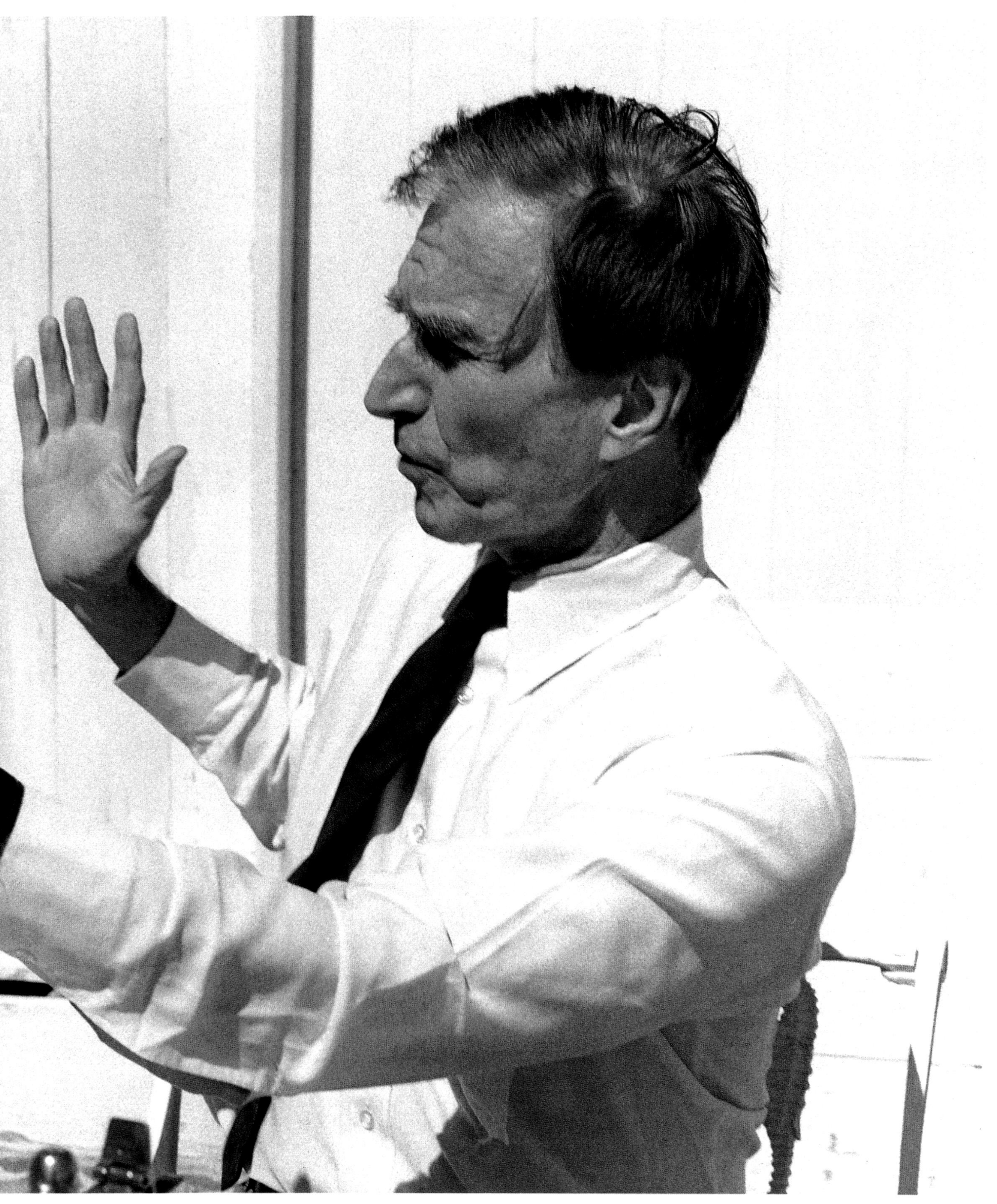

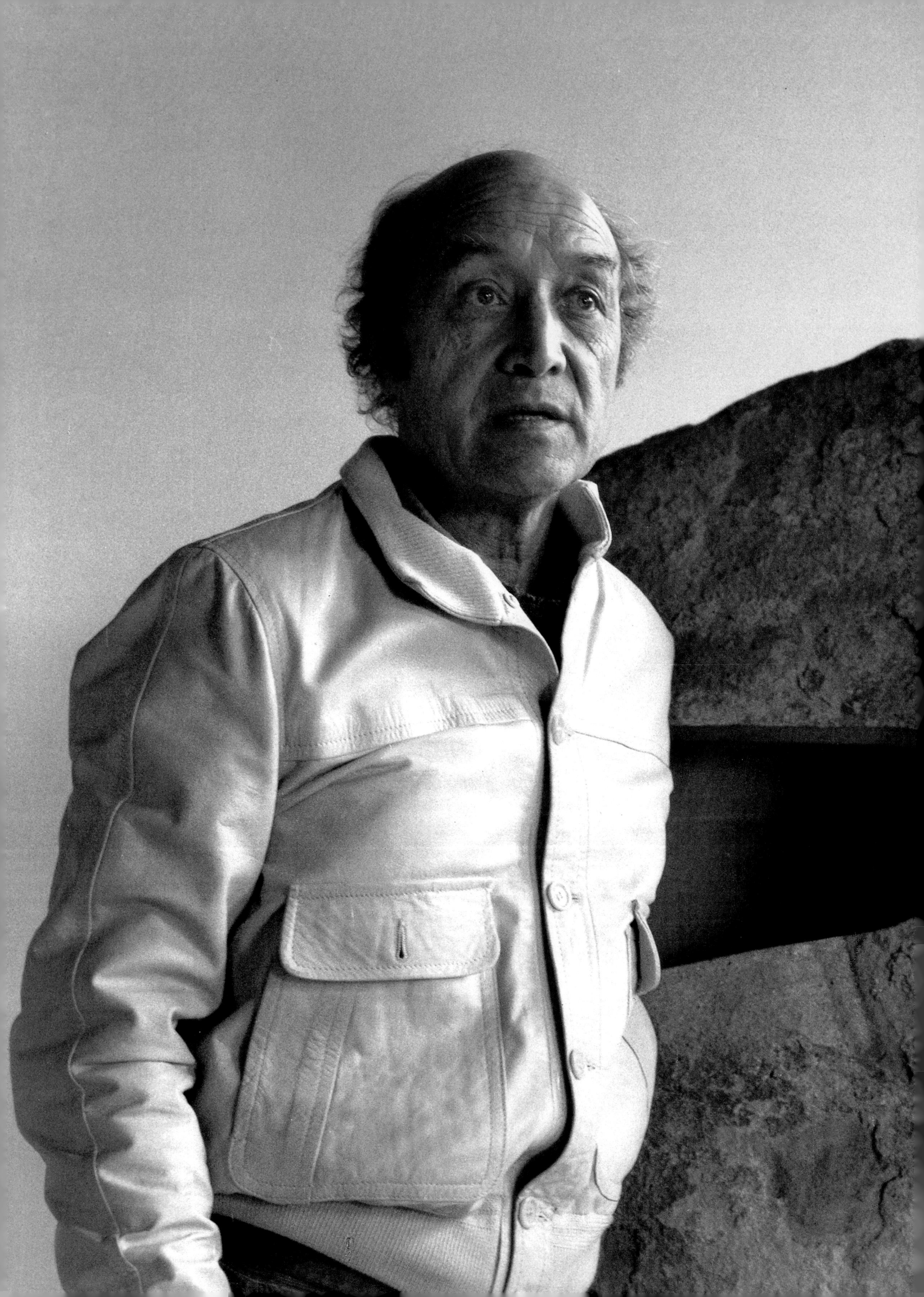

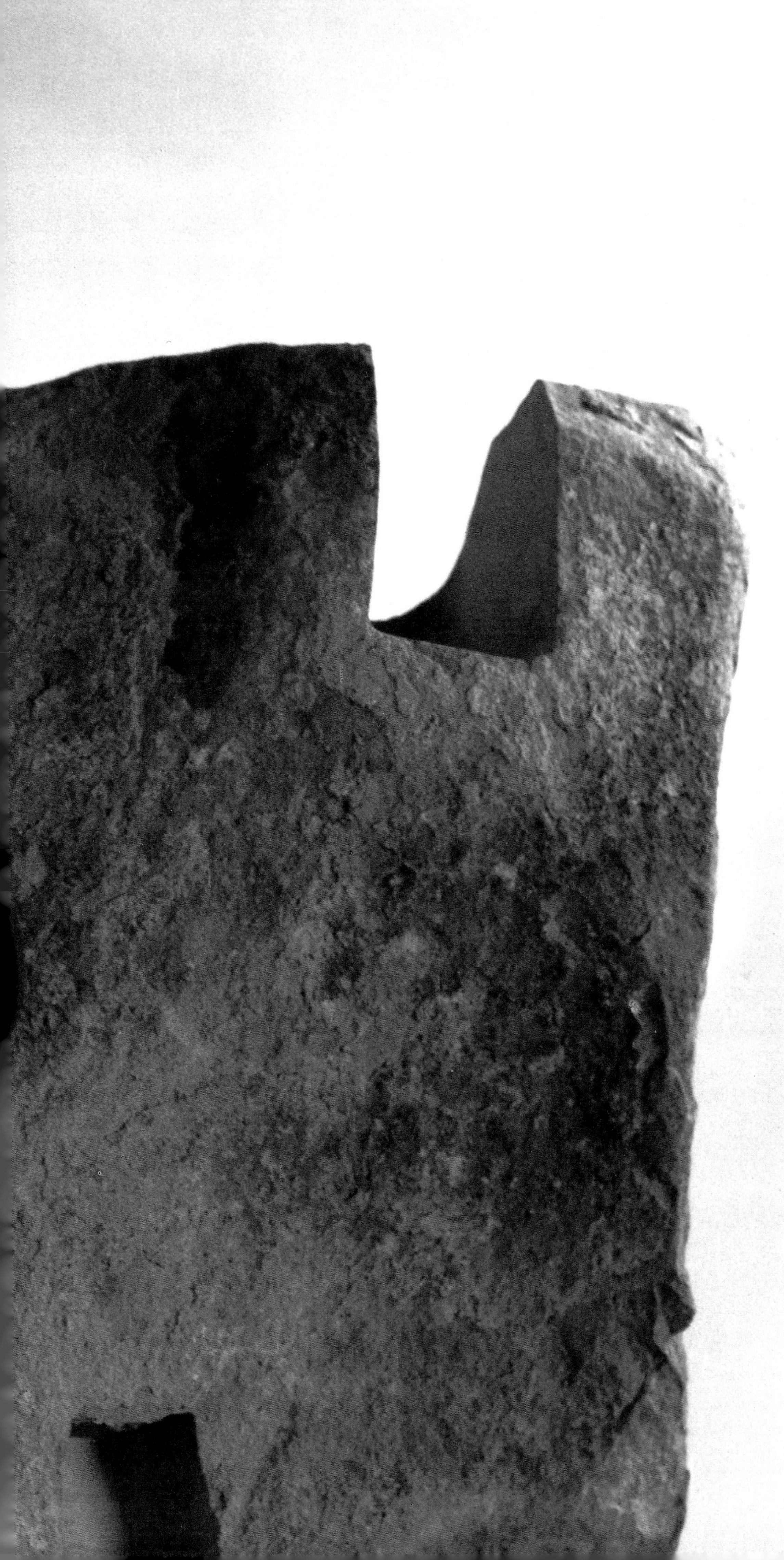

Isamu Noguchi   1977

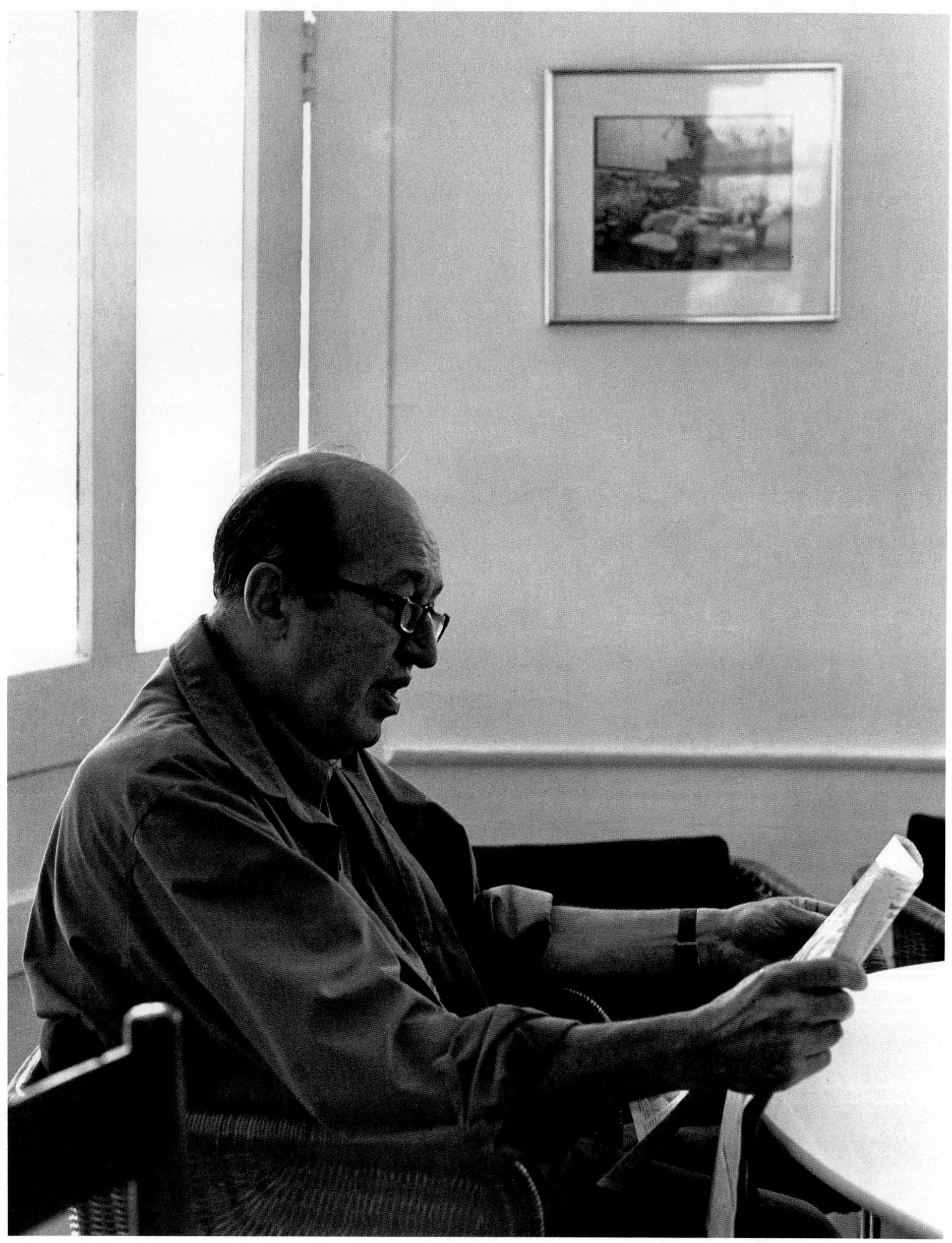

Clement Greenberg   1977

Lee Krasner   1977

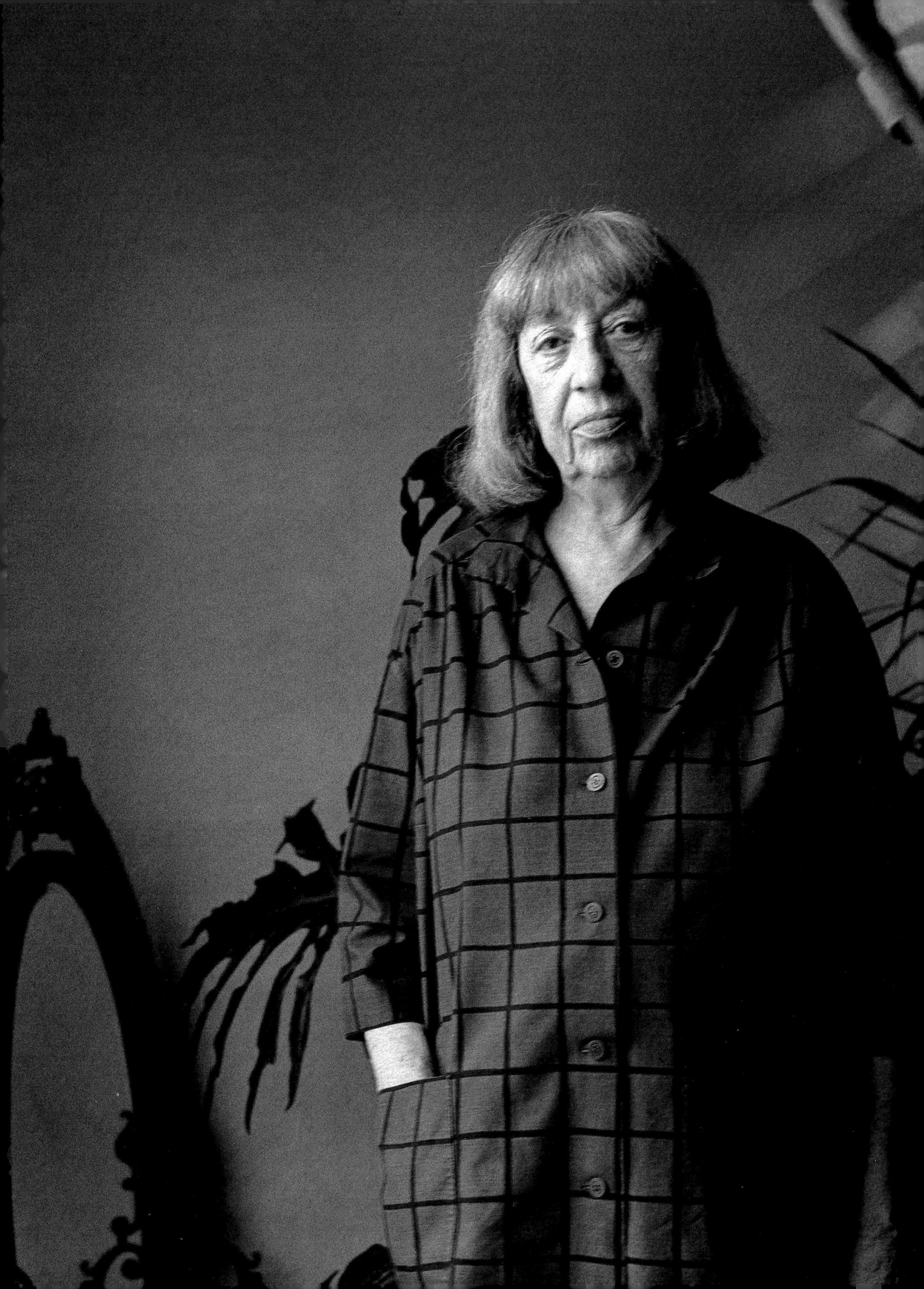

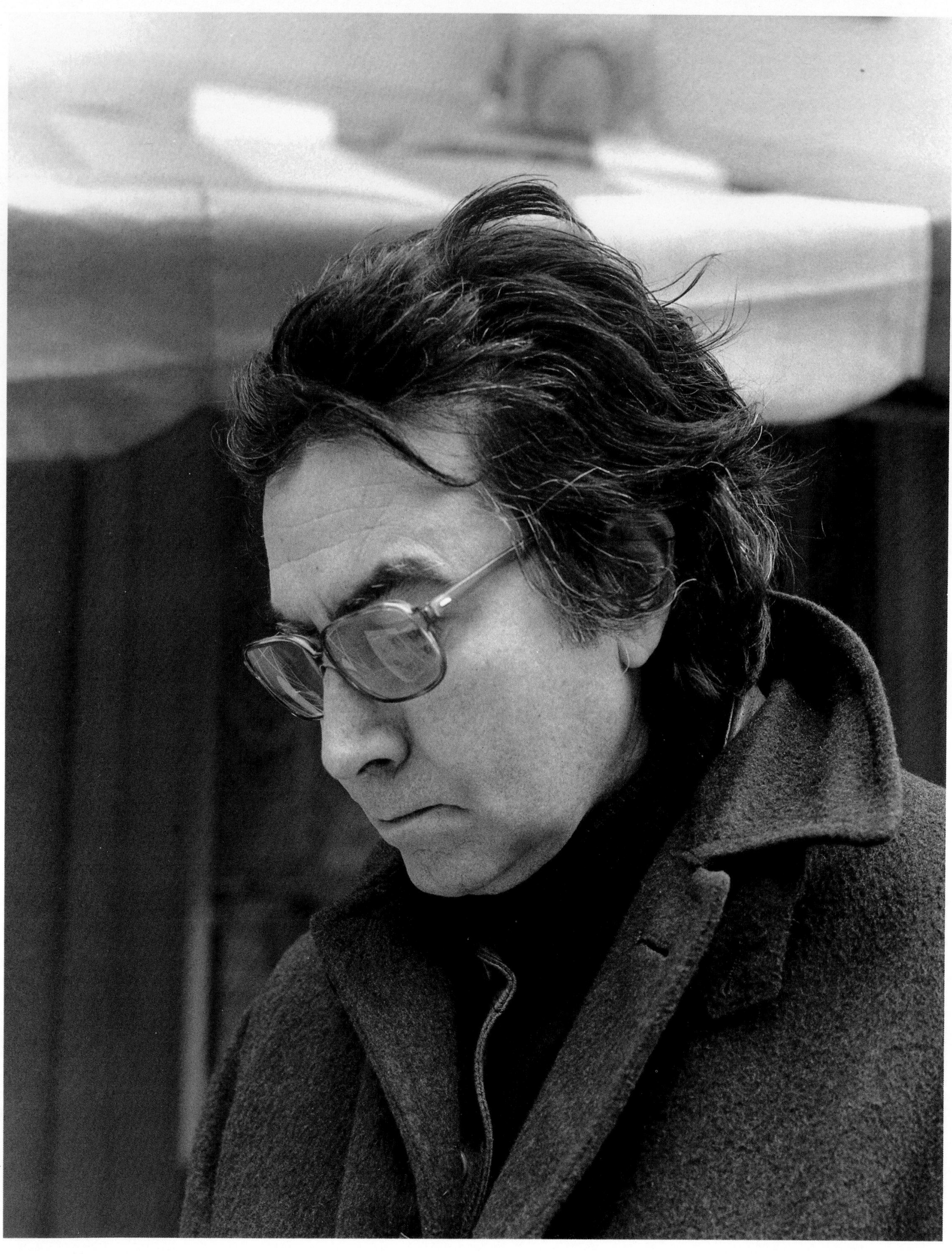

Antoni Tàpies   1978

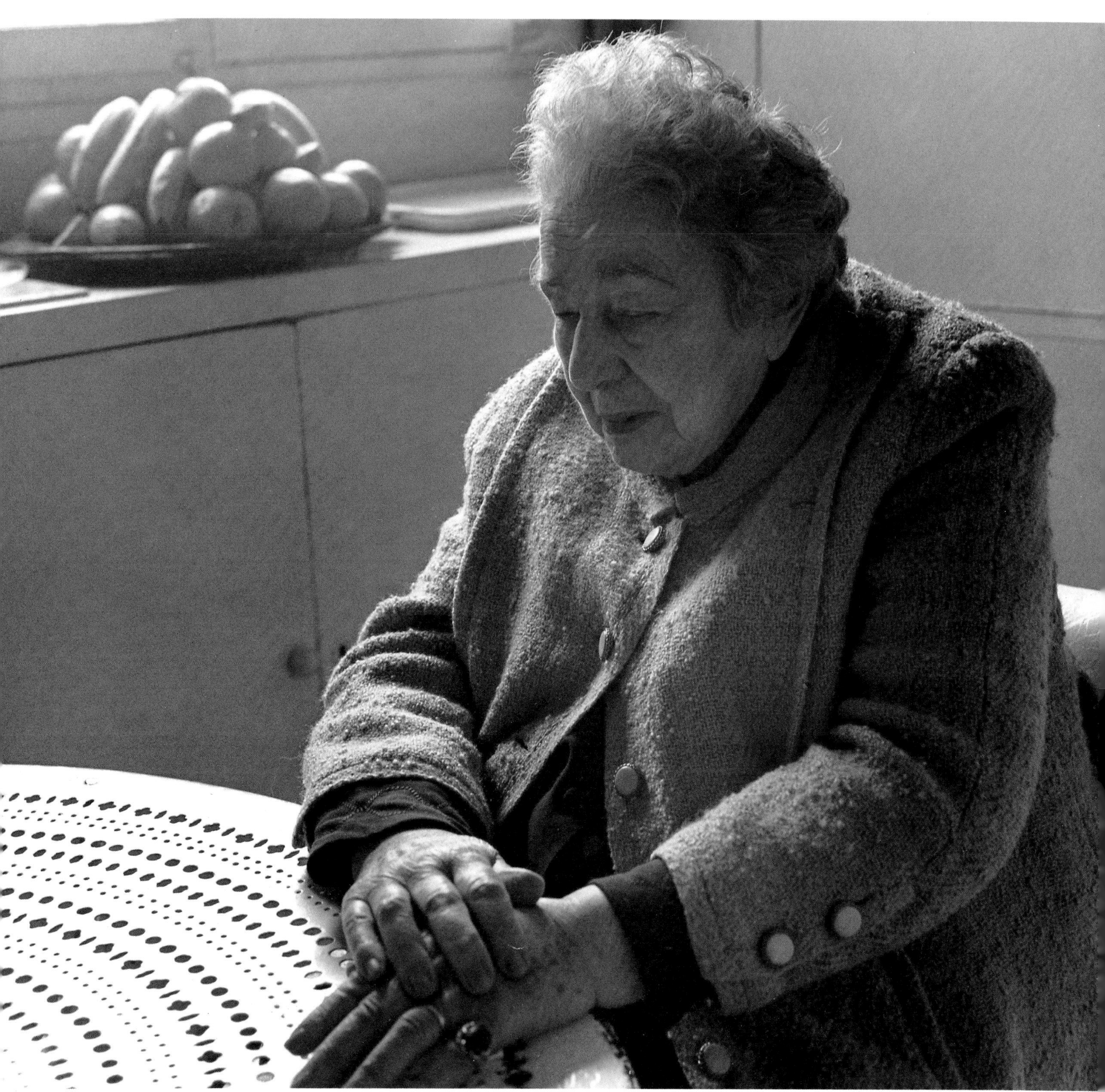

Sonia Delaunay   1977

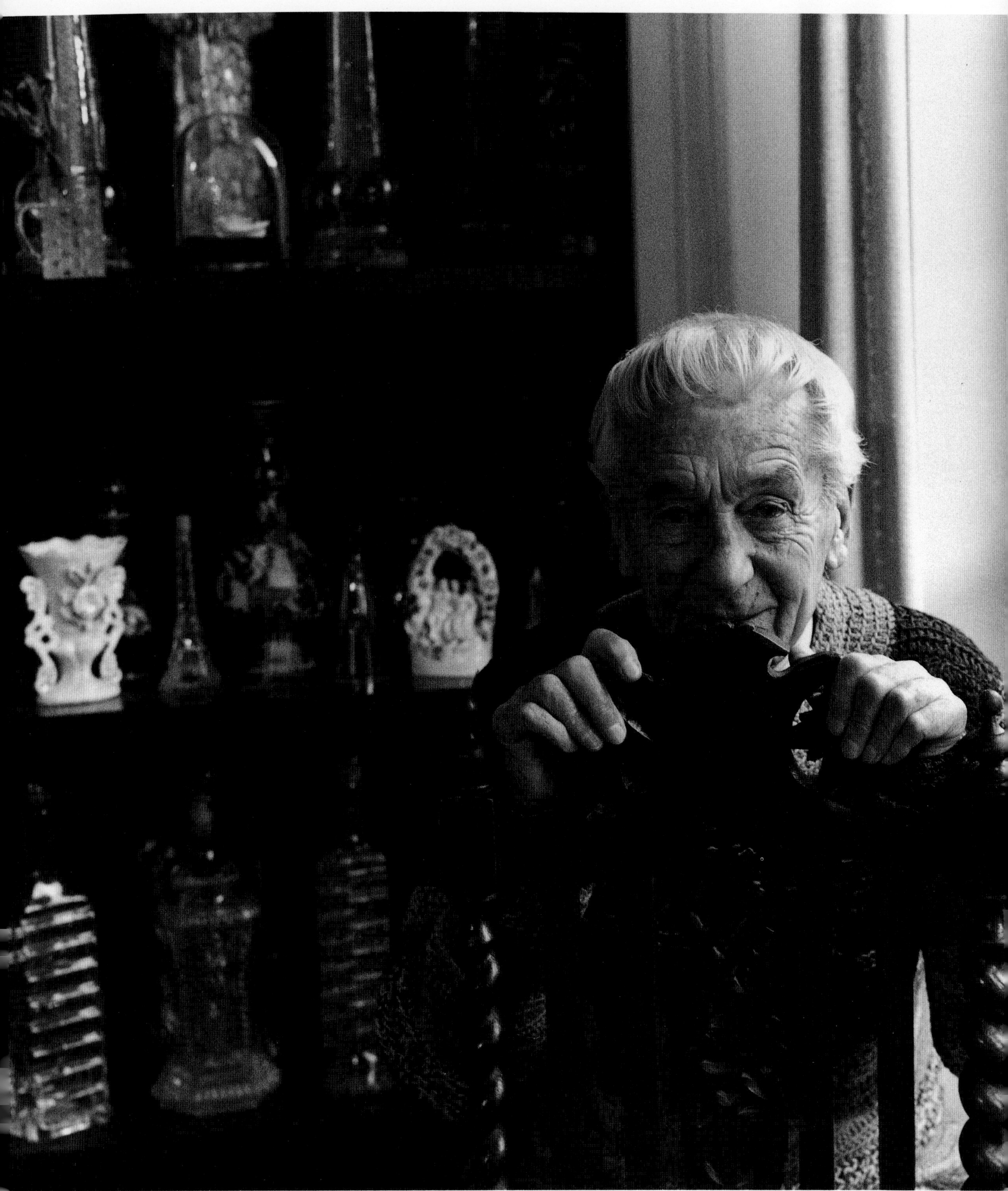

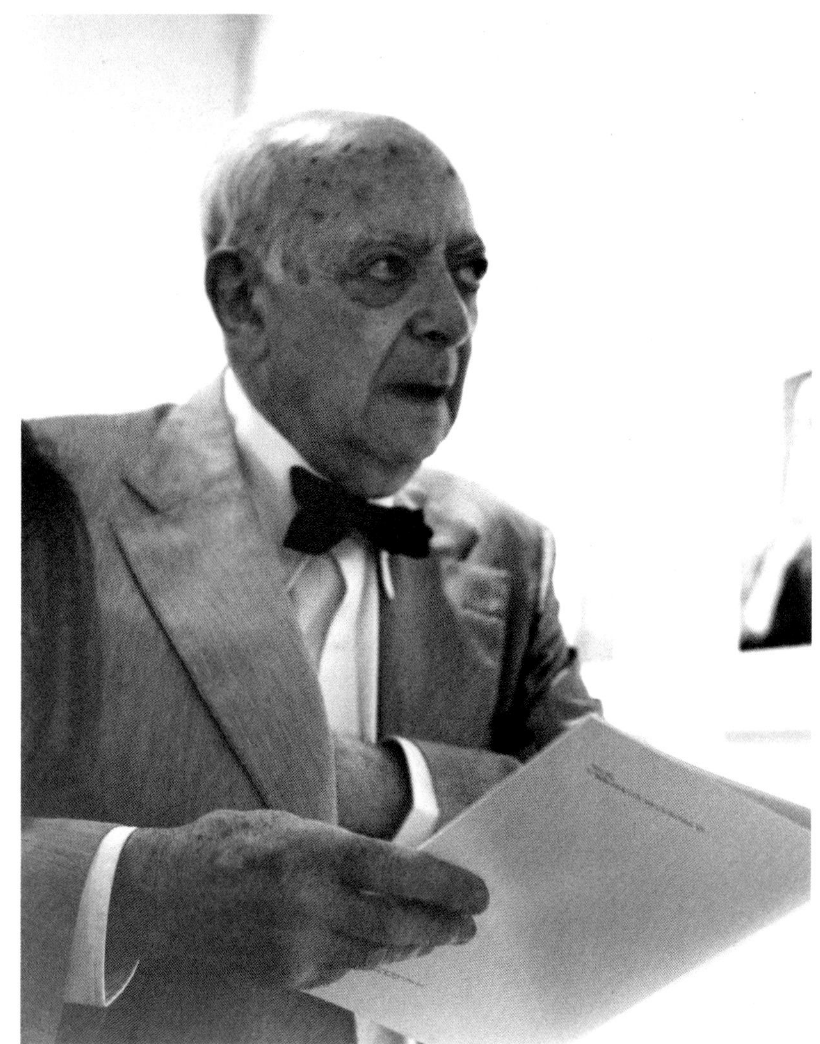

Brassaï   1979

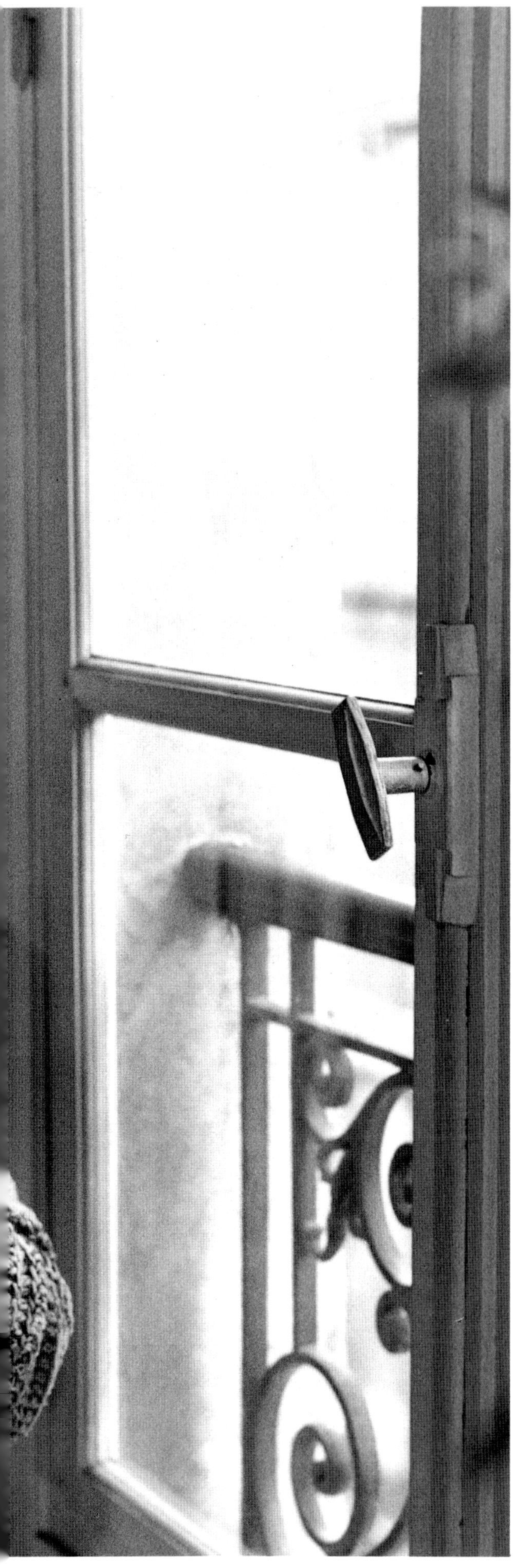

Jacques-Henri Lartigue   1978

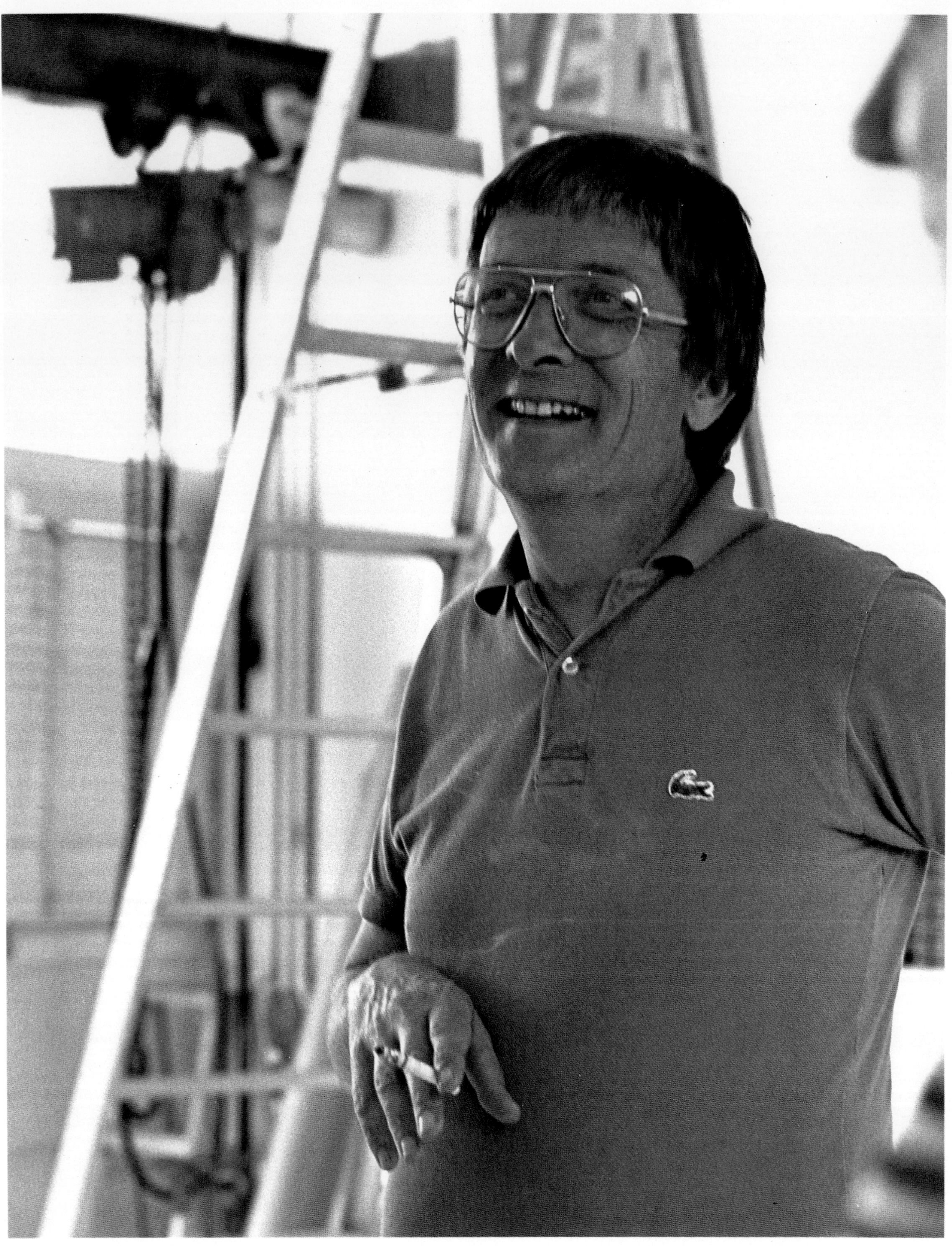

Kenneth Noland   1977

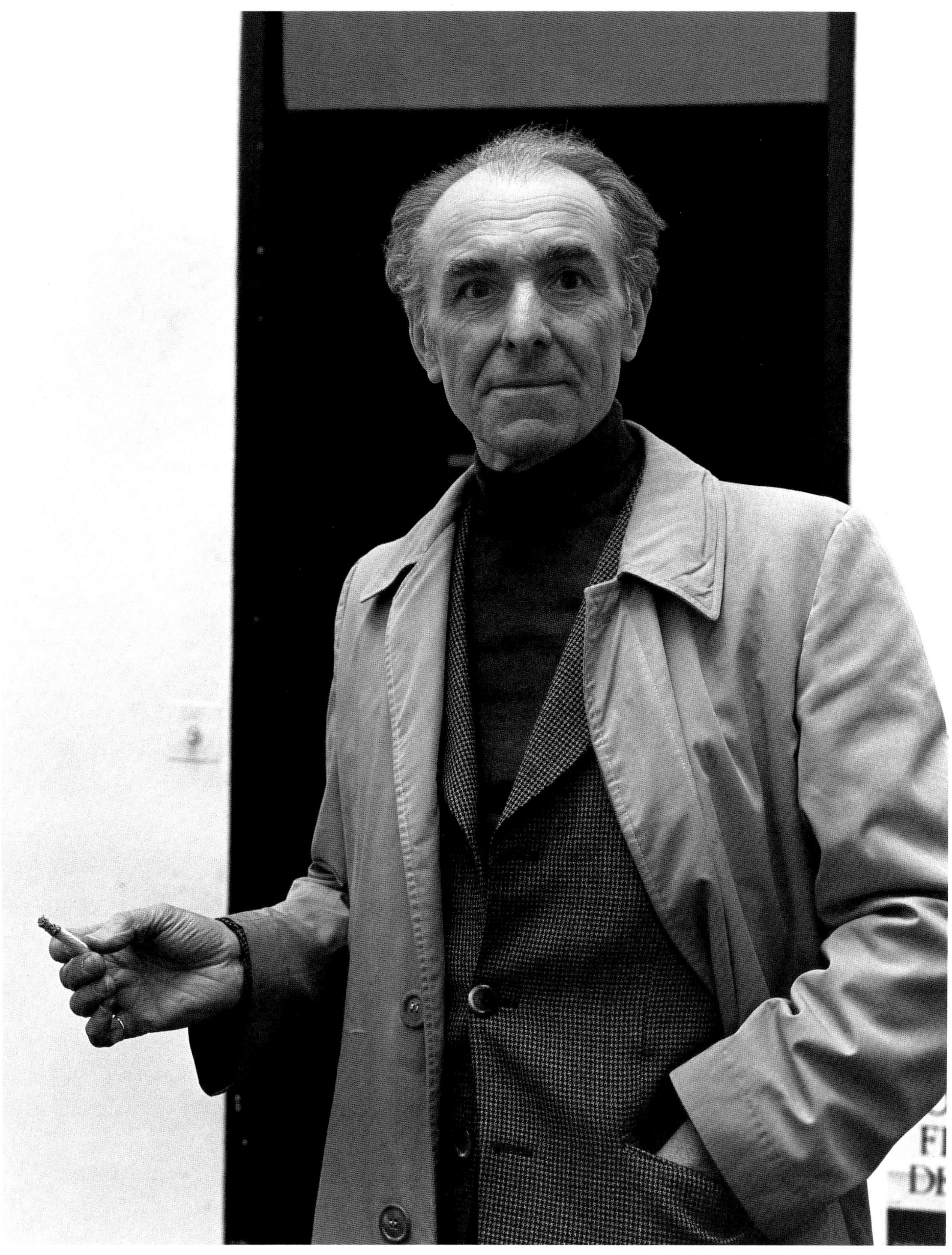

Robert Doisneau   1978

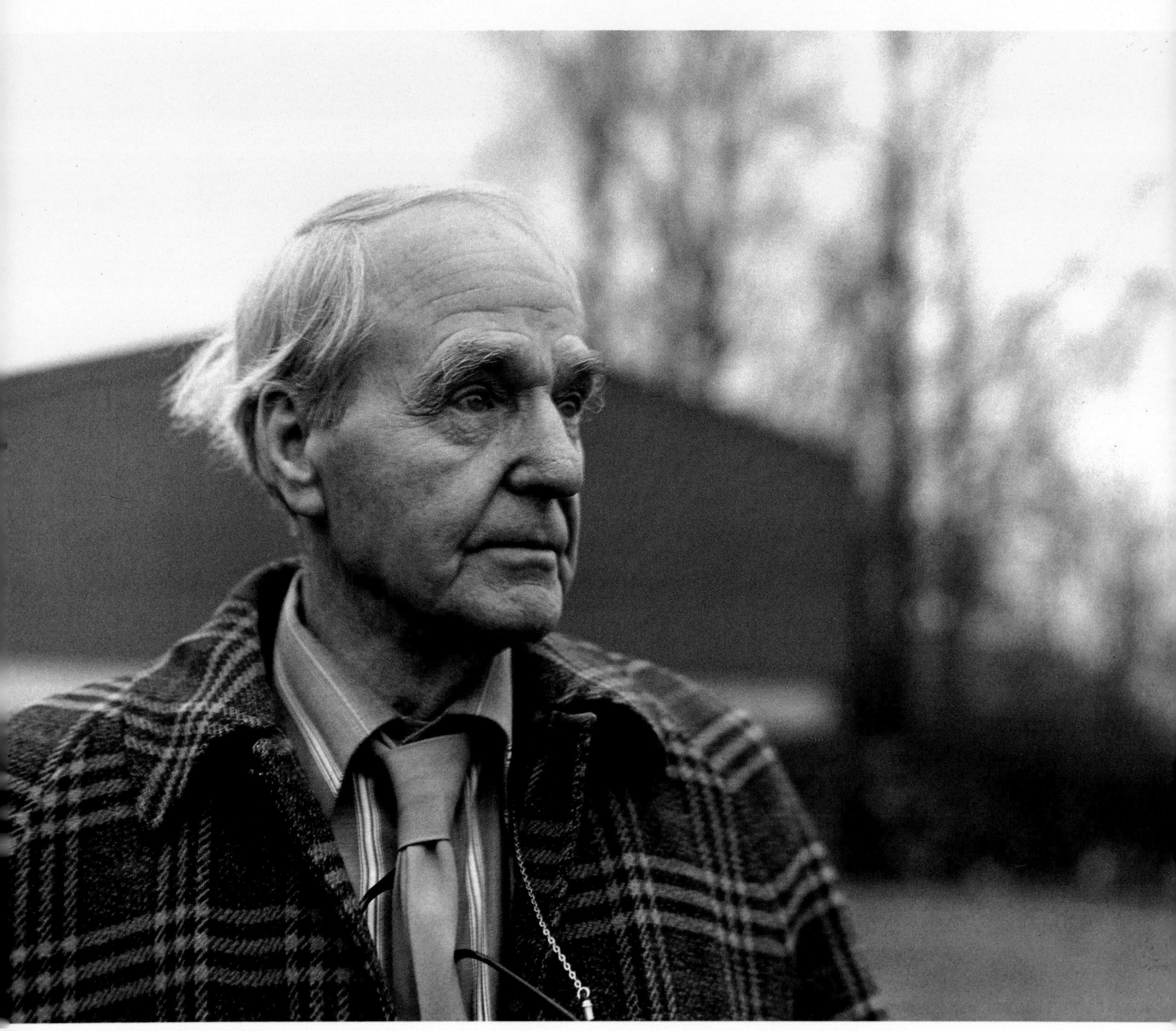

Henry Moore   1978

Tony Smith   1978

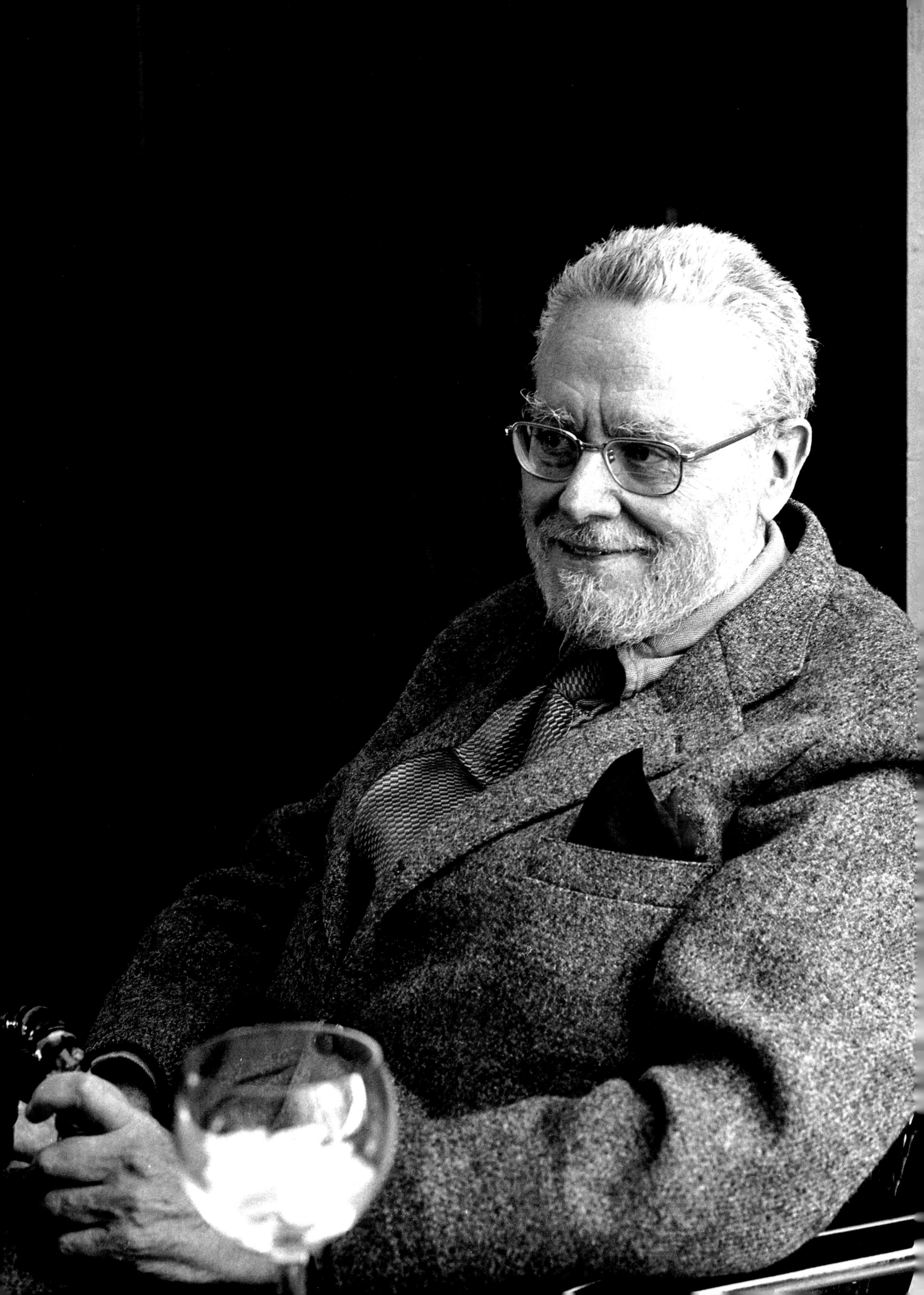

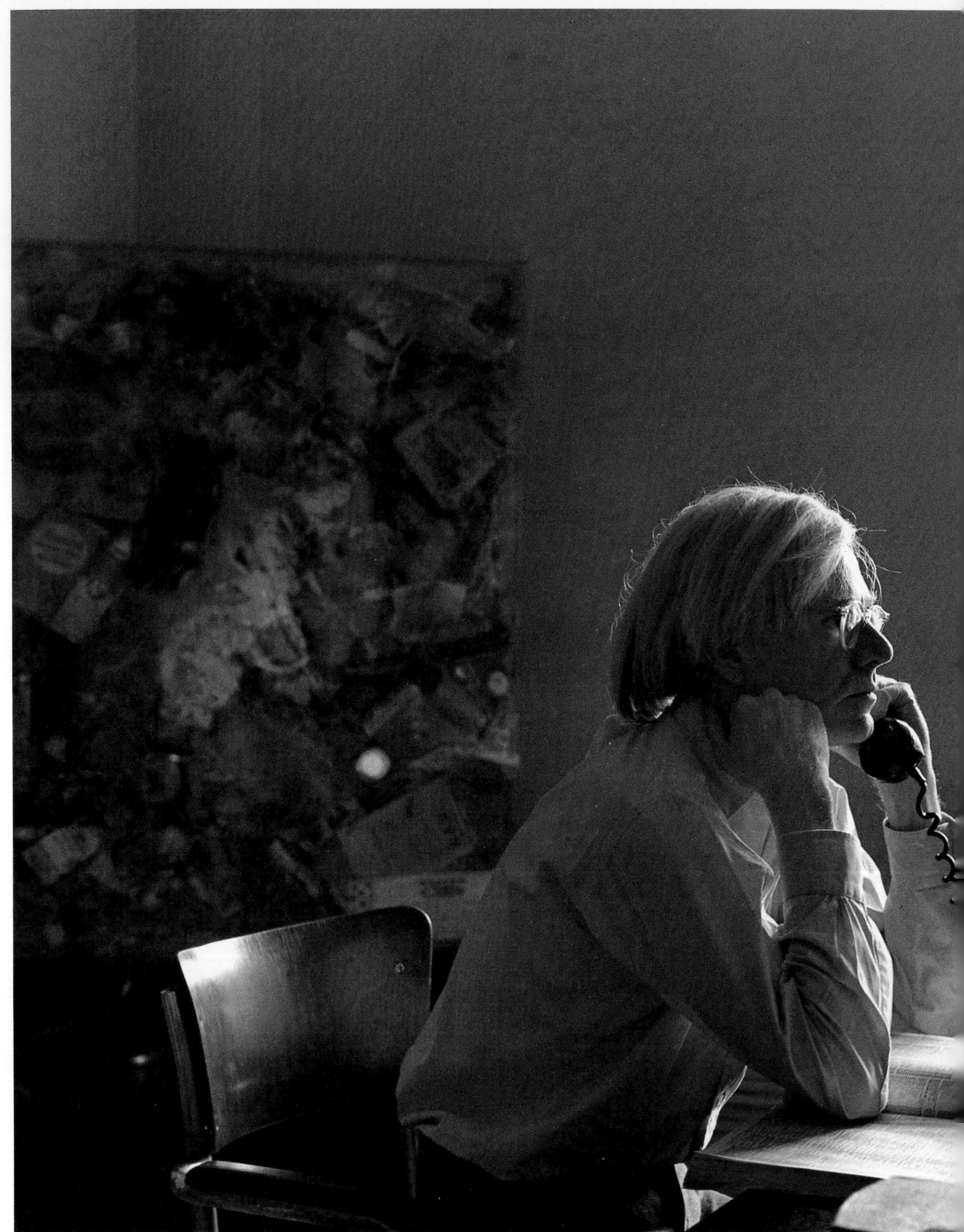

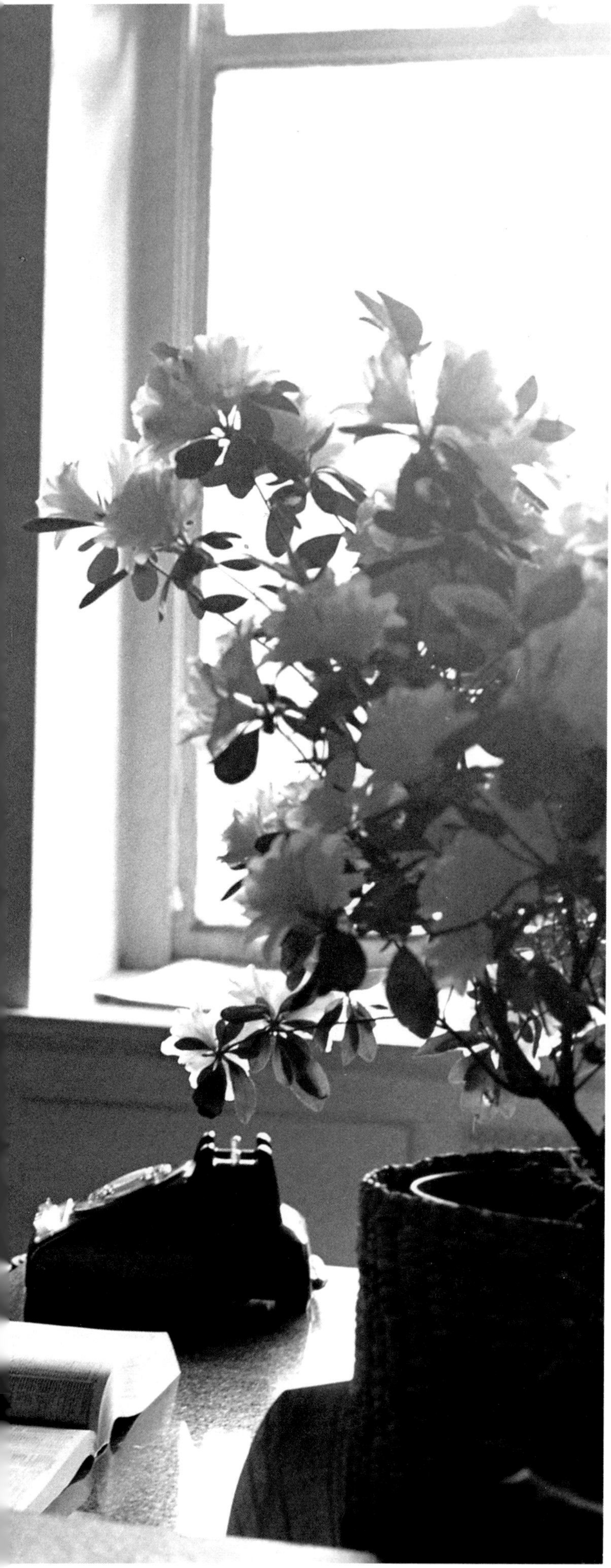

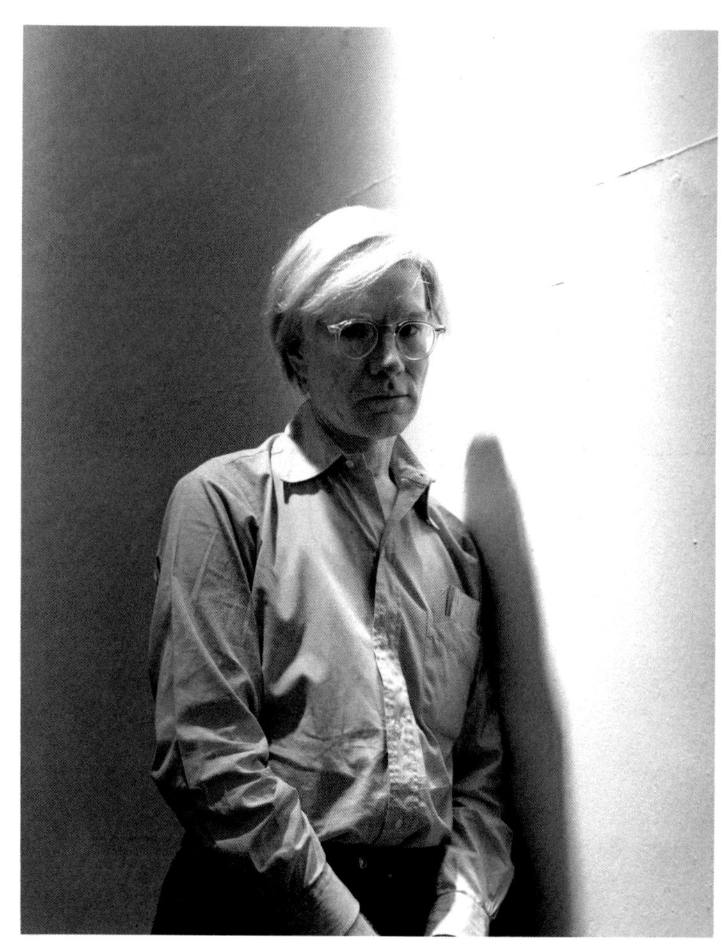

Andy Warhol   1978

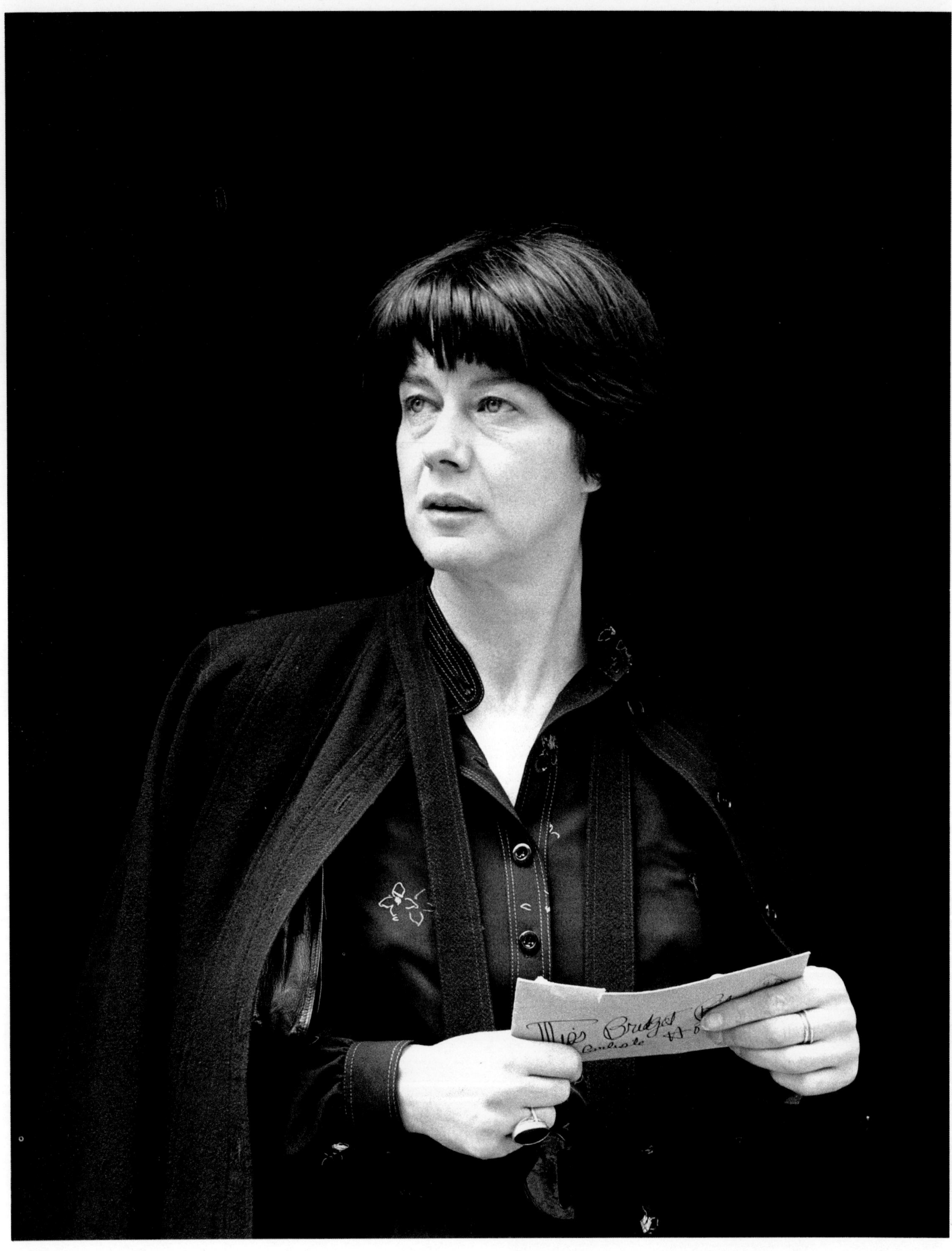

Bridget Riley   1978

Louise Nevelson   1979

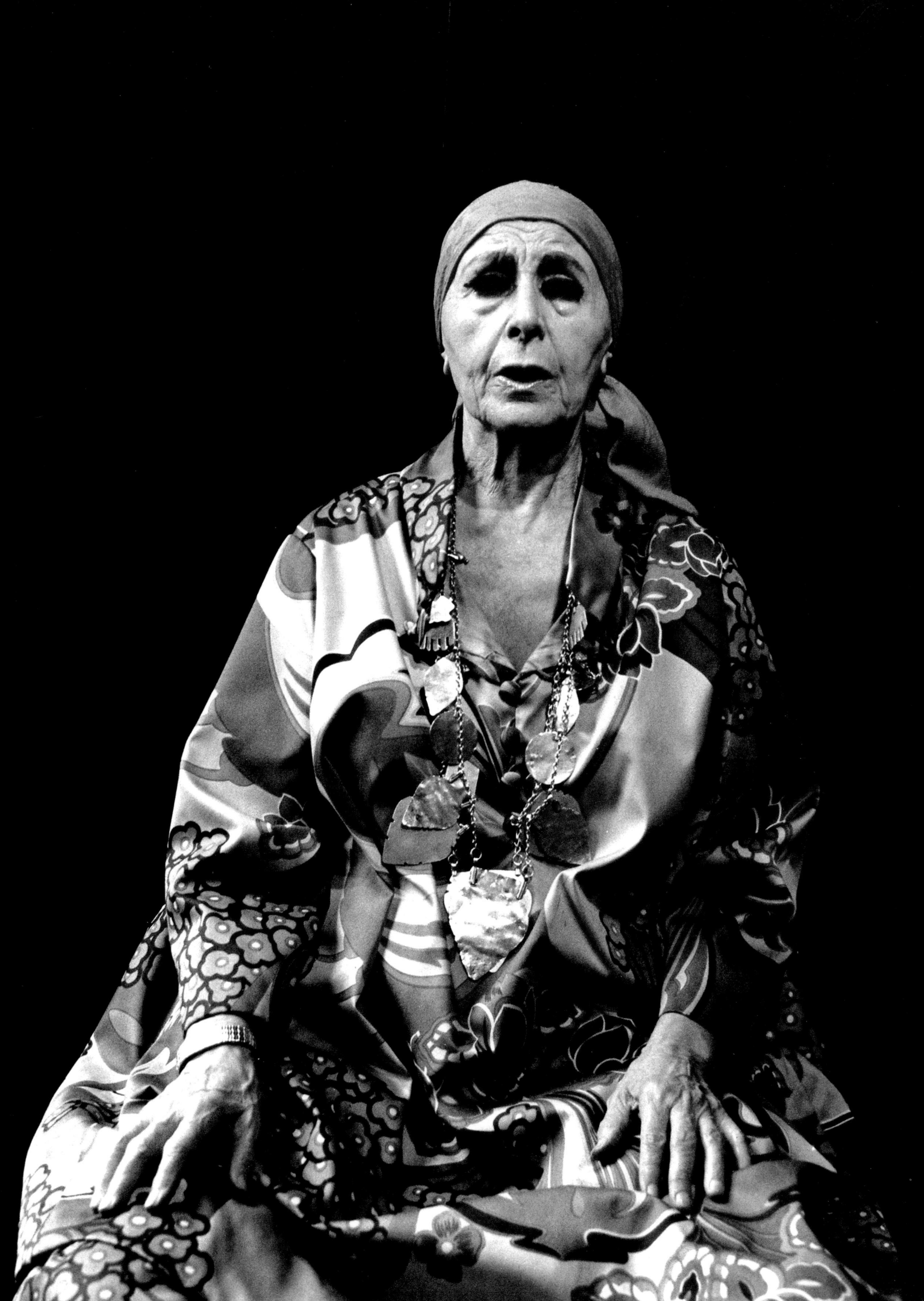

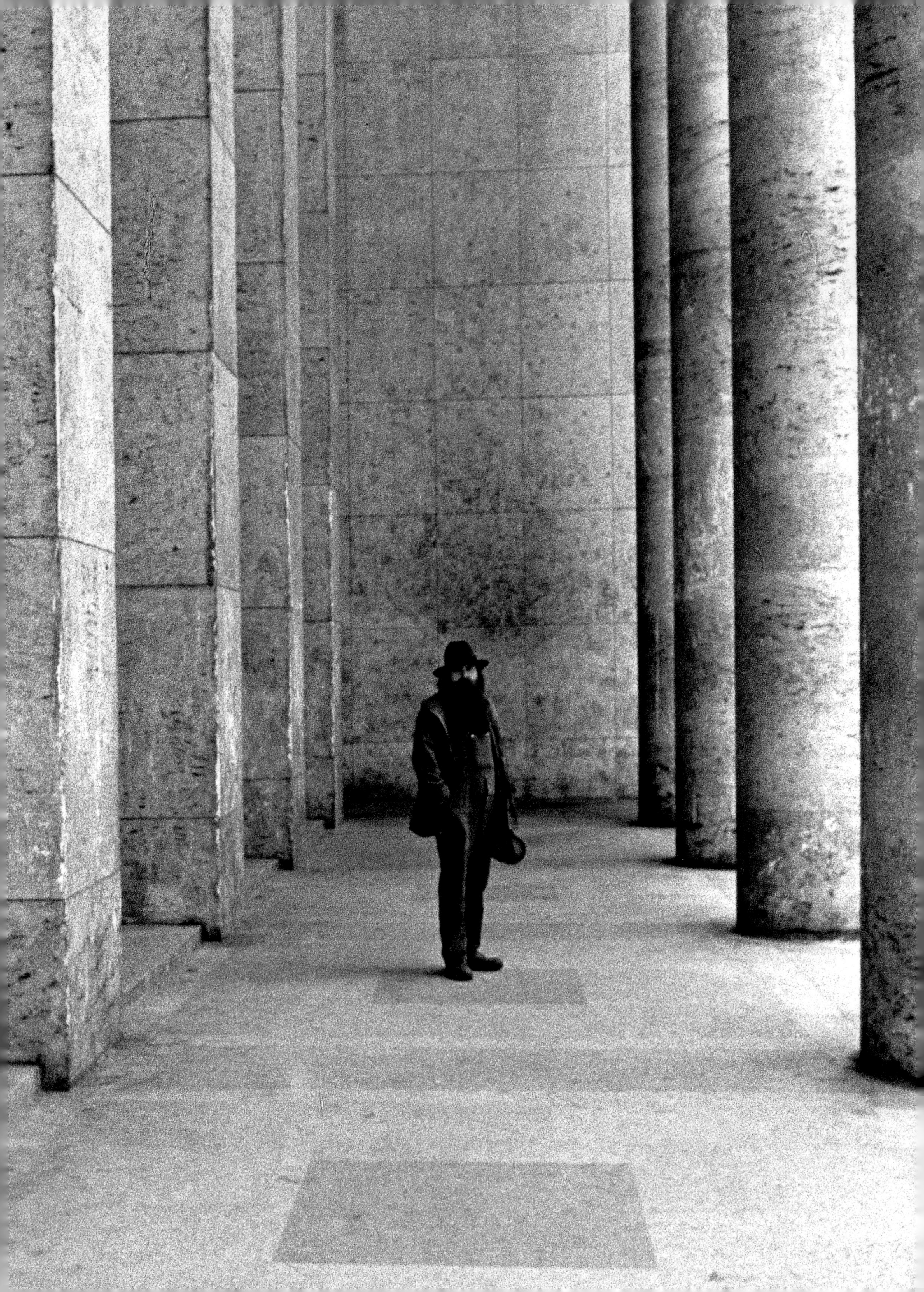

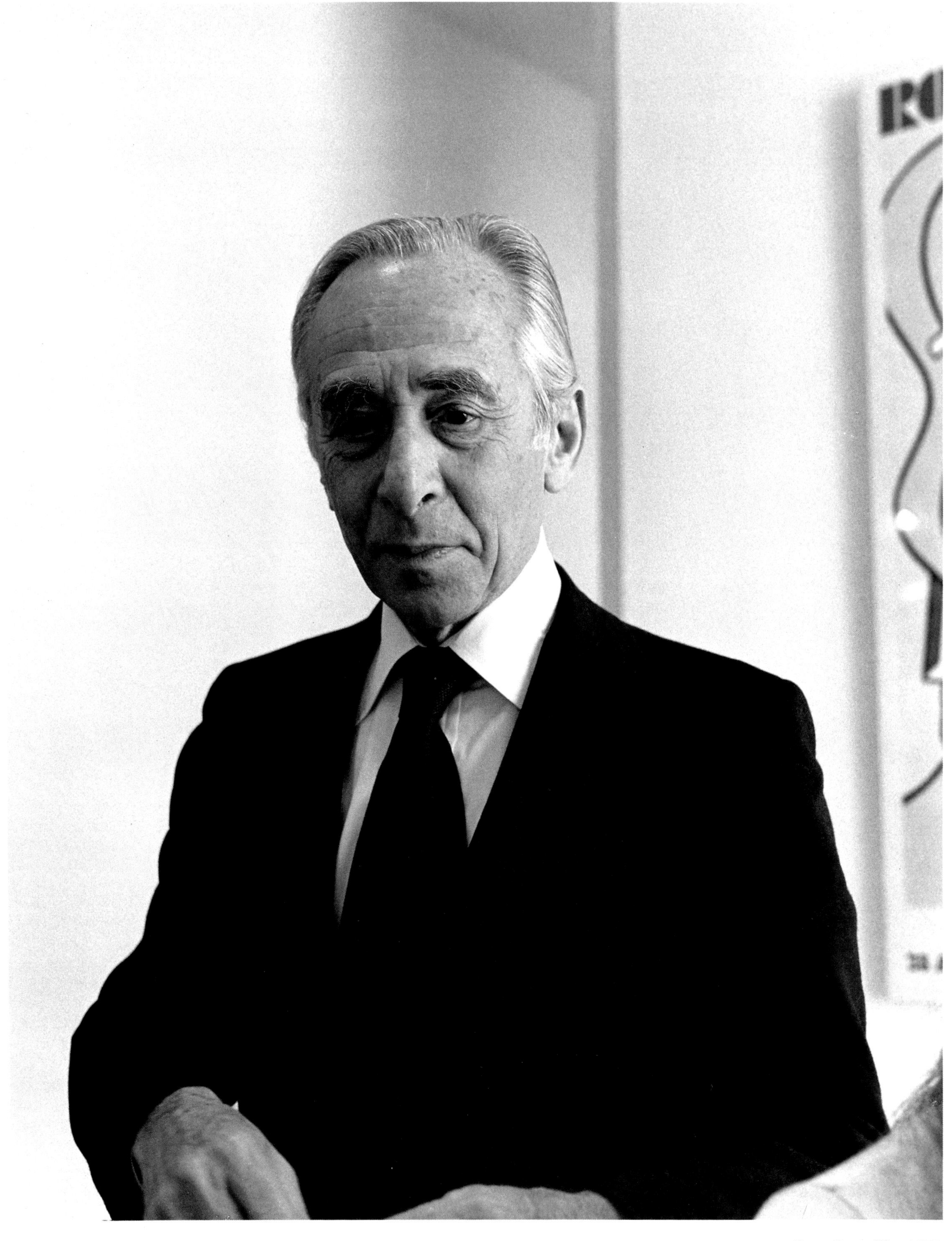

Leo Castelli   1979

Carl Andre   1979

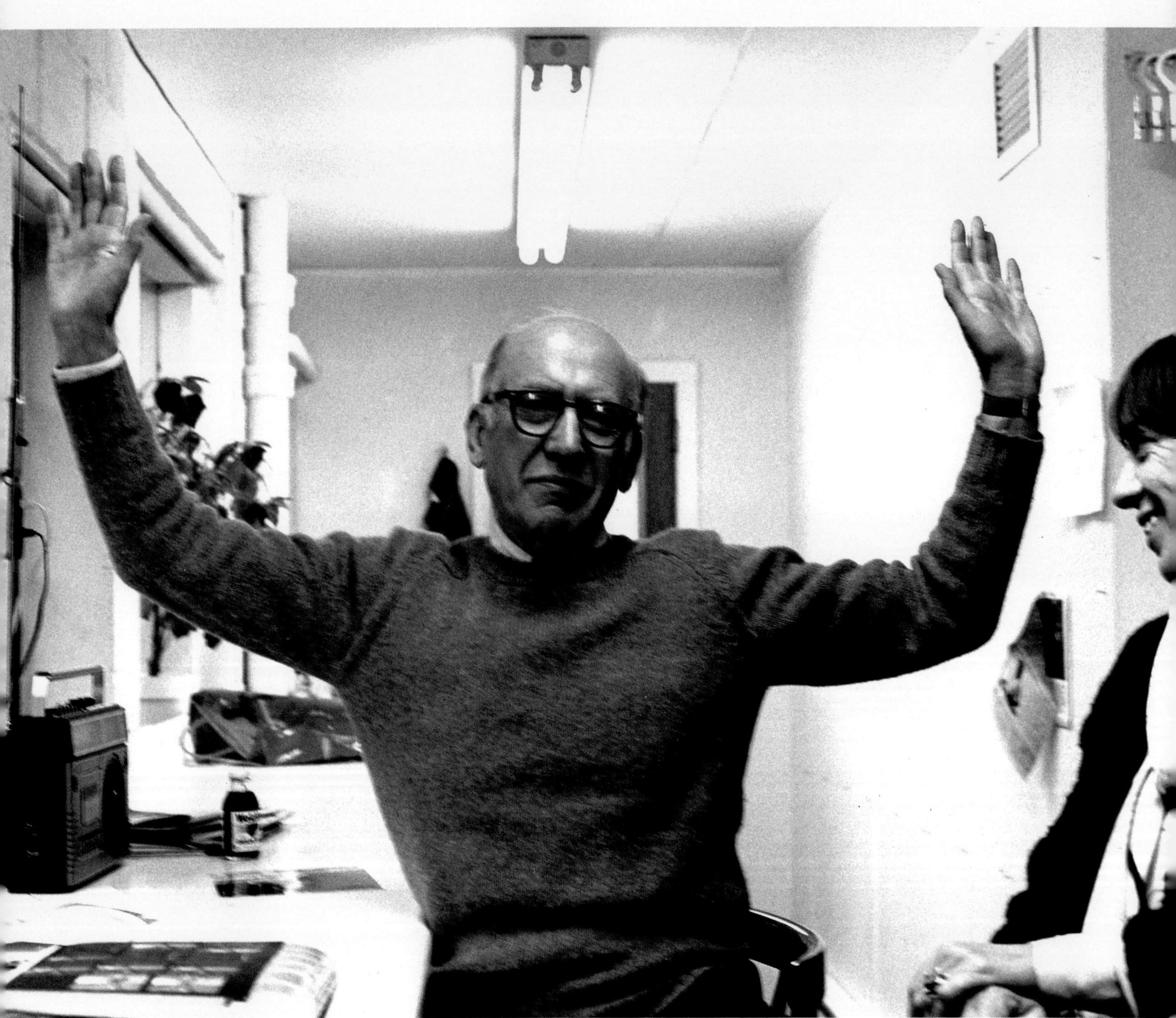

Saul Steinberg   1979

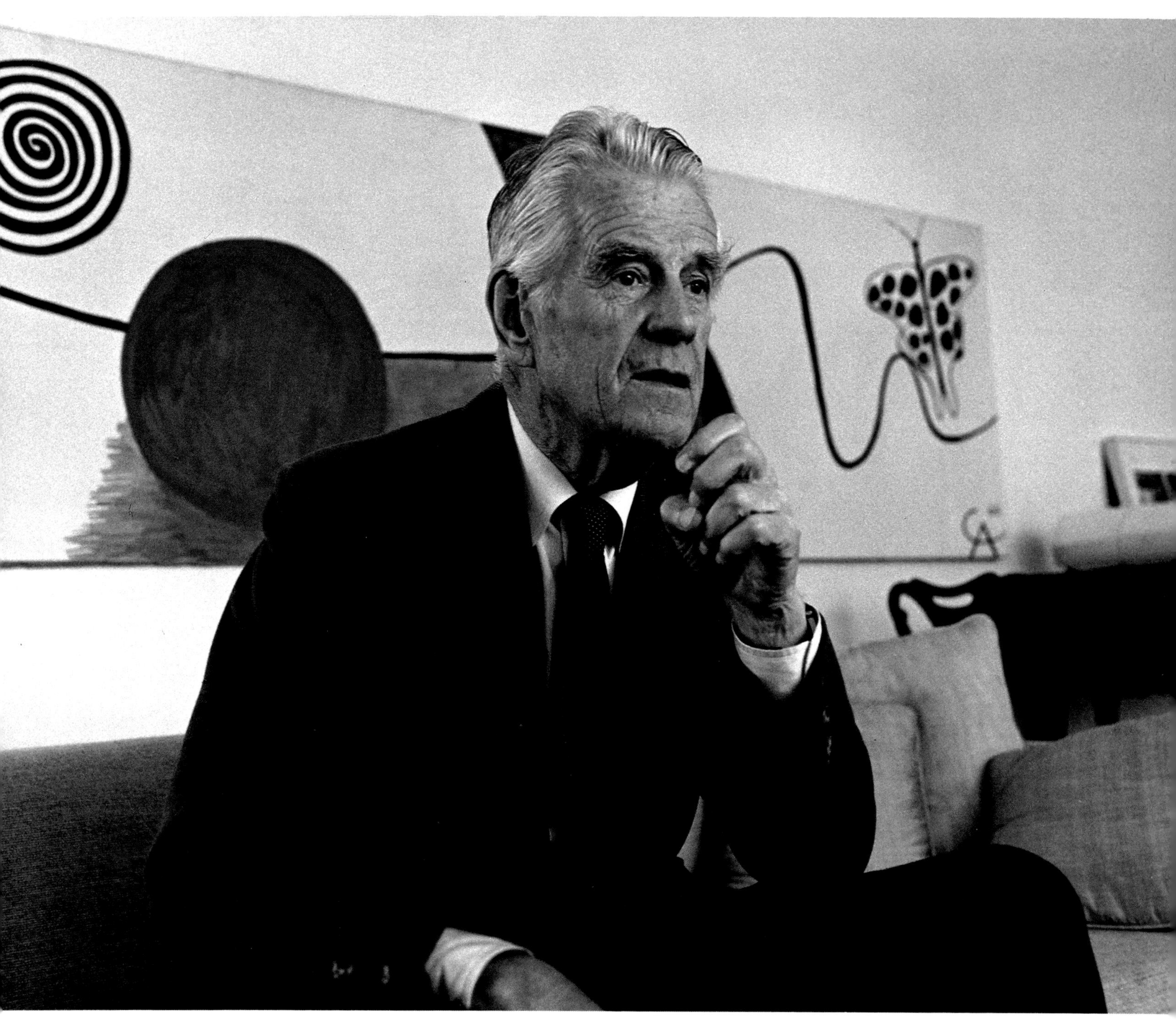

Robert Osborn   1979

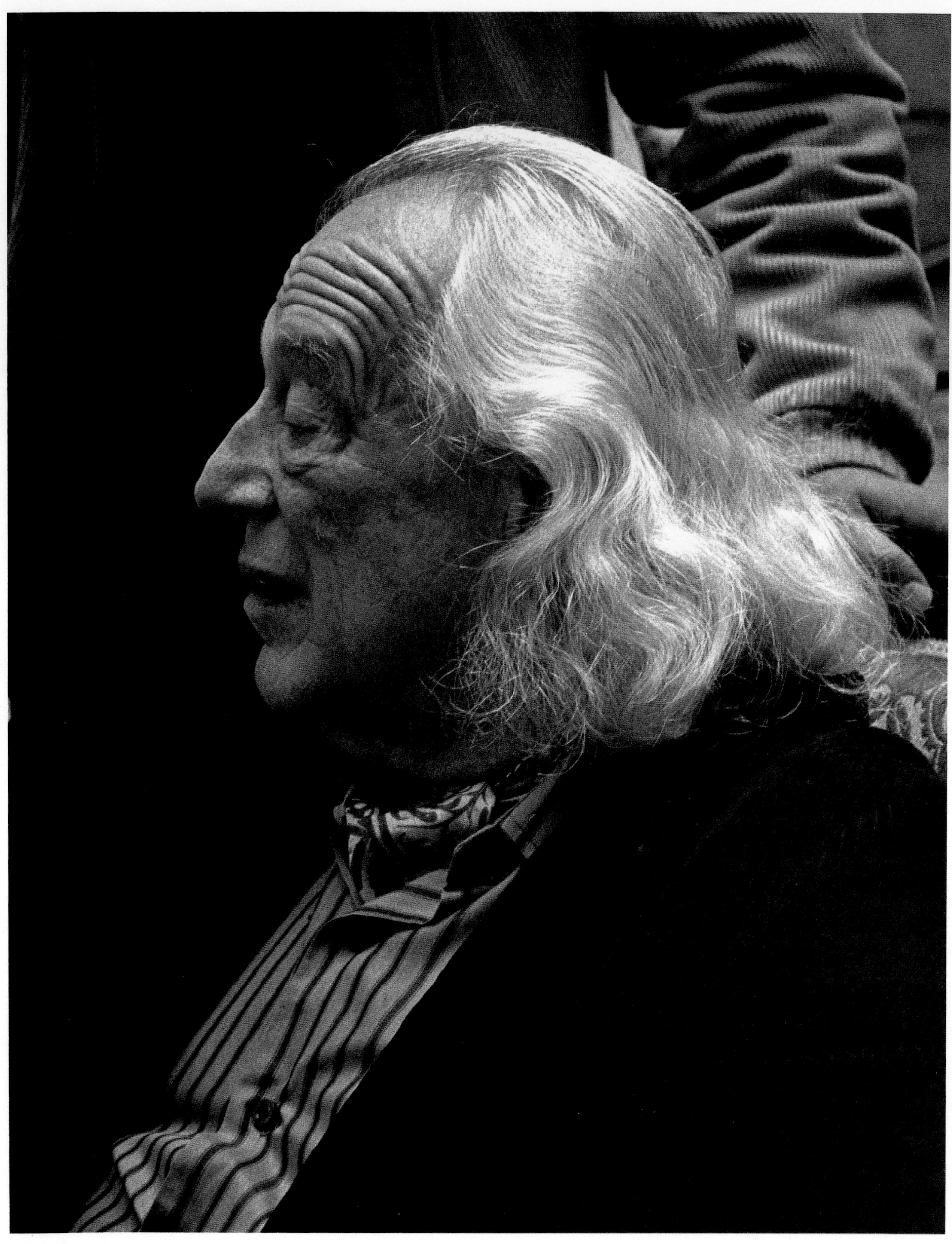

Rafael Alberti   1980

Eduardo Chillida   1980

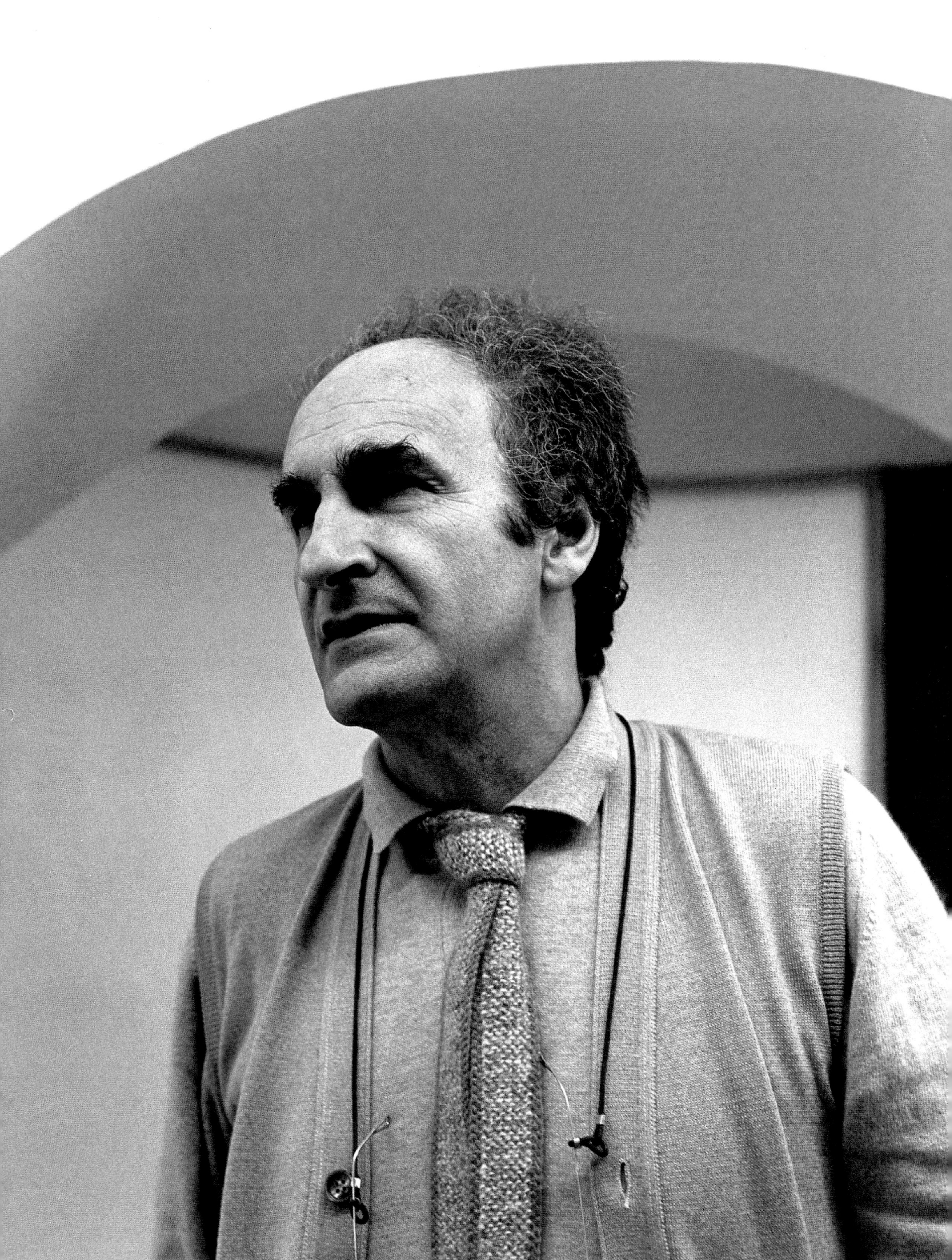

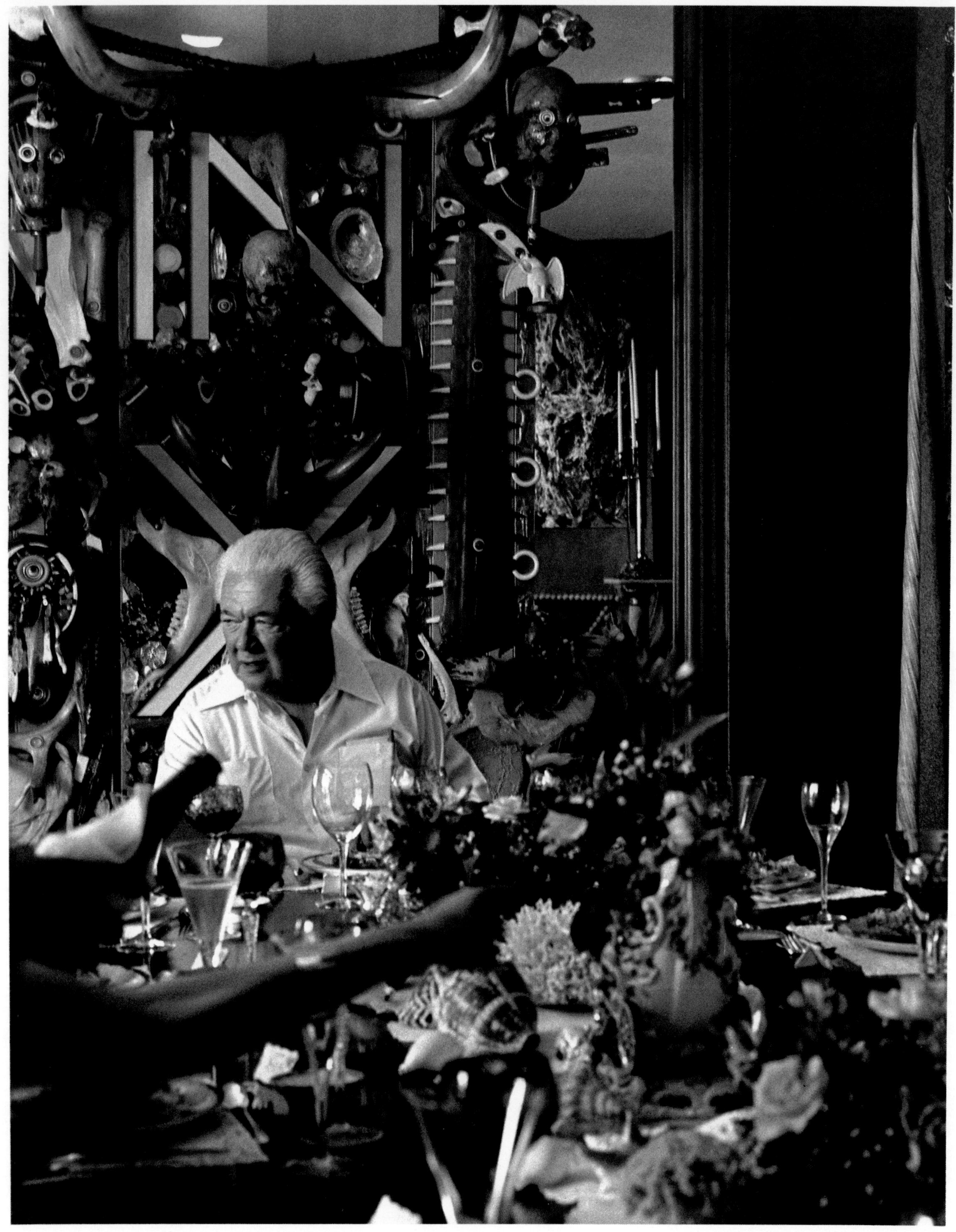

Alfonso Ossorio   1980

Christo   1980

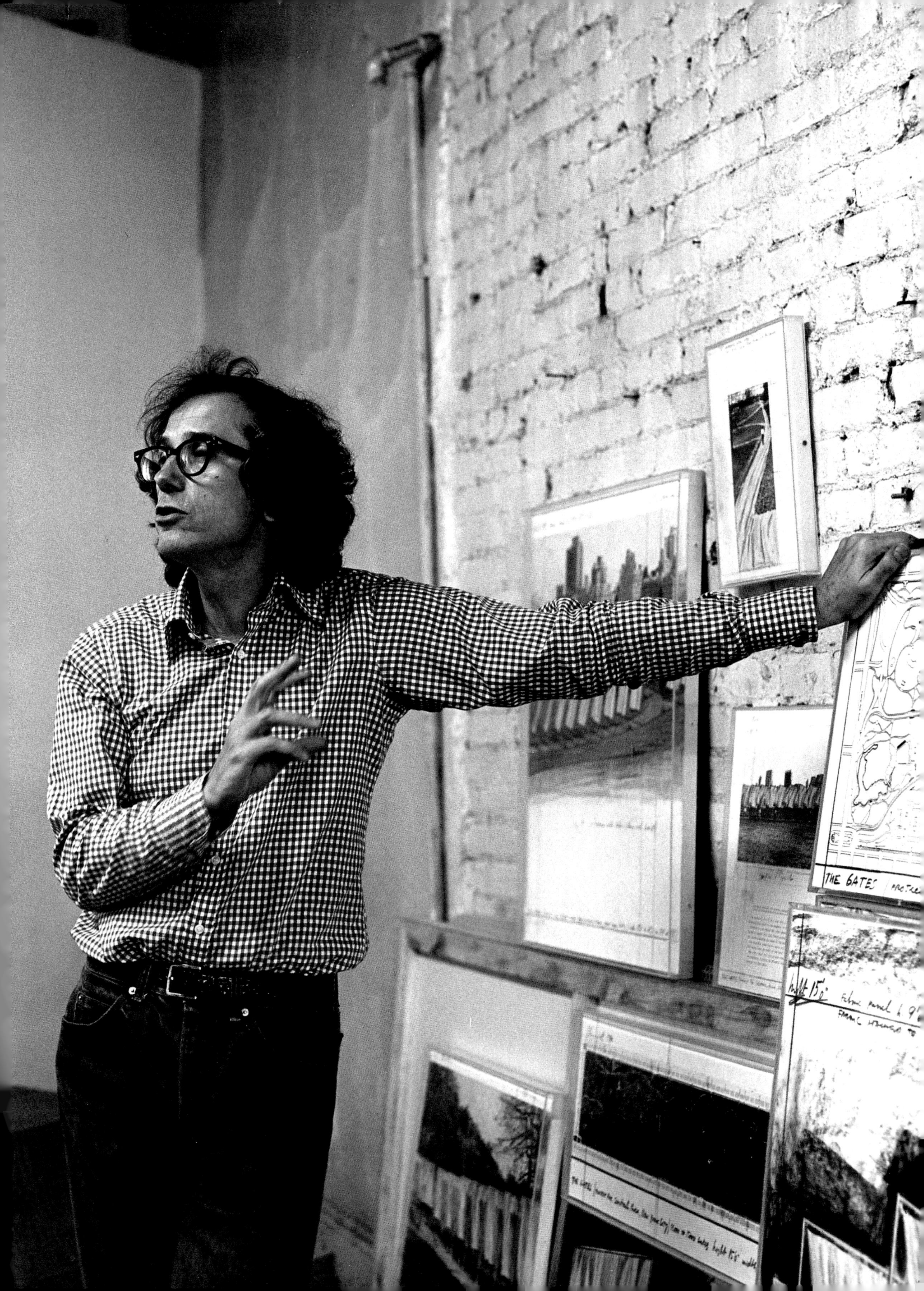

THE GATES

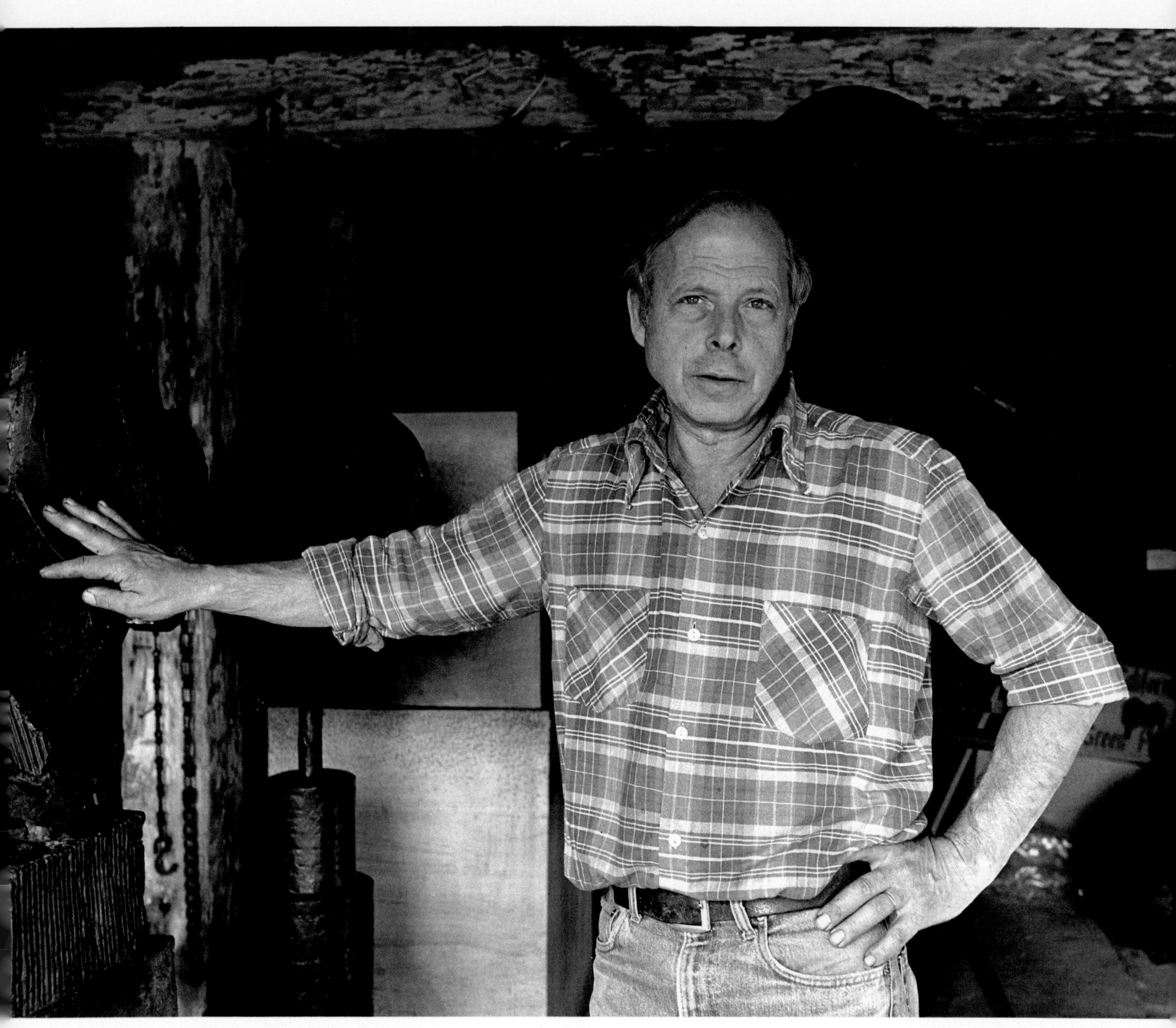

Edward Giobbi   1981

Elaine de Kooning   1981

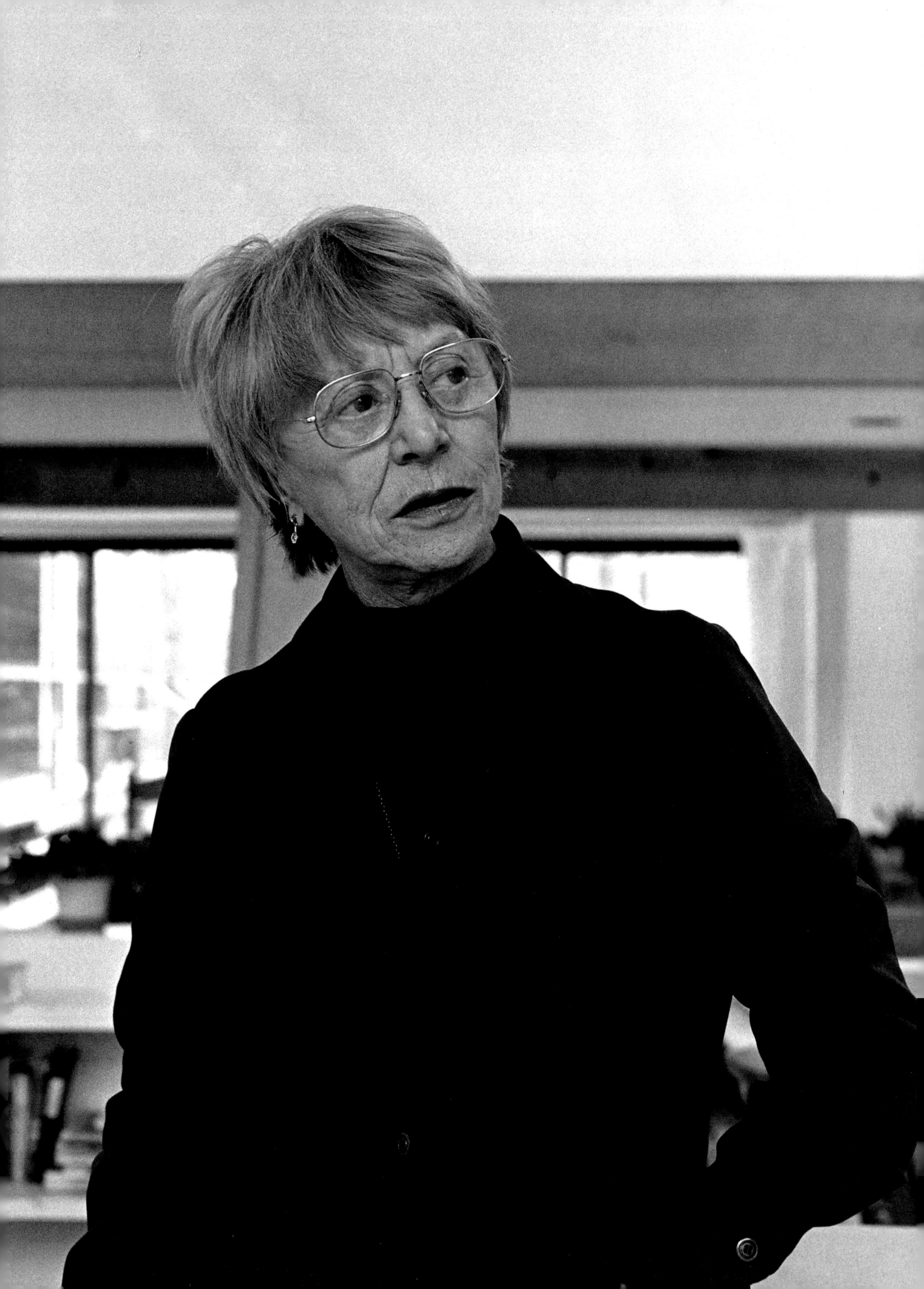

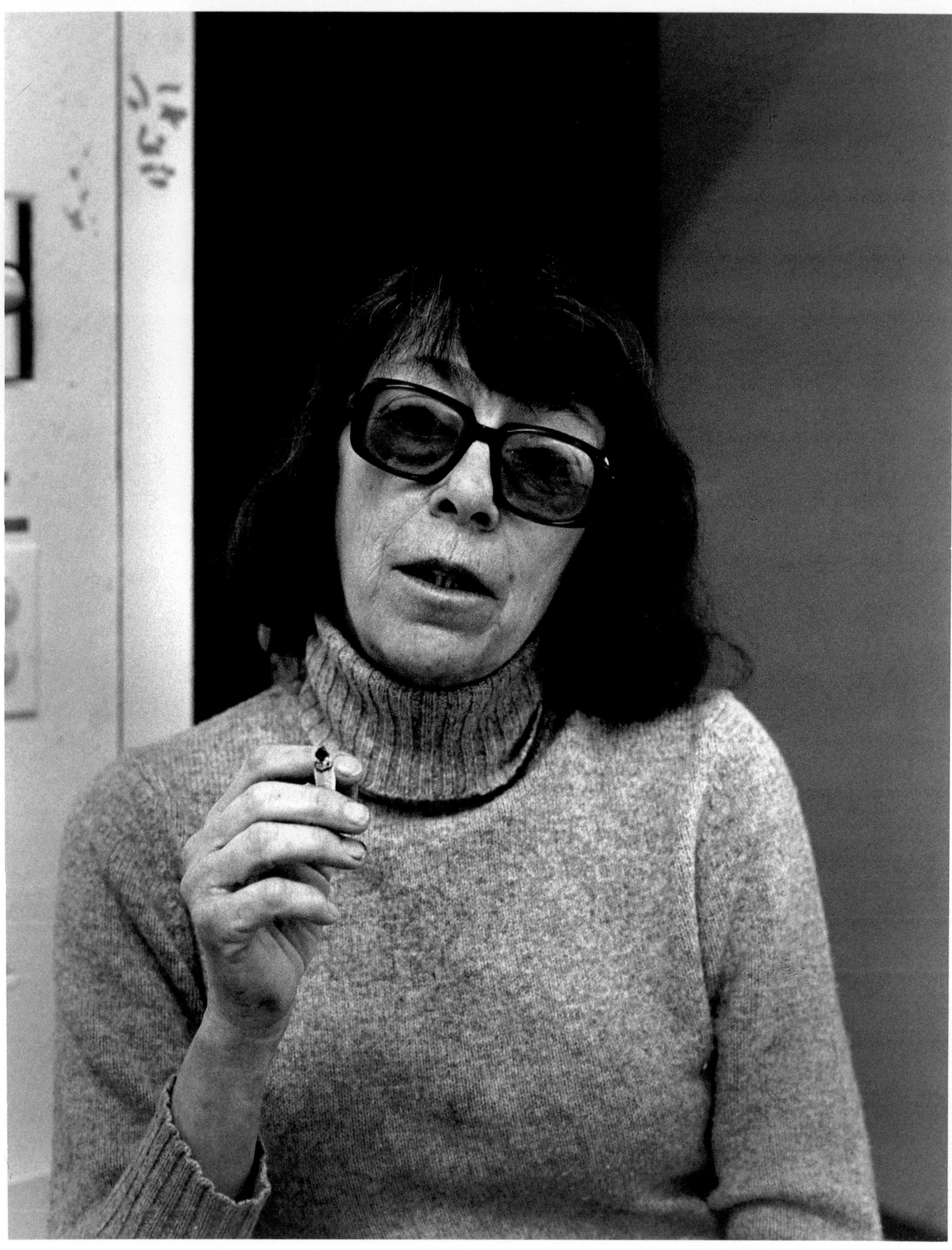

Joan Mitchell   1981

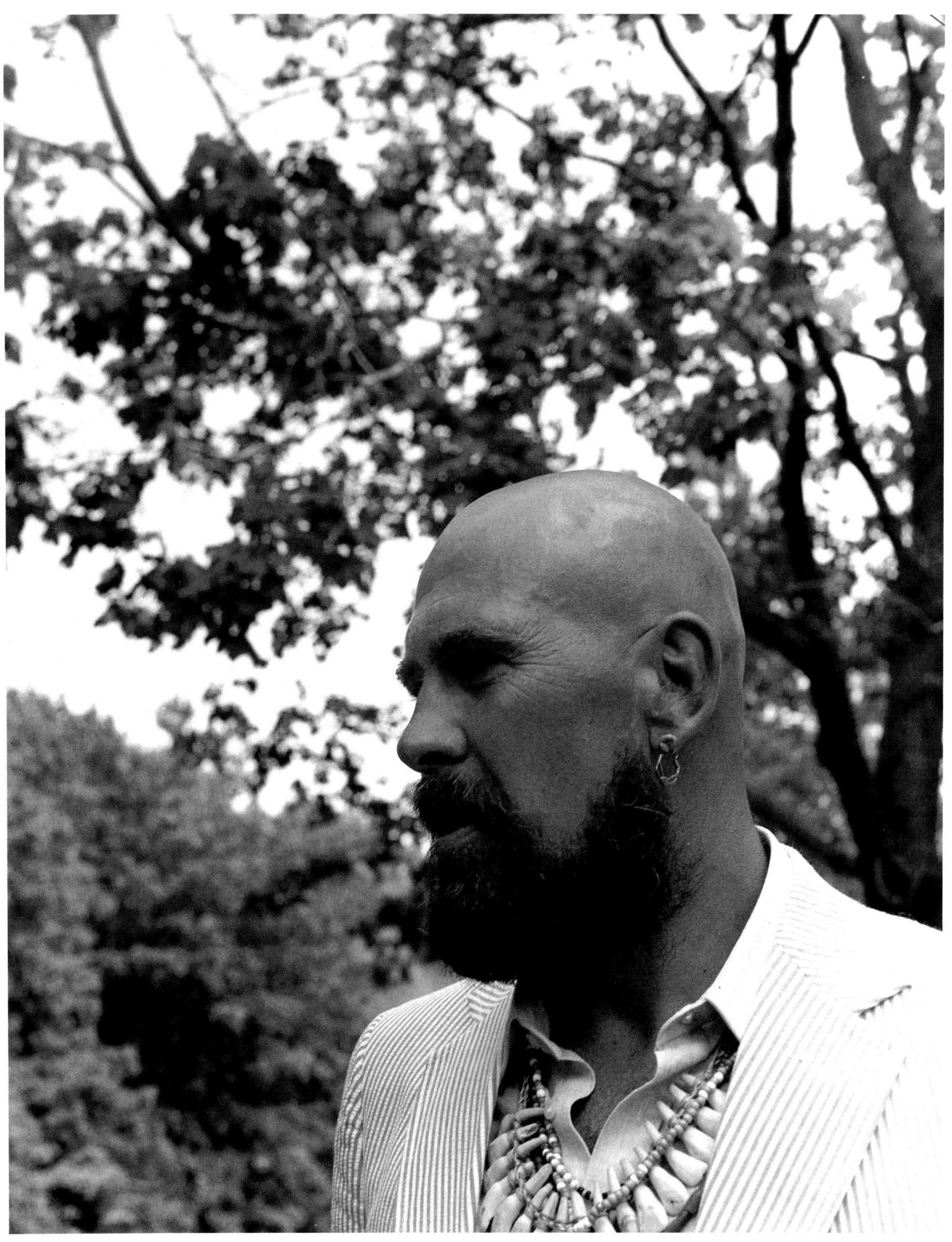

Alan Shields   1981

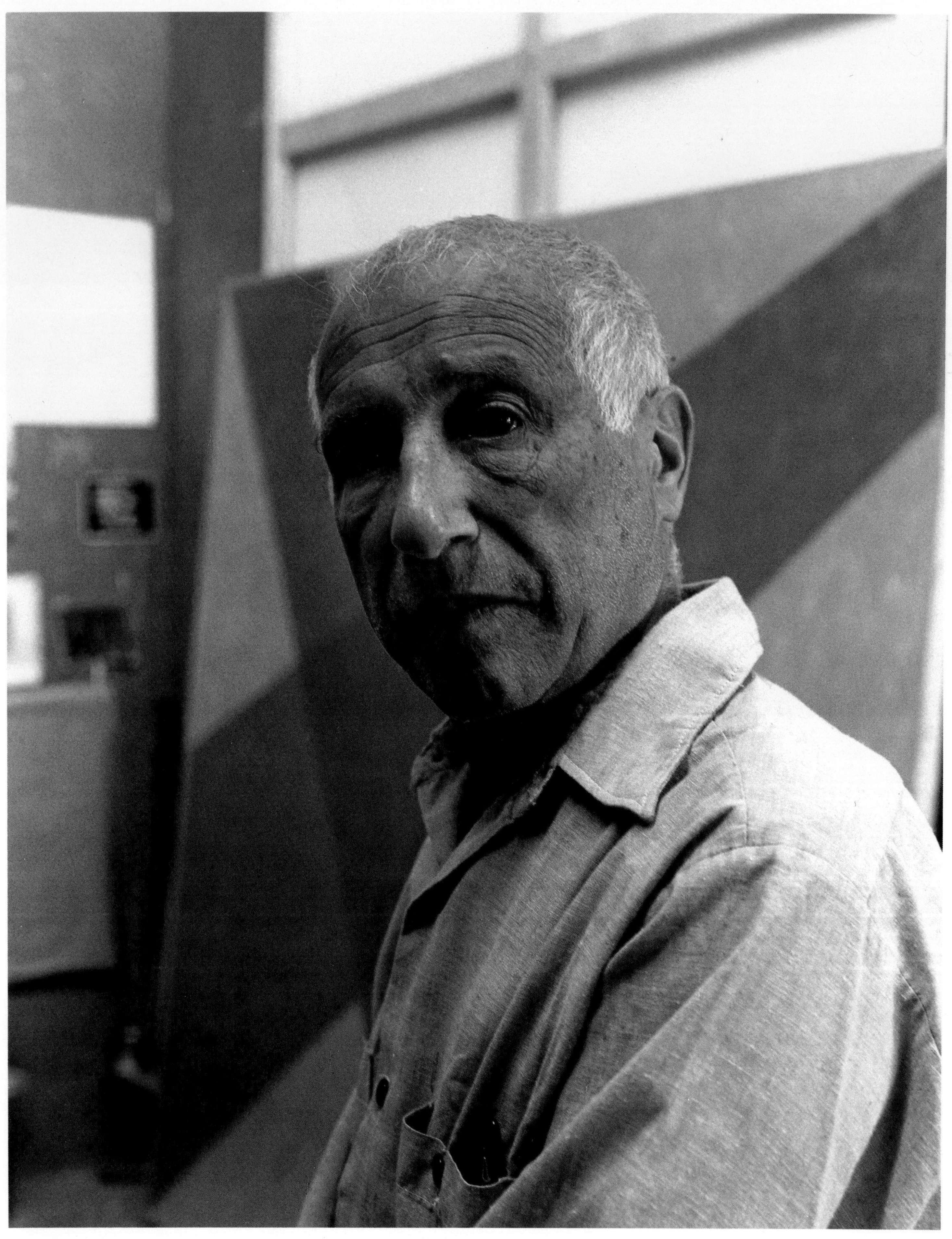

Jack Tworkov   1981

Jim Dine   1981

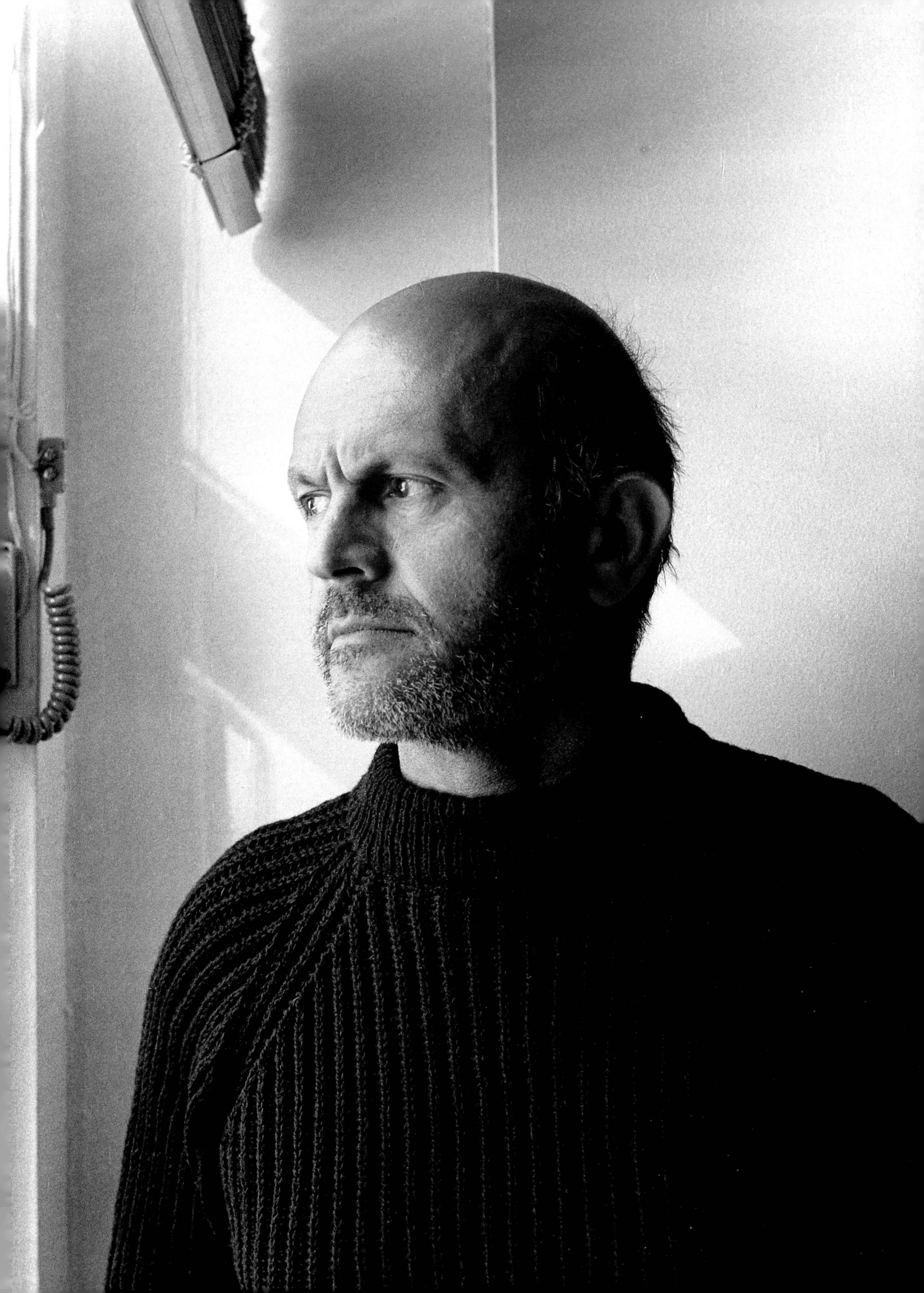

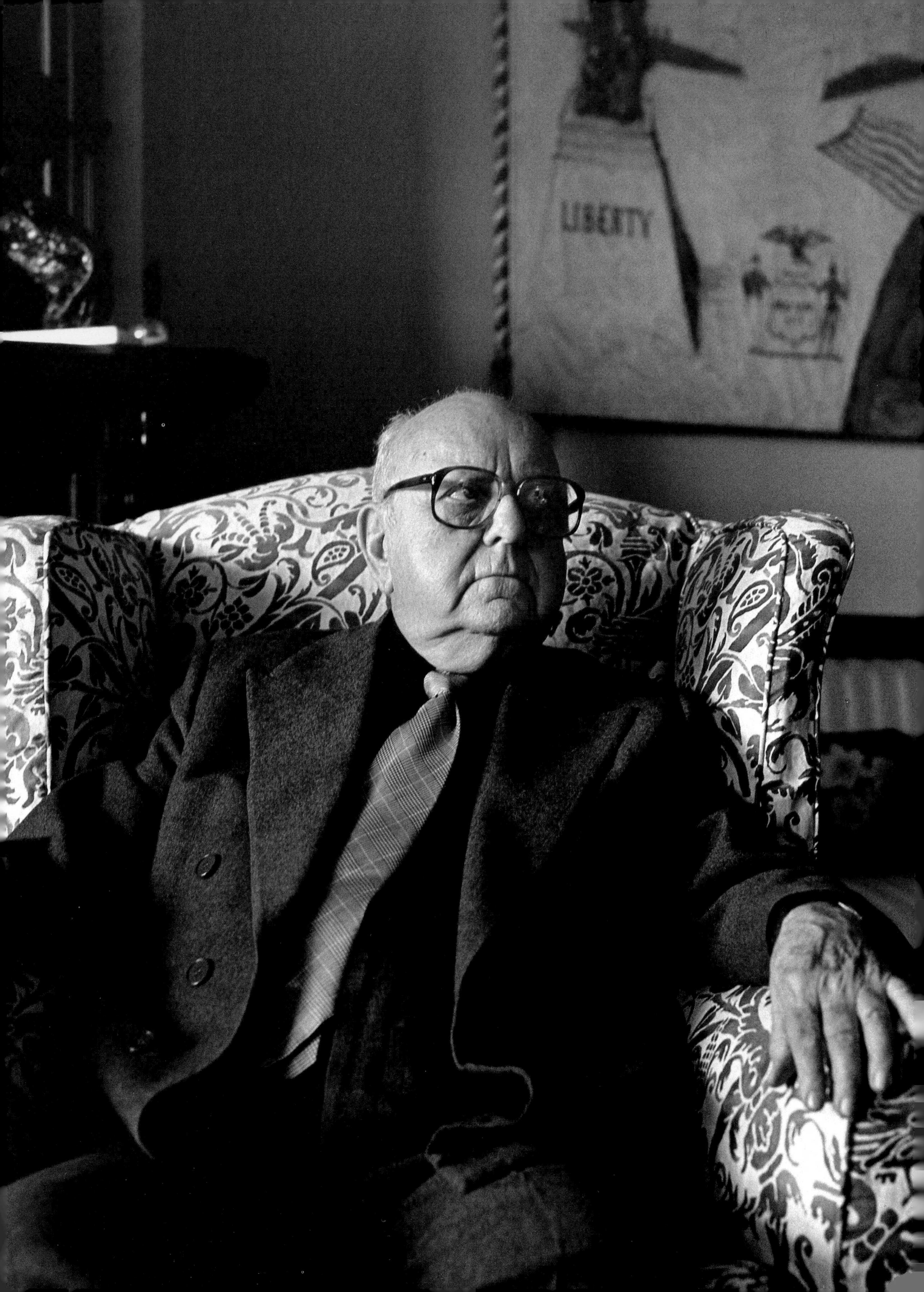
LIBERTY

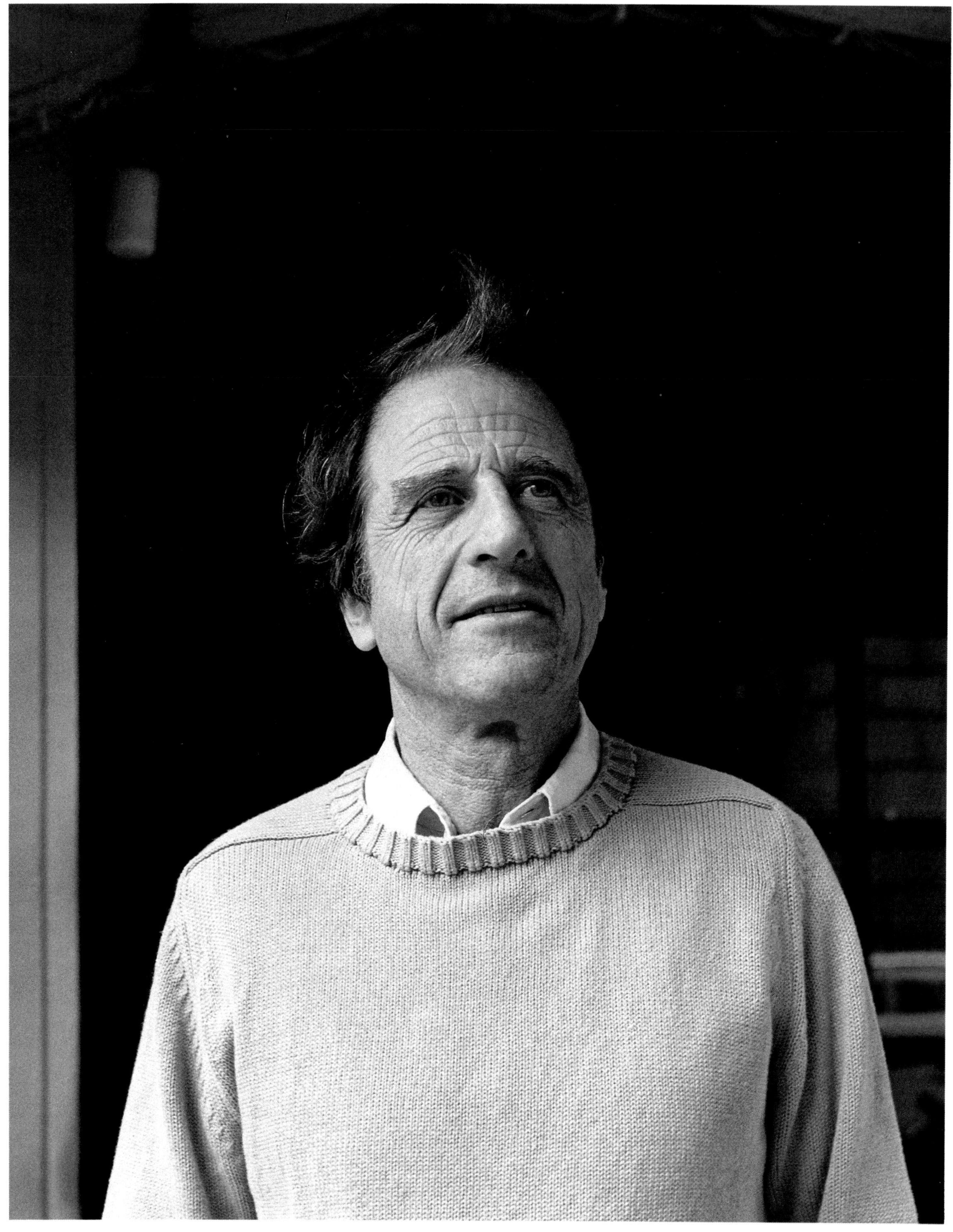

Lukas Foss   1983

Virgil Thomson   1980

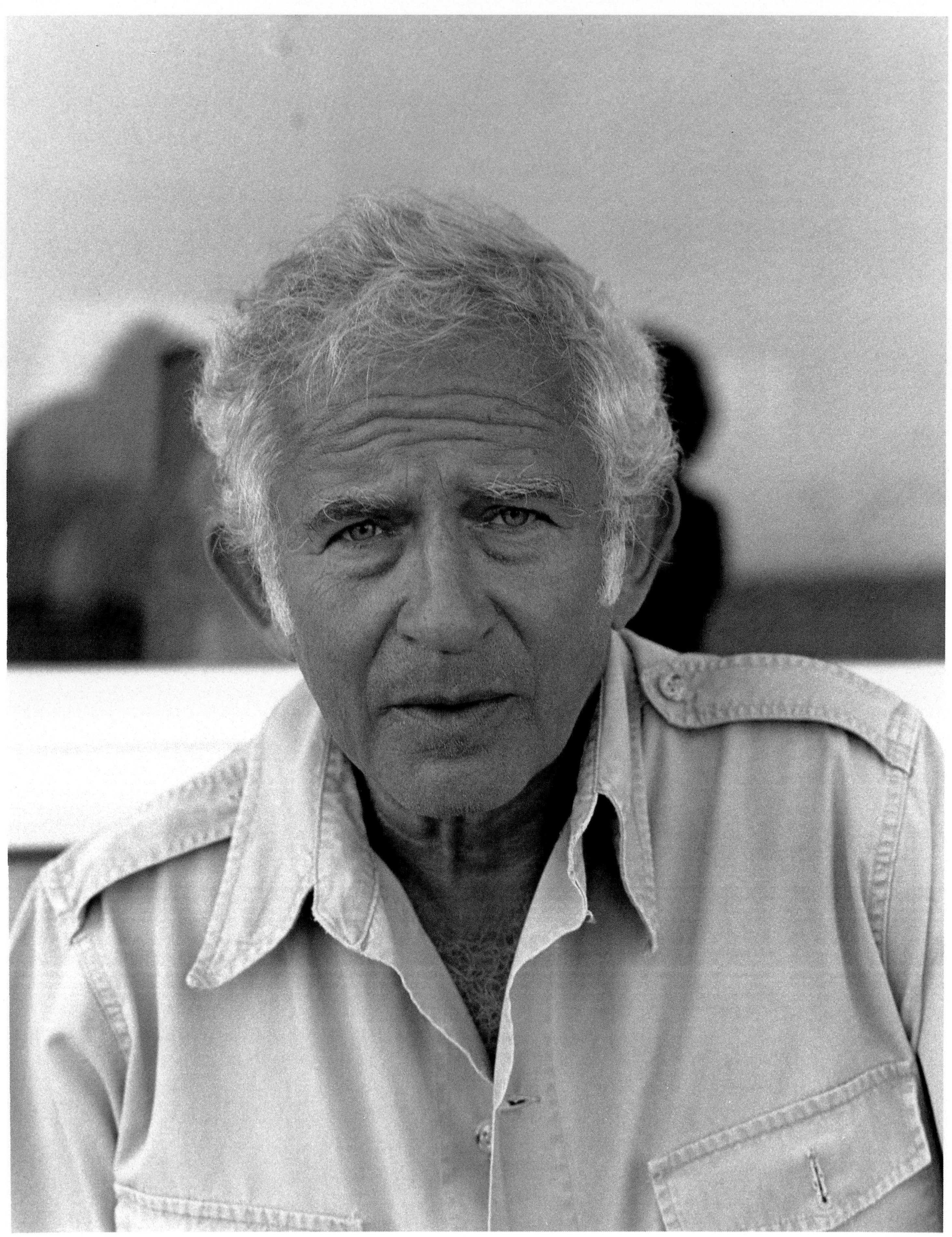

Norman Mailer   1982

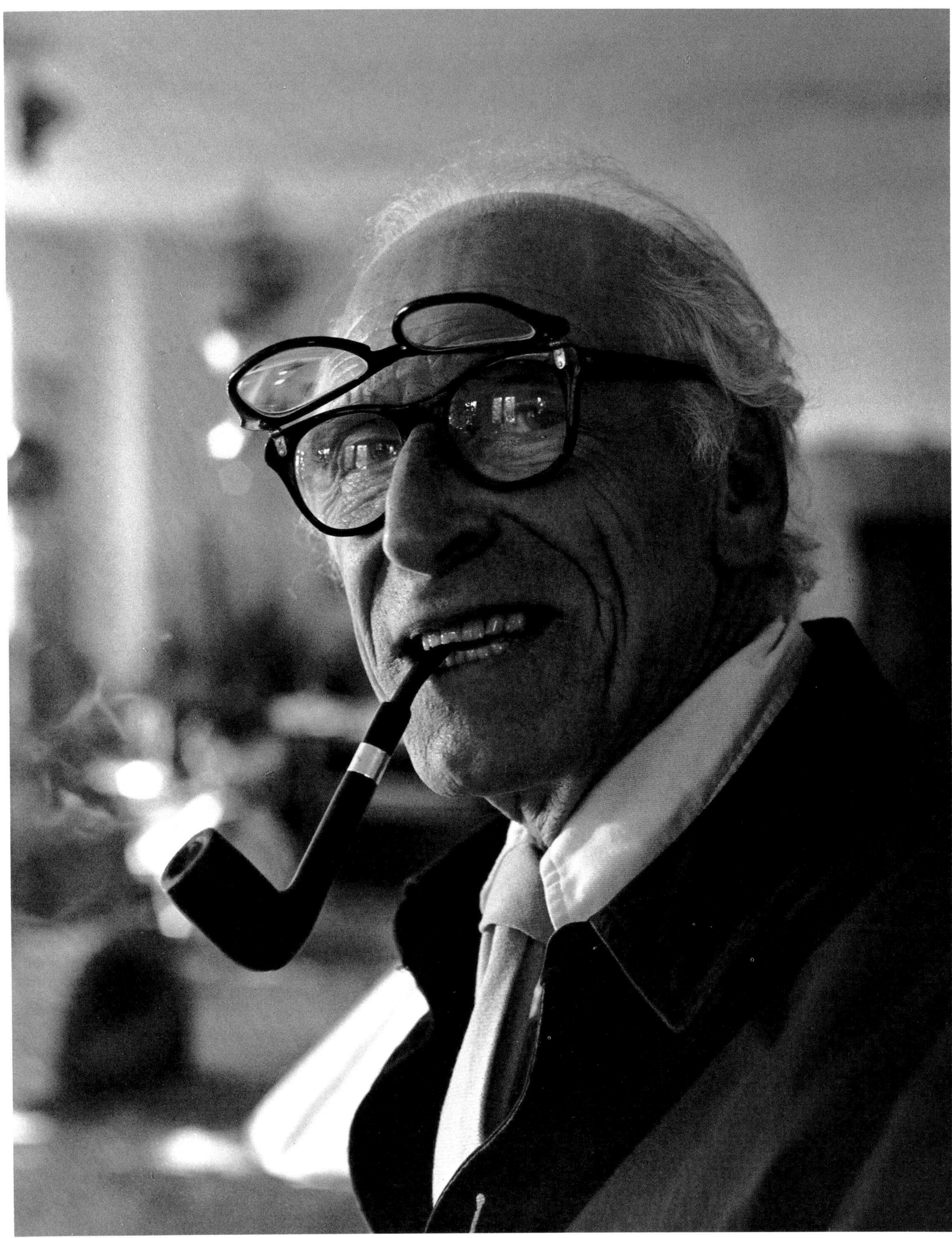

Harry Holtzman   1984

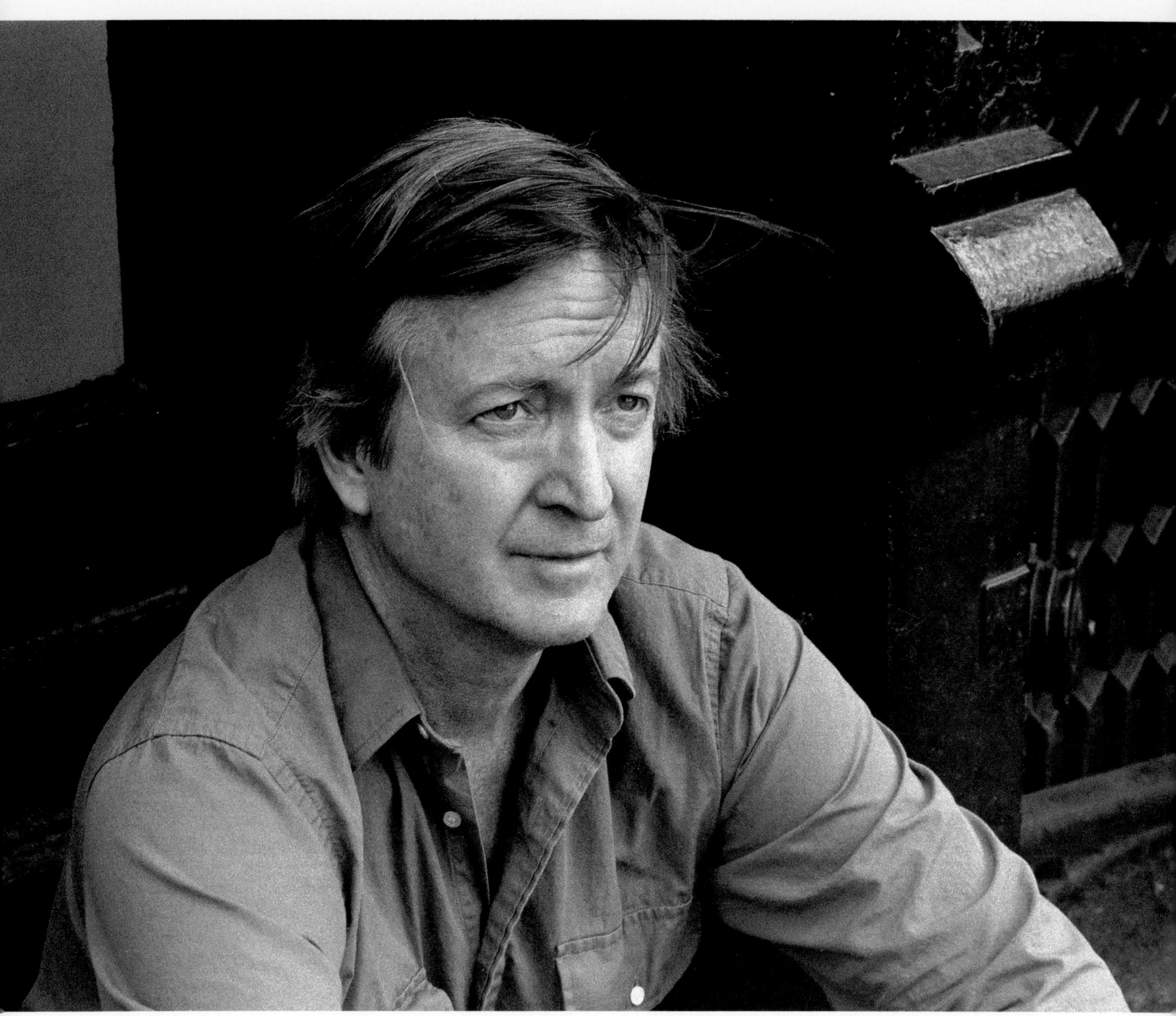

Jack Youngerman   1982

Myron Stout   1983

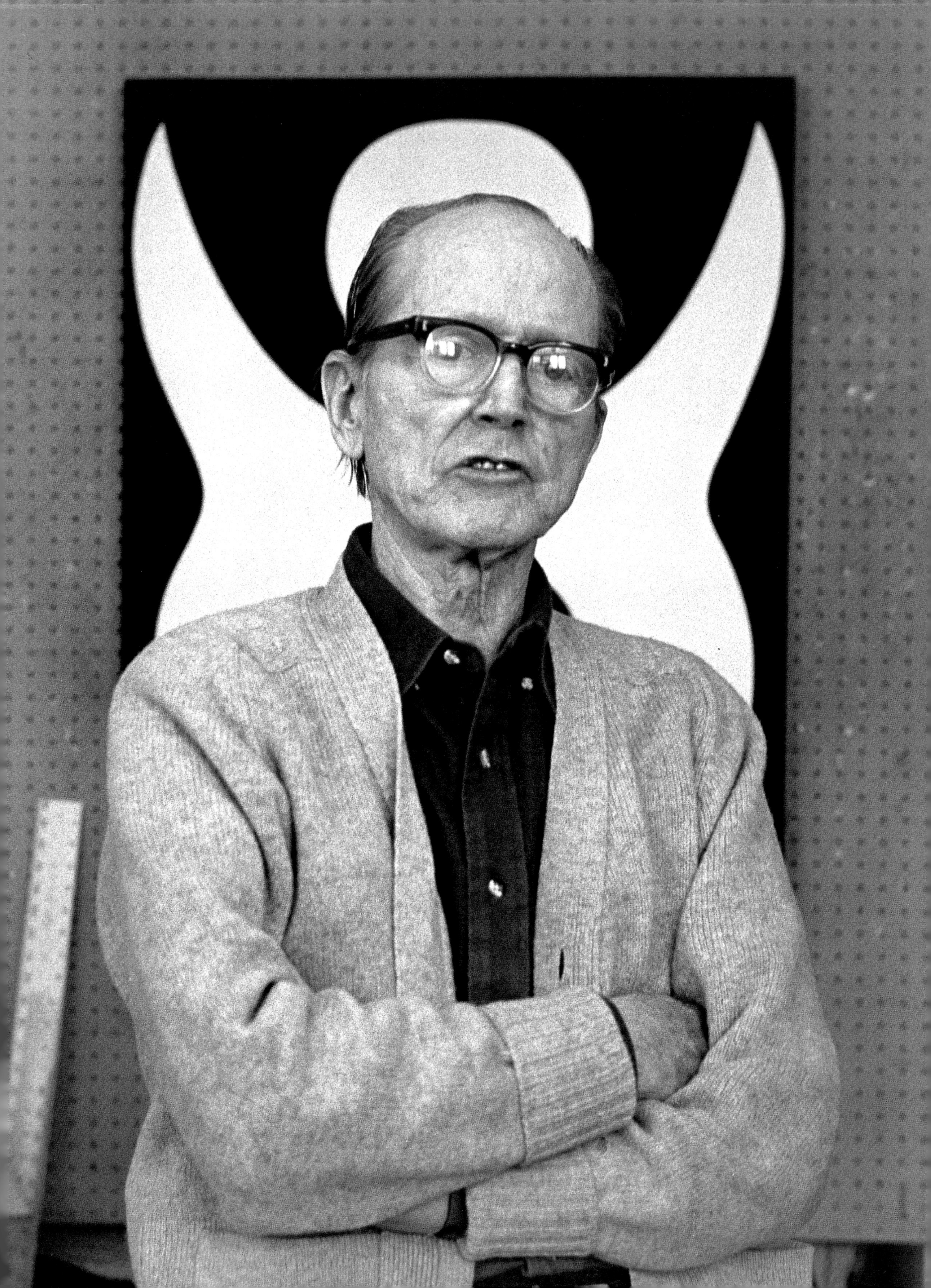

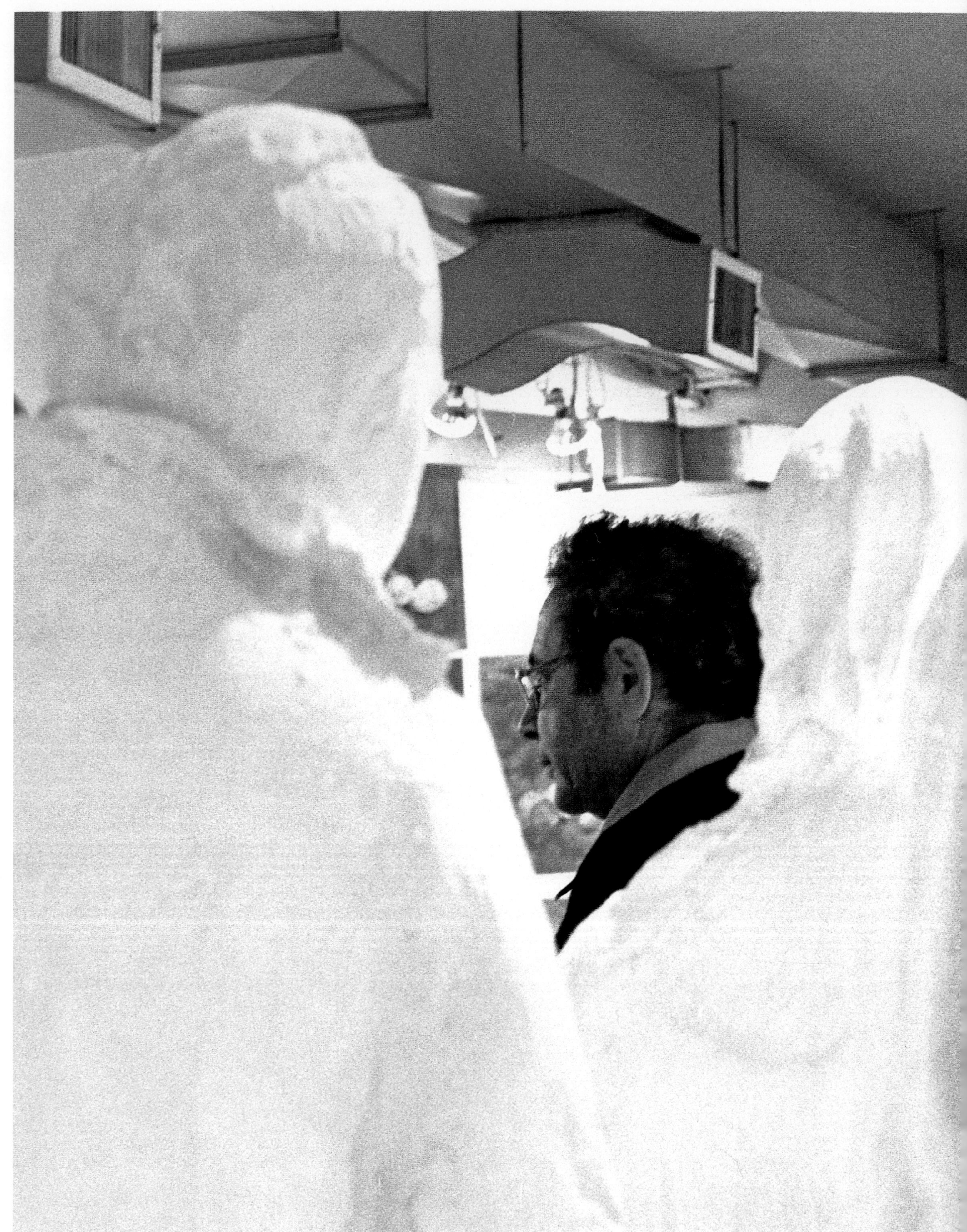

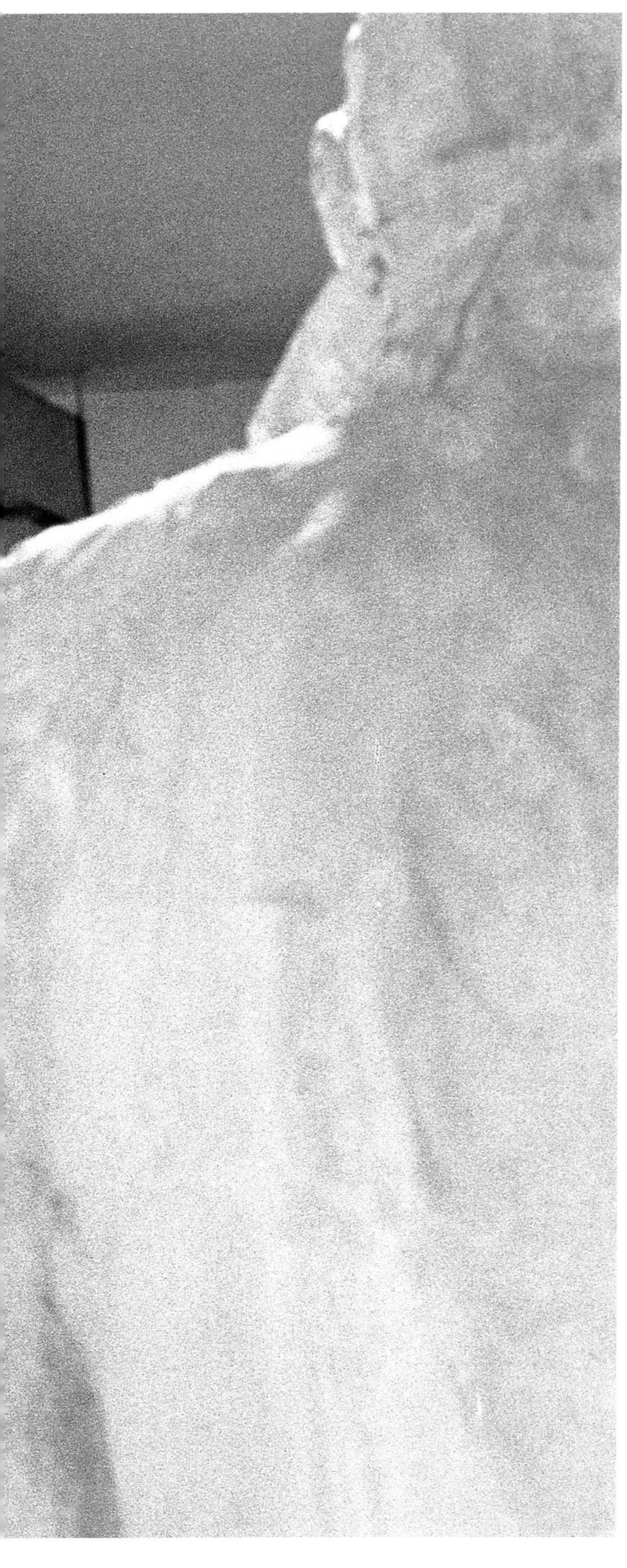

George Segal   1983

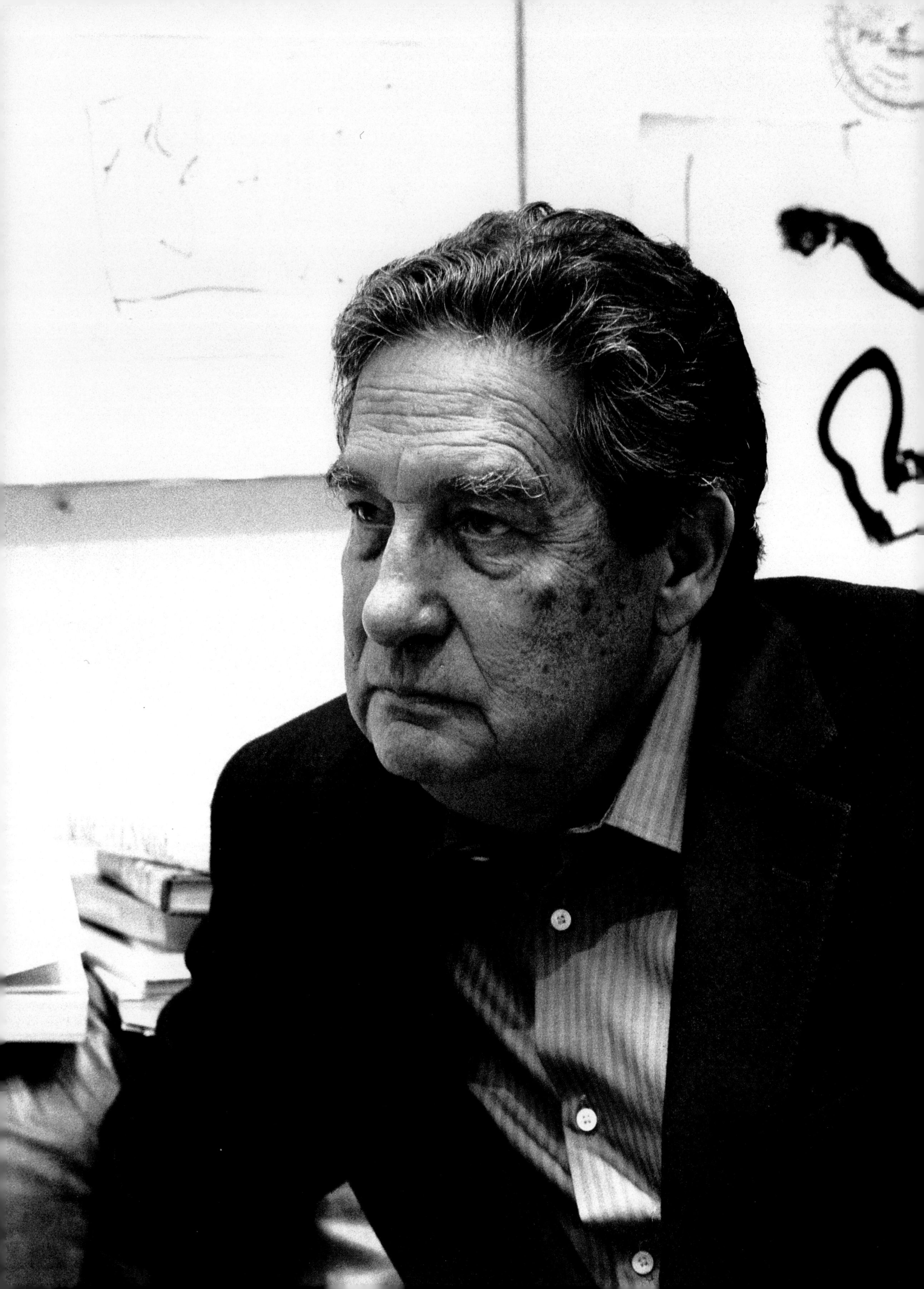

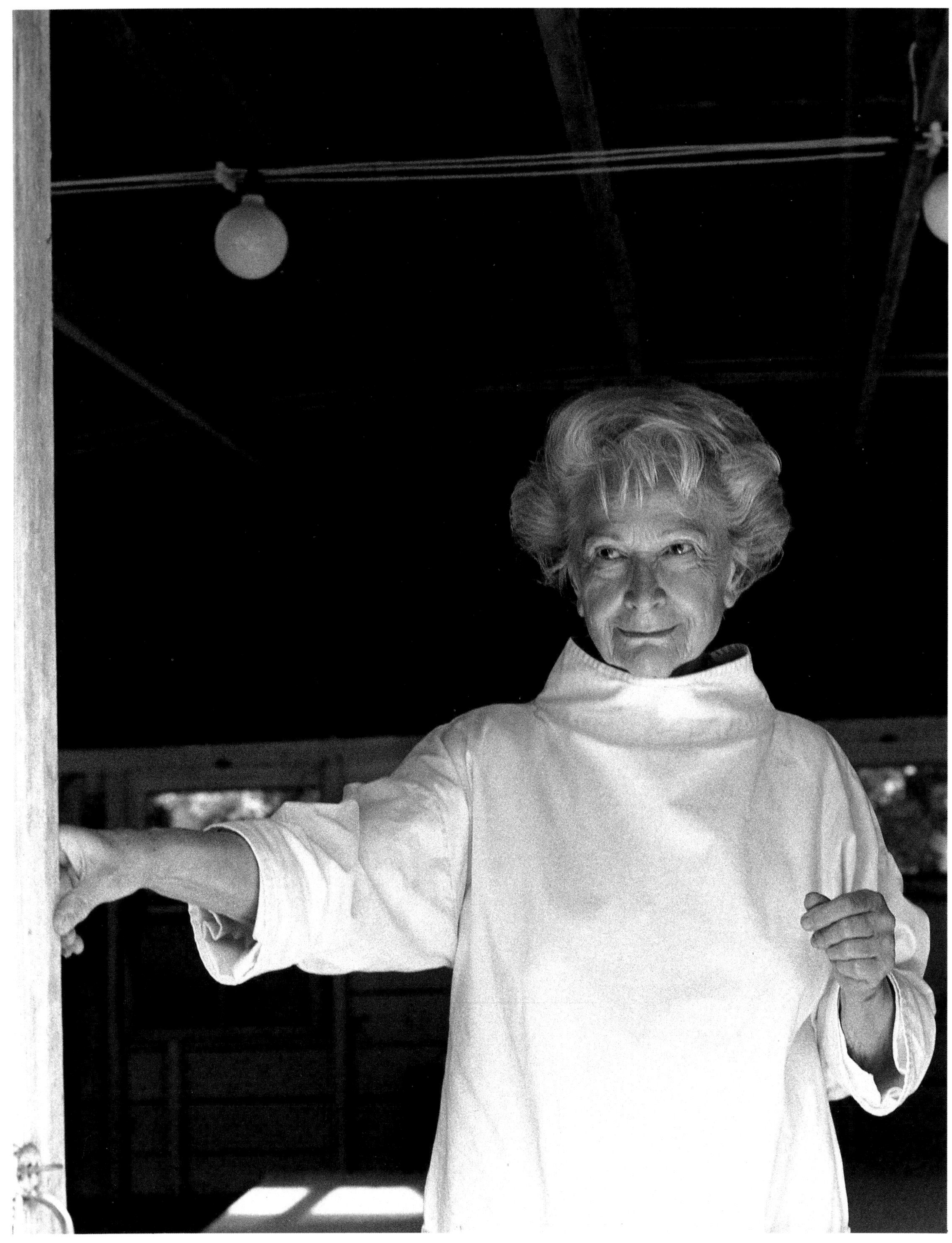

Hedda Sterne   1982

Octavio Paz   1984

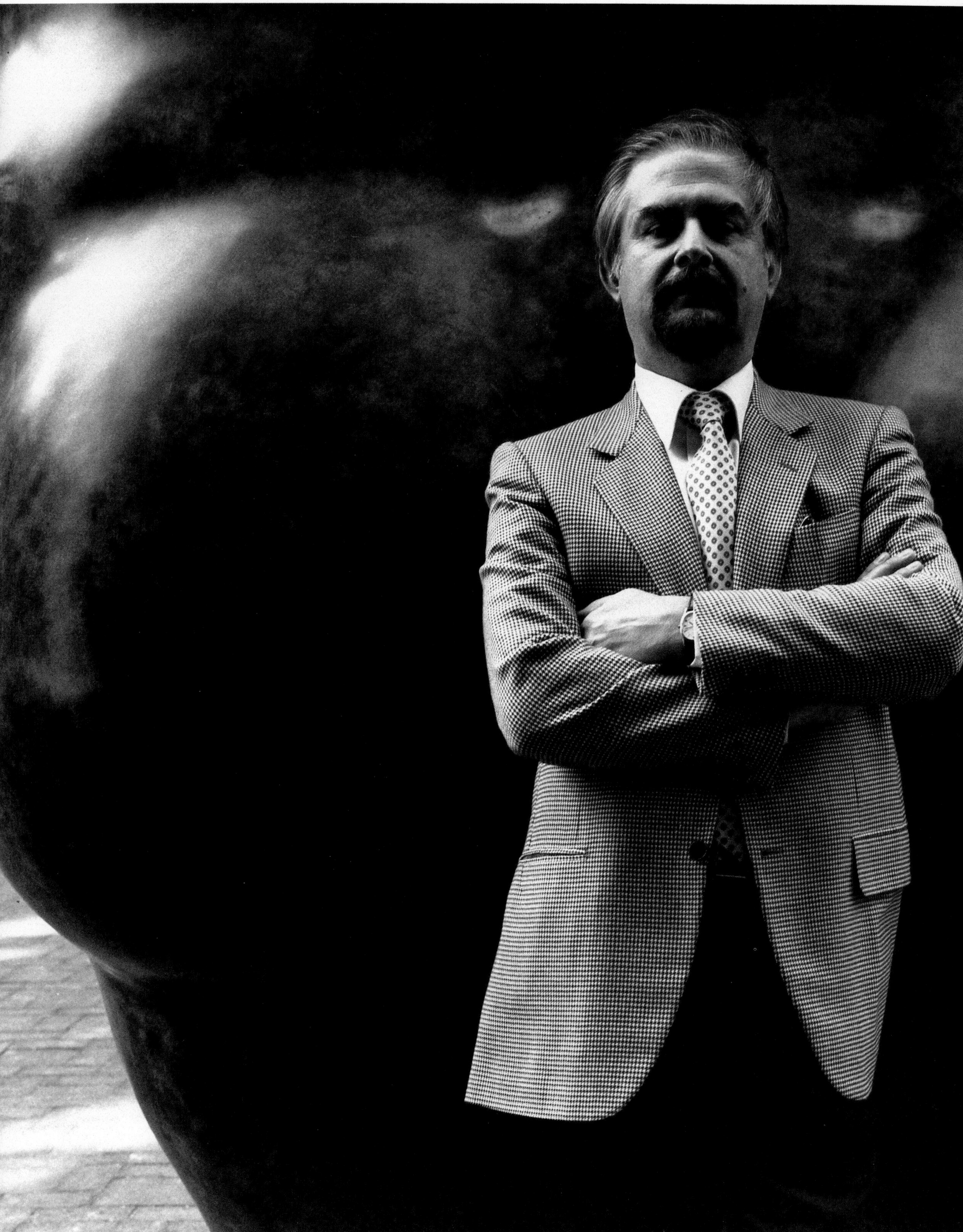

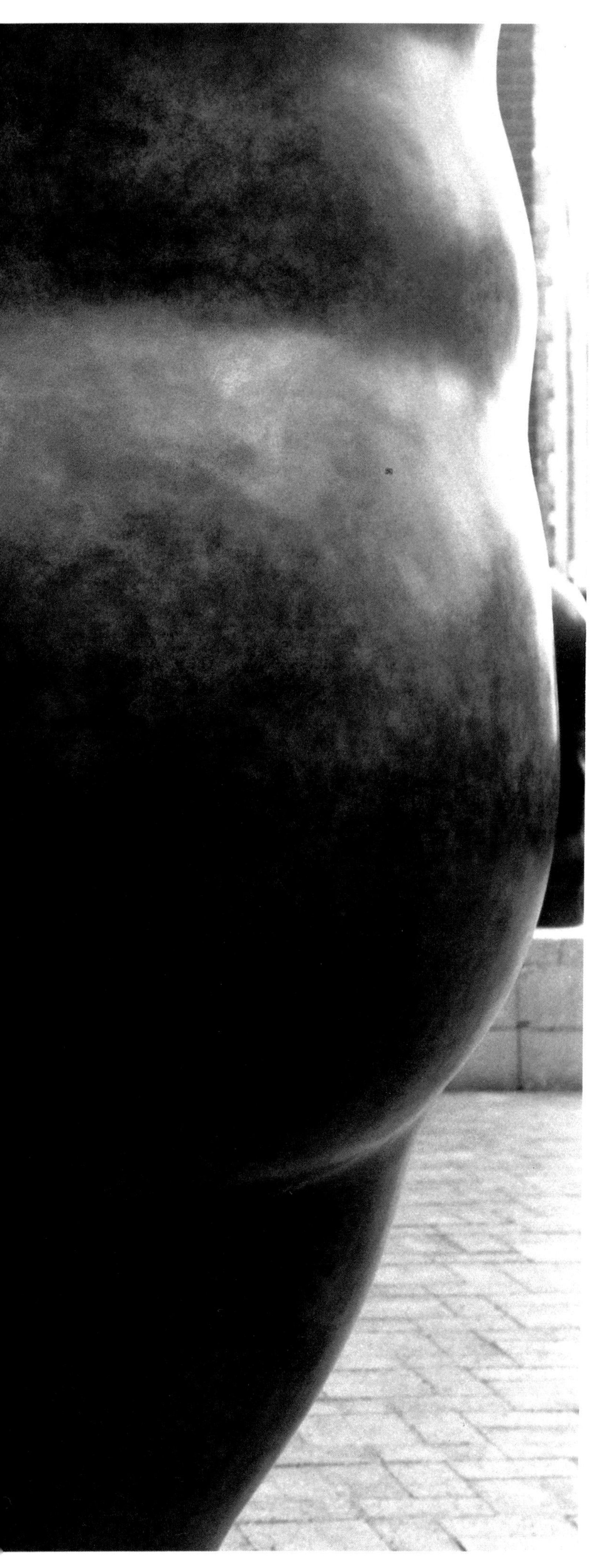

Fernando Botero   1985

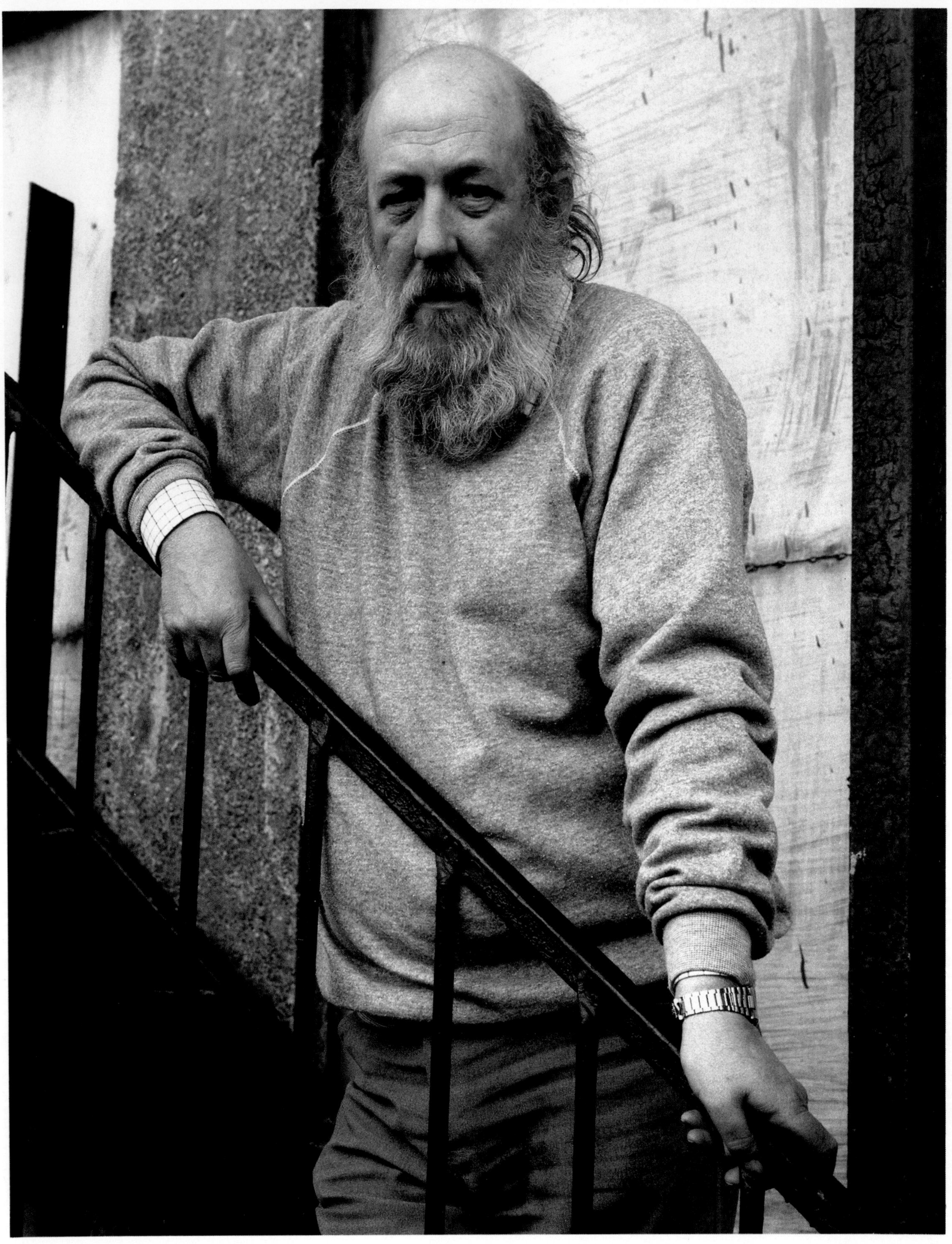

Jim Bird   1985

Gerry Mulligan   1986

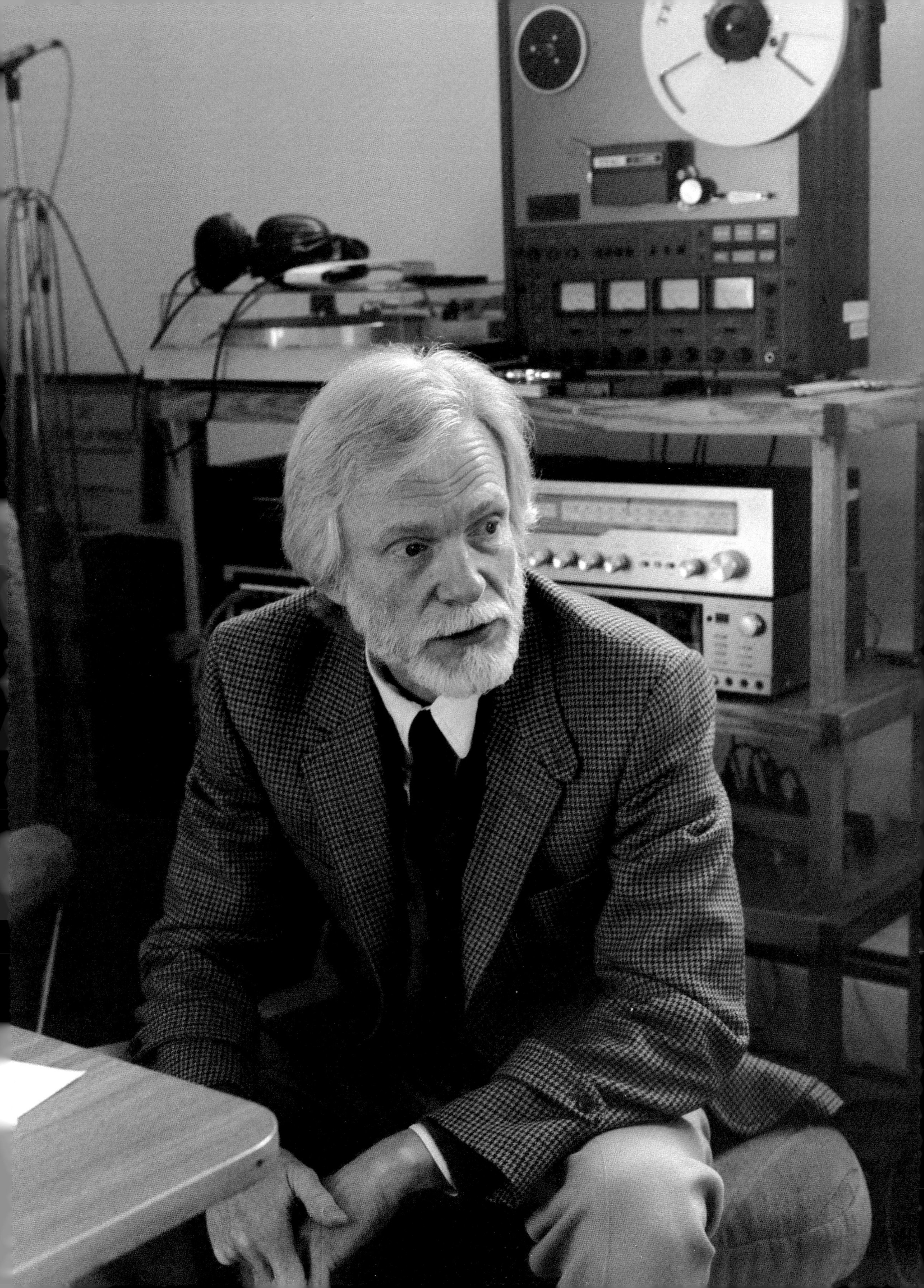

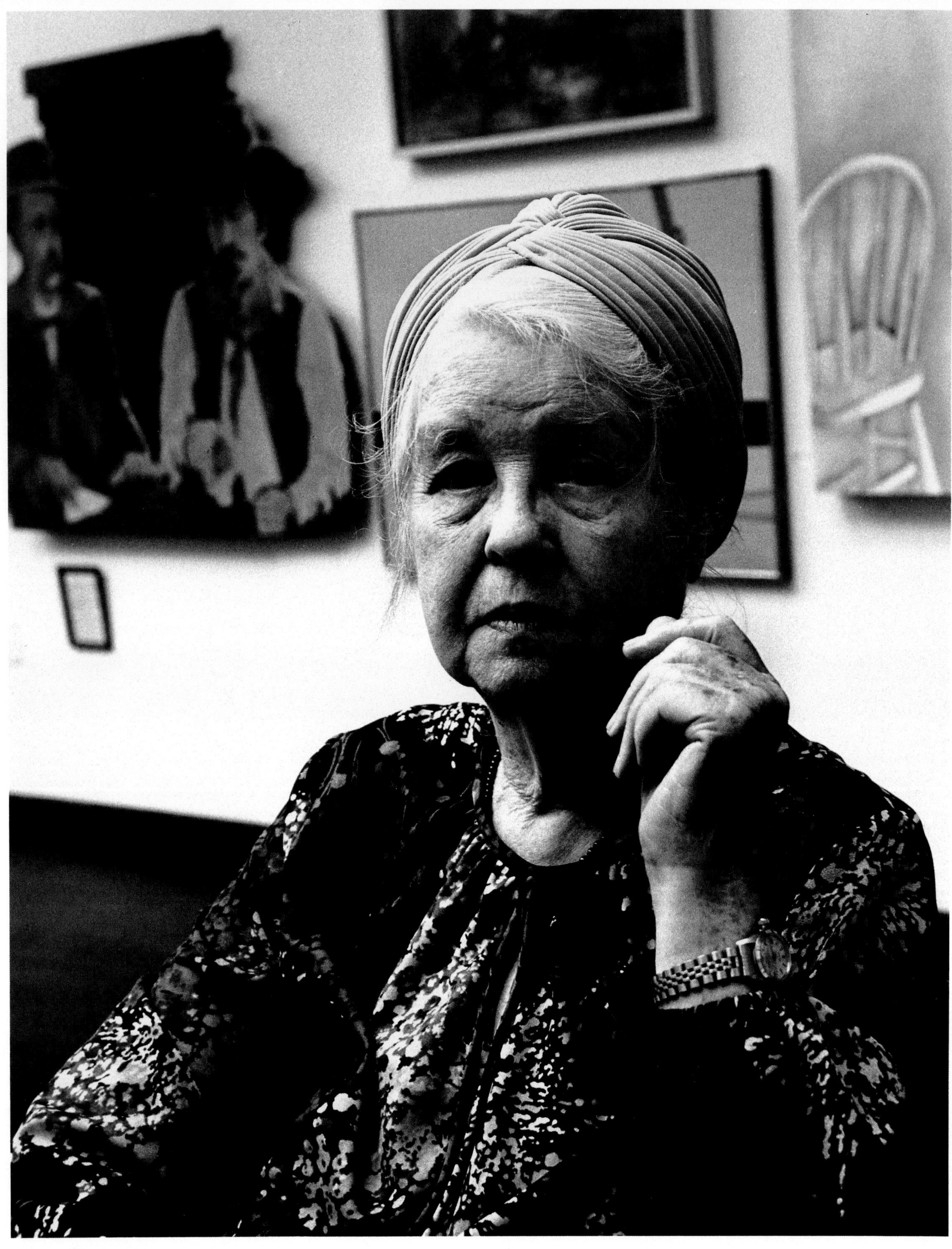

Alice Neel   1983

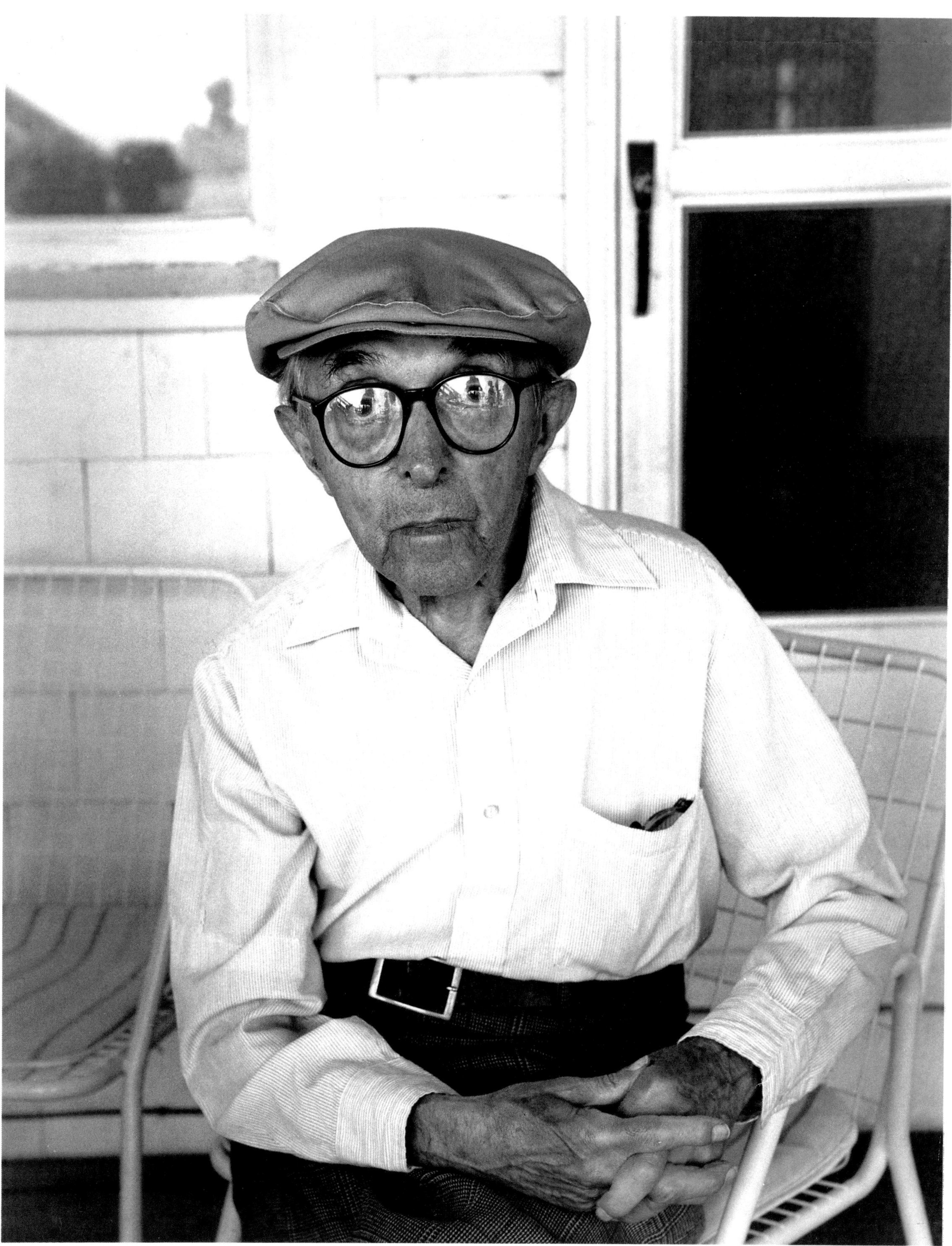

Raphael Soyer   1987

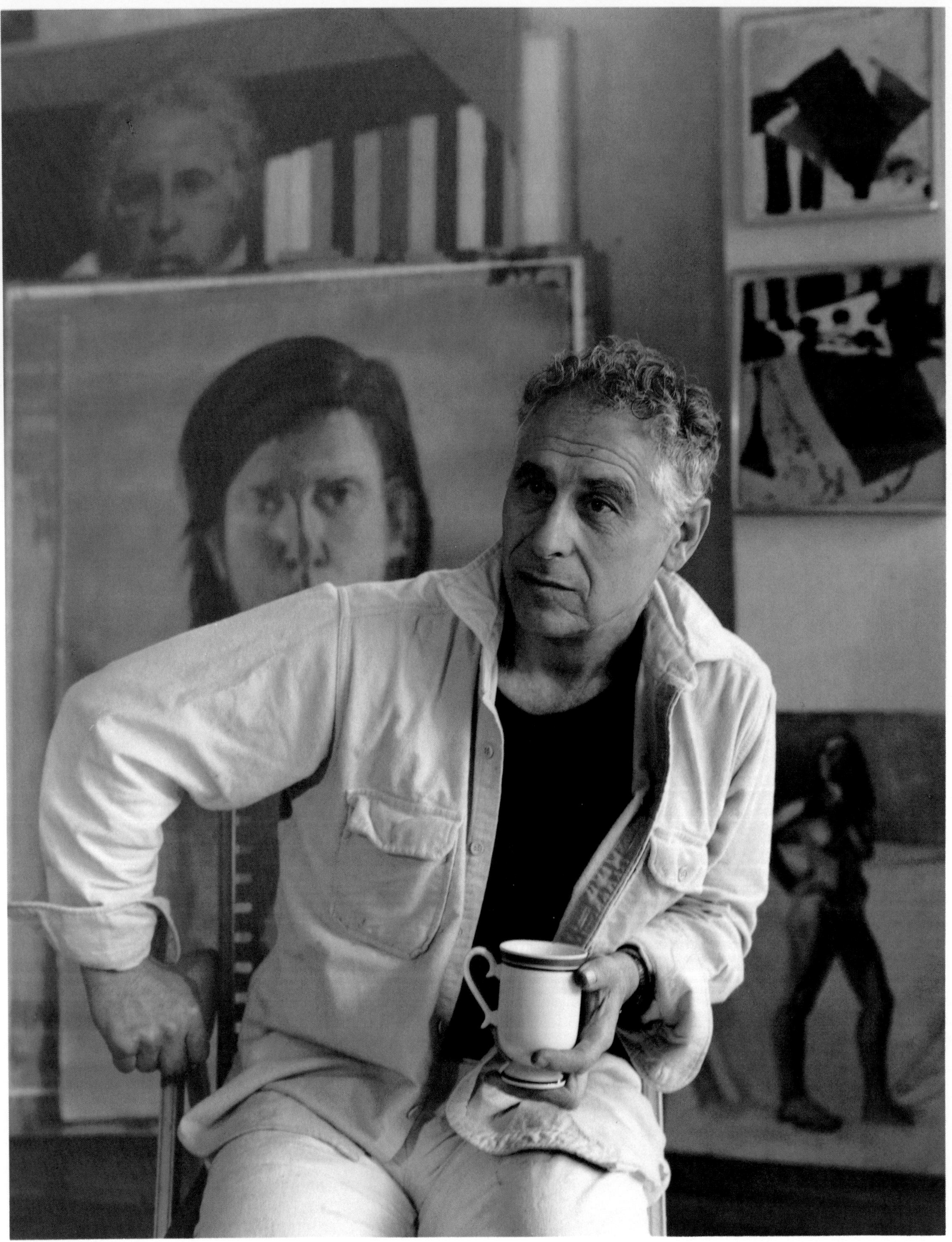

Alfred Leslie   1986

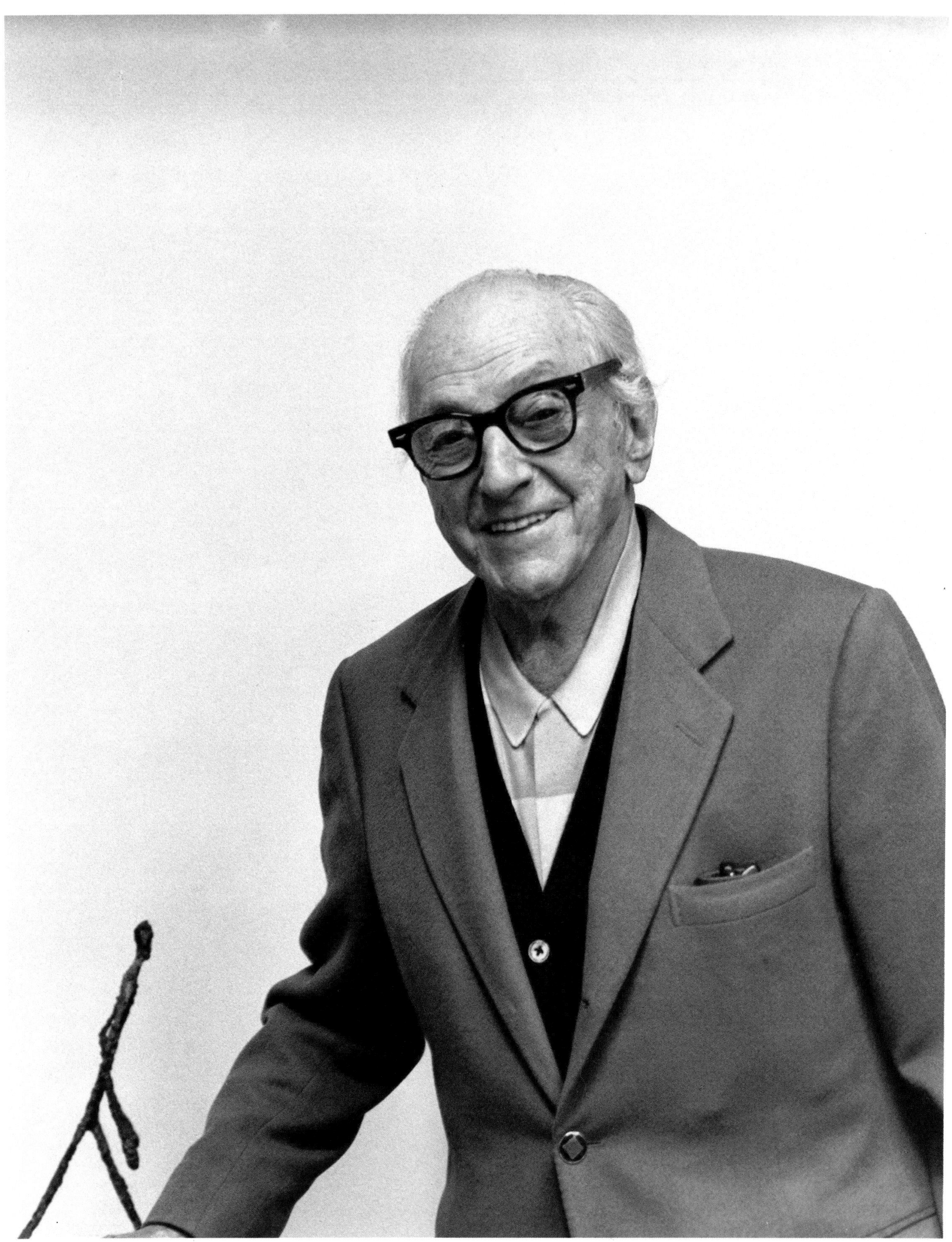

Sidney Janis   1988

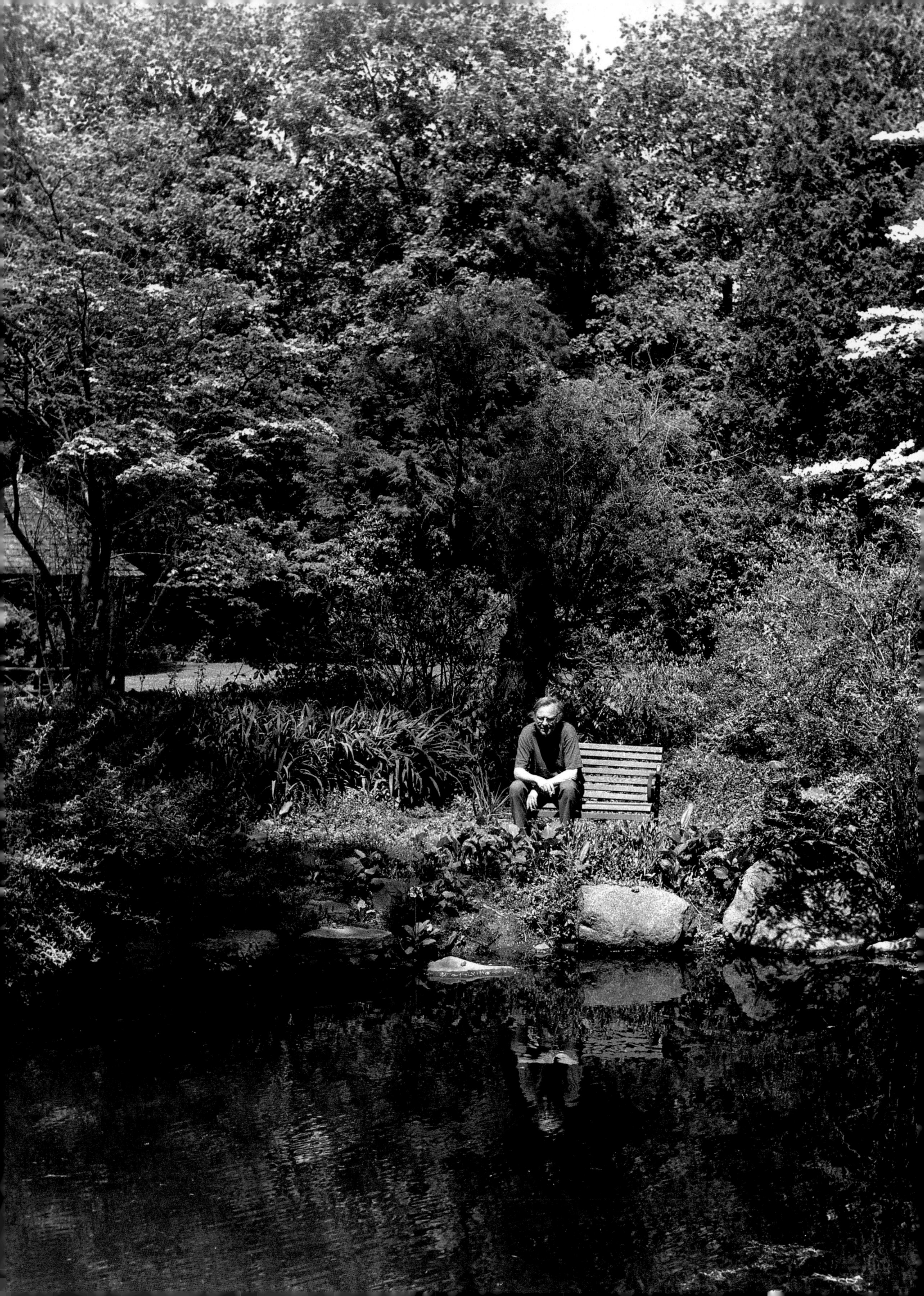

AFTERWORD

by ROBERT MOTHERWELL

There is little to add to Dore Ashton's sympathetic and penetrating portrait of my wife, Renate Ponsold. Dore knew her for a decade before Renate and I met in 1971, and knew me for at least two decades before that. Since we all moved in New York's world of modern art, it is perhaps surprising that Renate and I did not meet earlier. But just as well. When we met we were both free and independent, at that moment each reluctant to become deeply involved, yet both incapable of anything less. We were married in 1972—a year after our first chance meeting at a huge artists' party at a loft in Soho, the first such party that I had attended in over a year. I had been slowly moving from New York to an old stone carriage house in Connecticut, having lost my studio-house in New York. On pennies, I was making the carriage house livable, unheated and dark as it was when I found it, again by chance. (My accountant reminded me recently that in all of 1971, I sold a single picture.) I was then fifty-six; Renate was thirty-six. . . .

Renate had been a child in Germany during World War II and lived through its ultimate devastation. She was three when the war began. She could not have cared less about security when we met, after what she had seen and endured. Her spontaneous powers of improvisation are extraordinary. She has fear of neither life nor death, perhaps a necessity for survival during her youth. It is true that she still sleeps with a light on, and her fantastic hearing, like an animal's, is alert even in sleep. When she travels even a short distance in her beloved VW convertible, there is always something delicious on hand to eat and drink "in case." I used to joke with her that the war is over, but I slowly came to understand that even deeper than her awareness that everything can collapse is her life-affirming sense of celebration. What is usually routine can be made into an occasion, and should be, so she does.

Renate used to categorize people, in her personal shorthand, as creative or as "diplomats." She has no interest in the latter, though she is too well-bred to show it. She can listen to poets, composers, painters, and sculptors endlessly and with complete comprehension, because she herself is wholly creative, not only in photography but in everything on every level. (In all these years of days, there has not been one day when she has not in some way surprised me.) Her ear for classical music and jazz is faultless, as it is for poetry; she is my best critic as a painter, though she rarely speaks out without being asked; plants blossom under her touch; and in a flea market she sees what no one else does— lately, two nineteenth-century American soapstone chocolate egg molds as beautiful as Brancusi.

Unfortunately, her inhibitions regarding public statements have self-restricted her notes in this book to bare facts, so that her poetic use of language is absent, as though she were back in a strict German grammar school. No matter. What I am trying to express is that in the usual sense of the word she is not a "professional" photographer seeking to impose a "style" on a subject— posing, arranging lights, all those things that make being photographed an ordeal in the interests of a given photographer's logo mark. Instead, her creative intuition and culture—she knows by heart the oeuvre of her subjects— allow her the exact instant click (or more precisely, bang, since her Hasselblad sounds like a cannon). Her unposed subjects realize instinctively that they do not have to explain their work and obsessions, that she identifies, empathizes, and *knows*. Hence the "real" face (to the degree that there is one in any of us) feels free to show itself as itself, as though the photographer is not present. (It is rare that the culture of the photographer is as deep and genuine as that of her subjects.) I can imagine Renate never making a portrait again if not moved. But if moved, she improvises indomitably until looking at negatives in her darkroom she can say to herself, "Yes, oh yes."

May 1988

Robert Motherwell   1972

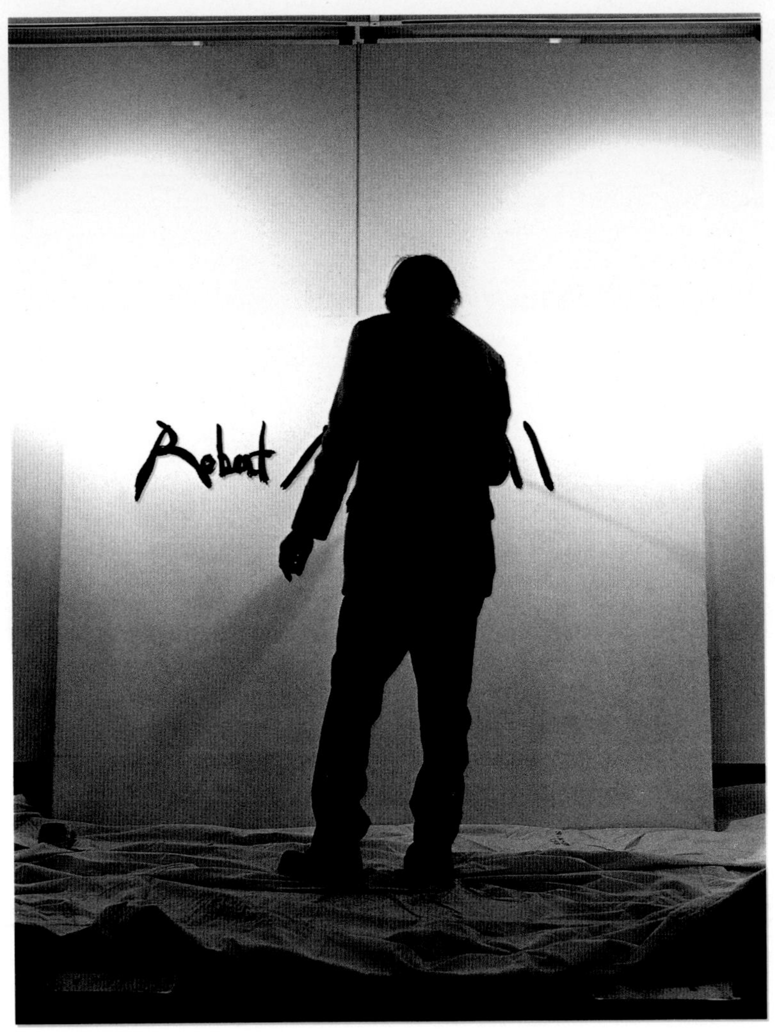

Robert Motherwell   1979

PHOTOGRAPHER'S RECOLLECTIONS

DORE ASHTON

Dore visited us for lunch in Greenwich to discuss an exhibition of Robert Motherwell's work for the Museo Nacional de Arte Moderno in Mexico City.

WILMA

Entering the Künstler-Klause (artists' pub) in Berlin in 1958 brought to life a glance into the past. Vivid stories came to my mind of what Berlin must have been like in the twenties. This character Wilma Stauber—the owner of the pub and once a star chanteuse of the underworld—received us students with straight vodkas and beer. I took this mirror image after Wilma had shown us "her" canvases, which looked like exact copies of Toulouse-Lautrec!

LOUIS ARMSTRONG

Louis Armstrong gave a concert in Munich where I was studying at the Bavarian State School of Photography. Colleagues rushed to the performance backstage, frontstage, wherever they could get near him. I had the good fortune to be invited to a private charity appearance at his hotel, the Regina, where he was cheered by a crowd of children left behind by American soldiers. I had a hard time getting through the mass of journalists and TV technicians. When I appeared in front of him, he gave me this disarming smile.

DUKE ELLINGTON

Duke Ellington was rehearsing at Madison Square Garden and two other jazz greats, George Shearing and Buddy Rich, were practicing for their evening concert when I was taken there by the wife of the Shearing Quintet's drummer. It was a rare privilege to witness this intimate collaboration.

KLAUS KINSKI

I photographed the German actor Klaus Kinski—yes, the father of Nastassia Kinski—in Berlin in 1958, after his dramatic poetry recital accompanied by a guitarist.

GAETANO POMPA

The studio of this attractive young painter from Rome was a meeting place for students at the Bavarian State School of Photography (which I attended from 1957 to 1959). He became our favorite model for our photographic portrait studies.

JULIO DE DIEGO

Julio de Diego was one of the first artists I was introduced to in New York in the early sixties. He invited me to his flamenco parties, took me to Roseland to dance, showed me his "Spanish Armada" paintings, and asked me to photograph him. He had a theatrical style, posing in a variety of hats and in his own handcrafted silver jewelry. He was once married to Gypsy Rose Lee and was still involved and surrounded by theater people.

OSCAR WILLIAMS

Oscar Williams seemed to know just about everyone in the New York art world. He often invited me to openings and to lunch downtown in his top-floor studio on Water Street, with a roof terrace and a magnificent view over the East River to Brooklyn Heights. He remarked, "That is where I was born." When I talked to him about my freighter journeys across the Atlantic, he pointed to the East River and said: "This is *my* Atlantic. I've never traveled farther than from Brooklyn to Manhattan and back." He always had gifts—a book, or dried flowers, or shells, or a record of poems by Dylan Thomas and Gene Derwood (Oscar's wife). Both died before I met him. He urged me to set up a darkroom in my fifty-four-dollar-a-month apartment on Sixth Street and Avenue D and bought me my first enlarger in New York for sixty dollars, which I paid back as soon as I got a job at the Museum of Modern Art. I phoned to invite him to the housewarming of my new apartment on East Thirty-fourth Street. He didn't feel well. Before I could find out what was wrong, I saw his photograph in the obituary section of the *New York Times*.

WILLEM DE KOONING, PHILIP GUSTON

Philip Guston wanted to see Bill's new studio-house in the Hamptons on Long Island. We knew vaguely where it was but couldn't find it. After driving around for an hour, we spotted Bill on a bicycle. He said, "Follow me." They talked about painting all afternoon.

PHILIP GUSTON
ADOLPH GOTTLIEB
SYD SOLOMON

During a weekend in the Hamptons at Syd Solomon's house, Hans Namuth had been asked to photograph Solomon, Guston, and Gottlieb for a brochure for an art school in Sarasota, where they had been artists-in-residence during the winter. I too took a shot just when they had all agreed to call it a day: "That's it, let's have a drink."

FREDERICK KIESLER

Philip Guston took me to Kiesler's studio to see his new sculpture. Kiesler asked me to lie down on the cowhide inside the belly of his "Trojan Horse" (the horse was lying on its side, so you could walk in) and to read the poems that were written all over the inside of the horse.

FRANK O'HARA

I met Frank O'Hara in the early sixties in Greenwich Village. When this photograph was taken we both worked at the Museum of Modern Art. That year, 1965, he curated a Motherwell retrospective there.

EDWARD STEICHEN

I never saw Steichen in daylight. We were introduced while I was printing in the darkroom downstairs at the Museum of Modern Art. This photograph was taken at a dinner for Sophia Loren in the museum garden, which was lit only by candles and dim spotlights. My negative looked too thin to print. At a later date Sidney Janis asked me if I had any portraits of photographers for a show he was thinking of doing someday to be called "Photographers Photograph Photographers." I thought that this thin negative might be worth a try. I liked what I saw!

SOPHIA LOREN

Working in the photography department at the Museum of Modern Art during the sixties not only gave me the pleasure of looking constantly at first-rate art; I could also attend many exciting evening events. One of them was a dinner party in honor of Sophia Loren. Camera at hand, I took this shot during her TV interview downstairs in front of her movie stills. I learned later that she had a miscarriage that very evening.

MAN RAY

Yvonne Hagen asked me to look up her longtime friends Man Ray and his wife, Juliet, during my Paris stay in 1970. A quiet, dark, late-November afternoon in his home-studio brought thin results on the negatives, which I decided were not worth printing. Five years later I was asked to include Man Ray in a portrait exhibition. They turned out to be among my best portraits.

KENNETH SNELSON

Snelson was installing his sculpture on the lawn behind the New York Public Library on Forty-second Street. His friend Marta Zogbaum asked me to join her there. I photographed him when he came over to greet us. He was exhausted from instructing technicians how to move his pipe-and-wire pieces into exact placement with a crane.

ALLAN D'ARCANGELO

An art historian and friend planned a book about talented New York artists who were well known but not established through a gallery. He asked me to photograph those he had in mind. One of them was Allan D'Arcangelo. The project was never completed.

W. H. AUDEN

I was introduced to Auden when he received a gold medal from the National Arts Club, which was an annual event that took place at their landmark building on Gramercy Park. I recognized him from having seen him on the subway, leafing through a pile of papers on his lap and wearing his famous felt slippers.

THORNTON WILDER

New York was full of the unexpected. One afternoon a Colombian friend called: "I want you to meet Thornton Wilder. Can we come over for tea?" An hour later Wilder, suffering from emphysema, appeared at the door of my fifth-floor walkup studio apartment on East Thirty-fourth Street with the most charming smile: "This is well worth climbing five flights!"

JAMES BALDWIN

I met Baldwin on some occasion in the early sixties in Greenwich Village in New York. In 1970, during a three-month job in Paris, I sat with writer friends in the bar at the Pont-Royale and recognized Baldwin at the next table. I photographed him the following day outside the bar.

ROBERT DASH

On one summer weekend visit to Long Island, Bob Dash invited me to lunch to view his much-admired garden, house, and studio. I started photographing him while he picked fresh greens for a salad.

YVONNE HAGEN, BOB FABIAN

Whenever I visited Yvonne in Bridgehampton, she had a house full of guests. A stroll on the beach was part of the Sunday morning ritual.

GALWAY KINNELL

After a long drive Yvonne Hagen and I arrived in Sheffield, Vermont, where Galway lived with his wife and two children in a wonderful old farmhouse. I started photographing the children. As soon as he entered the door, returning from a lecture tour, his children fell all over him, never giving me a chance to take a "serious" portrait of him. We dined at a beautiful handcrafted table. He smiled when we asked him where he found this perfect table. He had made it himself: "If I don't make money as a poet and teacher, I can always survive as a carpenter and furniture designer."

ALISTAIR COOKE

The occasion was graduation at the Maryland Institute College of Art, Baltimore, including honorary doctorates awarded to Alistair Cooke and Robert Motherwell. Cooke was the first one to sit down at the lunch table, a good moment to catch him, before he started his nonstop conversation.

HILTON KRAMER

Hilton Kramer and his wife, Esther, visited us in Province-town after they had enjoyed a restful week in Wellfleet. We had a relaxed, extended lunch, which helped me to capture this unguarded, peaceful moment.

EDWARD ALBEE

I stayed with Yvonne Hagen in Bridgehampton one summer weekend when she had invited many of her artist friends to a Sunday brunch. She told me later that Albee was surprised to see this portrait of himself when it was included in an exhibition at the Musée d'Art Moderne de la Ville de Paris.

ERICK HAWKINS

Erick Hawkins visited us one summer in Provincetown to discuss with Robert Motherwell the possibility of designing a stage set for a new ballet. (Unfortunately, the project was never realized.)

SONIA DELAUNAY

Robert Motherwell and I had a joint museum exhibition in Paris. We ran into our friend Arthur Cohen, who had just finished a book on Sonia Delaunay, then ninety-two. He said, "You have to photograph Sonia before she dies." I got an appointment the next day. She was quiet and tired. I had a hard time catching her with her eyes open.

BRASSAI

When I received the Marlborough Gallery invitation to Brassaï's exhibition, which announced that the artist would be present, I rushed to the gallery with my camera. Intimidated by this show entitled "Artists in Their Studios," I just snapped this one shot. When we were introduced, Brassaï asked me, "Which photograph do *you* prefer?" I took him to the one of Georges Braque in his Paris studio. I knew enough French to understand his enthusiastic response: "You are the one tonight who spotted *my* favorite!" This compliment was the catalyst for me to pick up my work in the darkroom again, after a long absence.

ANDY WARHOL

I visited Erika Billeter, then curator at the Kunsthaus in Zurich, who was preparing a retrospective of Andy Warhol's work. She asked me if I could photograph Andy for the catalogue. I had met him several times since the early sixties. I made an appointment immediately upon my return to New York and took a lot of photographs of him in his "Factory" on Union Square. Twelve of the pictures are reproduced in the Swiss catalogue.

CARL ANDRE

I like to return to the Musée d'Art Moderne de la Ville de Paris, where I had a show in 1977, to see my friends. On one occasion I was invited to lunch with Carl Andre, who was having an exhibition there at the time. I was pleased to find that he had one of my Roy Lichtenstein portraits in his personal collection.

EDUARDO CHILLIDA

I knew Chillida's work for many years but only met him in 1980, when he came with his very large family to New York for his Guggenheim Museum show. José Guerrero, a Spanish painter and good friend of Chillida, gave a party in his honor, where we arranged an appointment to photograph the next day.

NORMAN MAILER

As they are our neighbors in the summer in Provincetown, I see the Mailers quite often. I visited them one afternoon to photograph him outside on his deck. This photograph appeared on the jacket of his book *Ancient Evenings*.

JACK YOUNGERMAN

Usually I do not carry a camera with me while going to galleries or openings because the light is never right for "chance portraits." This day I was equipped and asked Jack to step outside the gallery. The light was good.

GEORGE SEGAL

Robert Motherwell and I had a delightful lunch at George Segal's house in New Brunswick, New Jersey. Afterward, he took us through his studio, a long row of what had been connected chicken coops.

OCTAVIO PAZ

I met Octavio Paz when he visited us with his wife to discuss a special publication of some of his poems illustrated with Robert Motherwell's lithographs.

HEDDA STERNE

I was preparing an exhibition for the CDS Gallery in New York. The owner, Clara Sujo, suggested that I include one of her esteemed gallery artists, Hedda Sterne, whom I had never met. We drove to Long Island to her place. I had my camera ready when Hedda, expecting us, opened her studio door. She is a radiant woman.

FERNANDO BOTERO

The same Colombian friend who introduced me to Thornton Wilder talked to me often about his old friend Botero. Many years later an appointment was arranged at the Marlborough Gallery for me to photograph him. His new paintings and large-sized sculptures were on view at the time. Meeting him was the most puzzling experience. I could not find any connection between him and his work.

JIM BIRD

Jim Bird, an English painter who has lived many years in Spain but also works in a Brooklyn studio, asked me to photograph him for a catalogue. A year later we had a joint exhibition (his mostly black-and-white monotypes and my portraits) in Barcelona and Mallorca.

INDEX OF PORTRAITS